PROFESSIONAL DISCRETION IN WELFARE SERVICES

Contemporary Social Work Studies

Series Editor:
Robin Lovelock, University of Southampton, UK

Series Advisory Board:
Lena Dominelli, University of Durham, UK
Jan Fook, University of Southampton, UK
Peter Ford, University of Southampton, UK
Lorraine Gutiérrez University of Michigan, USA
Walter Lorenz, Free University of Bozen-Bolzano, Italy
Karen Lyons, London Metropolitan University, UK
Joan Orme, University of Glasgow, UK
Jackie Powell, University of Southampton, UK
Gillian Ruch, University of Southampton, UK

Contemporary Social Work Studies is a series disseminating high quality new research and scholarship in the discipline and profession of social work. The series promotes critical engagement with contemporary issues relevant across the social work community and captures the diversity of interests currently evident at national, international and local levels.

CSWS is located in the School of Social Sciences (Social Work Studies Division) at the University of Southampton, UK and is a development from the successful series of books published by Ashgate in association with CEDR (the Centre for Evaluative and Developmental Research) from 1991.

Other titles in this series:

Social Work and Migration
Immigrant and Refugee Settlement and Integration
Kathleen Valtonen
ISBN 978 0 7546 7194 7

Indigenous Social Work around the World
Towards Culturally Relevant Education and Practice
Edited by Mel Gray, John Coates and Michael Yellow Bird
ISBN 978 0 7546 4838 3

UNIVERSITY OF
Southampton
School of Social Sciences

Professional Discretion in Welfare Services
Beyond Street-Level Bureaucracy

TONY EVANS
University of Warwick, UK

Routledge
Taylor & Francis Group
LONDON AND NEW YORK

First published 2010 by Ashgate Publishing

2 Park Square, Milton Park, Abingdon, Oxon OX14 4RN
711 Third Avenue, New York, NY 10017, USA

Routledge is an imprint of the Taylor & Francis Group, an informa business

First issued in paperback 2016

British Library Cataloguing in Publication Data
Evans, Tony.
  Professional discretion in welfare services : beyond
  street-level bureaucracy. -- (Contemporary social work
  studies)
  1. Social service--Moral and ethical aspects. 2. Social
  work administration--Moral and ethical aspects. 3. Lipsky,
  Michael. Street-level bureaucracy.
  I. Title II. Series
  361.3'068-dc22

Library of Congress Cataloging-in-Publication Data
Evans, Tony.
  Professional discretion in welfare services : beyond street-level bureaucracy / by Tony
Evans.
    p. cm. -- (Contemporary social work studies)
  Includes bibliographical references and index.
  ISBN 978-0-7546-7491-7 (hardback) -- ISBN 978-1-4094-0848-2 (ebook) 1. Social
work administration. 2. Administrative discretion 3. Social workers. 4. Social service. I.
Title.
  HV41.E964 2010
  361.0068--dc22

                                                           2010007091

ISBN 13: 978-0-7546-7491-7 (hbk)
ISBN 13: 978-1-138-25601-9 (pbk)

Contents

Er cof am fy rhieni Blodwen a Richard Evans

List of Figures

Figures

Table

Introduction

Professional discretion has re-emerged as a key issue in current social work. It encapsulates the tension in current policy between the increasing regulation of practice and the need for practitioners' initiative and creativity in policy implementation. In this book I want to explore professional discretion in the context of contemporary welfare services; specifically the example of social work in social services.

This book reflects the development of my thinking about discretion in welfare bureaucracies and the roles played by managerialism and professionalism in the structuring of discretion. My interest in professional discretion has developed over the past two decades, in the context of a developing management culture in public services, and reflects my critical engagement with key ideas encountered as I struggled, first as a practitioner and then as a researcher, to understand discretion in contemporary social service.

A key approach to the study of discretion is Lipsky's 'street-level bureaucracy' theory, and this perspective has re-emerged as a significant point of debate in the analysis of the impact of managerial reforms of public services. An important aspect of these reforms has been the attempt to curtail professional discretion in the organisation and delivery of services. New Labour's Modernisation programme, for instance, has seen an intensification of this aspect of managerial reform but, at the same time, there has been a growing political and academic debate about the problems of centralised control and direction of services and its impact on local responsiveness and professional autonomy.

My starting point, then, is a critical examination of Michael Lipsky's account of discretion in his seminal study of street-level bureaucracies (Lipsky 1980). His work challenges a significant strand in the contemporary analysis of social work discretion in that he points to the continuation of extensive day-to-day discretion of street-level bureaucrats such as social workers (Evans and Harris 2004a, Turbett 2009). While I start with Lipsky, I seek neither to defend nor to dismiss the street-level perspective, but rather aim to use it to stimulate critical thinking about the extent and basis of professional discretion within social work, as the introduction to an empirical study of discretion.

There is a growing recognition that social policy research needs to be grounded in street-level experience (McDonald and Marston 2005, Mead 2005) and, accordingly, this study reports empirical research the goal of which has been both to evaluate ideas of discretion in the field and, recognising the role of serendipity in research, to be sensitive to: '… the complexity of what one learns in the field [and to be open to] ideas … that fall outside the existing literature' (Mead 2005: 543).

Investigating Discretion

Discretion is a difficult idea to pin down. The term is used in different ways in different contexts (Smith 1981, Evetts 2002). One possible approach would be to examine the full range of definitions and to choose one as 'correct'—though this raises the further problem of how to determine a correct definition. Furthermore, Smith warns against attempts at extended *a priori* definitions of the term, pointing out that the: '… apparent supposition that we can settle upon a definition, before research begins in social work, [is] unhelpful' (Smith 1981: 60). Within the different uses of the term, he argues, there is a general sense of concern with the freedom to make decisions in a work role, but beyond this it is difficult to provide a robust or precise definition (*ibid.* 47–48). Avoiding definitional debates, then, Smith prefers to see discretion as a topic for exploration. Rather than using it as a conceptual tool to be specified and applied to all situations, he looks at '… the language of discretion in relation to the action of discretion' (*ibid.* 60). As a topic, discretion is concerned with the extent of freedom a worker can exercise in a specific context and the factors that give rise to this freedom in that context (*ibid.*).

Discretion—as freedom—is seen as a key characteristic of professional workers (Freidson 1994). Social work as a profession is relatively new in Britain. While its origins can be traced back to the late nineteenth century (Lymbery 1998a, Parry and Parry 1979), its creation and recognition as a professional role are often associated with the Seebohm reforms and the creation of Social Services Departments in the early 1970s (Marshal and Rees 1985, Lymbery 1998a, Foster and Wilding 2000, Harris 2003). Almost since the point of social work's professional consolidation, the idea of social work discretion has been contested, because of the close link between Social Services as an organisation and the idea of the professional status of social work (Parry and Parry 1979, Jones 1983). Paradoxically, what might be seen as the apotheosis of the social work professional project, in terms of the consolidation of social work and Social Services, was quickly followed by the increasing criticism of professional discretion, including that of social workers (Langan 1998). In a post-war welfare state professionals were recognised as playing a significant role, not only in delivering services but also in developing and implementing service policies (e.g. Marshal and Rees 1985). However, from the 1970s professionalism within the welfare state was increasingly subject to a range of criticisms (Foster and Wilding 2000). Academic analysis questioned the functionalist view of professionals as ethically committed and altruistic experts, pointing instead to their self-interested occupational strategies. This analysis was also related to a radical critique which saw professional collusion with dominant forces in society. The developing consumer movement was critical of perceived professional arrogance, and the resurgent New Right offered an economic analysis of the producer power of professionals, restricting efficiency and choice, capturing public services and operating them in their own interest. The election of a Conservative government in 1979 gave particular emphasis to this latter analysis, which regarded professionalism as a problem, the solution to which was the introduction of focused techniques of management and market disciplines derived from the business world into public services as a means of controlling professional freedom (Alaszewski and Manthorpe 1990, Clarke 1996, Harris 1998a, Jones 1999). Over the past 20 years the debate within the social work literature on discretion has largely focused on the decline of discretion (Evans and Harris 2004a). This literature has emphasised the rise of managers and managerial ways of thinking and the increasingly intense and effective control of welfare professionals. However, alongside this picture of the decline of professional discretion, there has also been a developing literature influenced by Lipsky's work on street-level bureaucracy, arguing that social work discretion continues to be significant (Baldwin 1998, 2000, 2004, Ellis *et al.* 1999, Newton and Brown 2008, Ellis 2007, Halliday *et al.* 2008, Dunkerley *et al.* 2005). This literature contests the view that the impact of managerialism is all-powerful and pervasive and points to the need for further investigation of discretion in terms of how much discretion social workers still exercise, the form discretion takes and the means by which it is structured and controlled.

Discretion and Street-Level Bureaucracy

The core of Lipsky's argument is that discretion is not only inevitable but also necessary in welfare bureaucracies. Public service organisations are necessarily complex and unwieldy bodies with vague and conflicting policy goals and limited resources. Discretion arises from the need to turn broad goals into practical policy, and to decide how to use limited resources to achieve those goals (Lipsky 1980). In presenting this argument, Lipsky challenges formal accounts of policy implementation as clear policy issued from the centre and carried out locally, without problems, by street-level practitioners.

Lipsky developed his theory in the context of urban politics in North America in the late 1960s and 1970s (Hawley and Lipsky 1976). His approach reflects both his disciplinary perspective—political science—and the range of issues within urban politics. He examines street-level bureaucracies—public organisations delivering services to citizens—in relation to street-level bureaucrats' interaction with citizens receiving services and their relationship with politicians and the electorate. However, the focus of his analysis of discretion, as the subtitle of his book—*Dilemmas of the Individual in Public Services*—suggests, is on the relationship between street-level bureaucrats and their managers within public organisations and the dynamics of discretion which it generates. This is also the focus of the treatment of Lipsky's work in this book.

Why Start with Lipsky?

In Britain Lipsky's work was initially well received and seen as an insightful account directly applicable to the analysis of social work practice (Hill 1982). After this initial interest, the street-level bureaucracy perspective received little attention (Hudson 1993), but there has been renewed interest in the last few years, particularly in relation to social work (Evans and Harris 2004a). Lipsky's account shares the general view found in the social work literature of the increasing significance of management's attempts to direct and control day-to-day street-level practice. However, it also offers a counterbalance to the main body of this literature, which tends to characterise managers as omnipotent and capable of suppressing discretion. Accordingly, his work has been subject to criticism by some of the authors who adopt this stance (Howe 1991a and Cheetham 1993).

Lipsky's work has largely been used to underline the continuation of practitioner discretion, while acknowledging the increasing role of managers (Baldwin 2000, Ellis *et al.* 1999). I will argue that Lipsky's scepticism about managerial control is an important contribution to the debate about professional social work discretion but I will also point to its limitations in terms of its characterisation of management, particularly front-line management, and its general disregard of the role of professional claims in the construction of discretion for some street-level bureaucrats.

Lipsky's work continues to be relevant to debates about discretion in social work, and, as such, offers a useful starting point in examining the topography of professional discretion in Social Services. In line with Smith's emphasis on approaching discretion as a topic for investigation, Lipsky's analysis is useful because of both its strengths and its weaknesses. It provides a set of hypotheses about discretion that facilitates 'the uncomfortable process of moving from theory to data and back again', which Smith sees as a crucial process in the analysis of discretion (Smith 1981: 48).

Any exploration of such an issue inevitably brings ideas and presumptions to the investigation (Gadamer 1975). In embarking on this research I have used Lipsky's work as my starting point. However, this study claims an uncommitted, rather than a partisan, use of the street-level perspective. To support this claim, I will outline the origin and development of my interest in Lipsky's perspective.

Encountering Lipsky

My first encounter with Lipsky's work was in the early 1990s, as a graduate trainee social worker. Before commencing social work training I worked in policy implementation, and Lipsky's account of street-level bureaucracy seemed to me a convincing account of the ability of professionals to influence the nature of the policy implemented at street level. In the context of the Griffiths reforms in health (National Health Service Management Inquiry 1983) and then in social care (Griffiths 1988), it also seemed to me to pose interesting questions about the claims being made for the effectiveness of management techniques in controlling and directing services.

My interest in the critical examination of Lipsky's work developed through my experience as a qualified social worker in the period following the implementation of the NHS and Community Care Act (1990). I qualified in 1993 and started work in a Mental Health Team soon after the introduction of the new community care framework. According to Lipsky's argument, street-level workers such as social workers retain discretion despite their managers; however, I also felt that I was given a wide degree of freedom in my practice by managers—social work professionals who had moved into management roles. In part this may have been due to my lack of previous experience as a social worker; certainly some practitioners in the team regarded the new community care framework as limiting their professional freedom. However, other practitioners believed that recent reforms had helped remove some of the interference that they had experienced before the reforms.

I moved to another social work team, where my experience was of continuing professional freedom. At the same time I encountered a situation described by Lipsky: that is, an organisation seeking to use resources and procedures (such as eligibility criteria) to control access to services; but creating uncertainty and confusion, which both generated discretion and required its use to make systems work.

As a social work teacher and academic I have found Lipsky's work prescient and a counterweight to the view that social workers no longer exercised discretion (Evans and Harris 2004a). As mentioned above, the literature on social services organisations points to a significant change in their underpinning structure over the past two decades, in the form of the growing influence of managerialism. In preparing this book I returned to Lipsky's original work and found its contemporary relevance reinforced. While Lipsky writes about American public services in the 1970s, his account of these organisations and how they were managed reflects contemporary accounts of managerialised Social Services—for instance, in terms of the ethos of management control and the language of eligibility, performance measures and outputs etc. (Harris 1998a). Accordingly, his work offers an interesting starting point from which to explore arguments about the impact of managerialism on Social Services, because it challenges key claims of managerial capacity and effectiveness. However, the perspective's limited analysis of the nature of management and of the influence of professional status on discretion points to areas for further investigation. Managerialism's emphasis on formal systems of management and the effectiveness of managers in controlling staff relates to the view within much of the literature identifying and analysing the impact of managerialism on Social Services: that workers no longer have discretion. Commentators looking at the impact of managerialism on professional discretion often share this view. However, on closer examination the literature examining the impact of managerialism on social work staff suggests two different analyses with differing implications for understanding discretion.

Lipsky's work can be seen as a challenge to accounts—which I refer to as 'domination managerialism'—of the success and power of managers in running organisations and curtailing practitioner discretion. His account of discretion is in terms of the day-to-day ability of street-level practitioners to influence and change policy, which is often more extensive than formal (organisationally acknowledged) discretion. While Lipsky and domination managerialism disagree on the effectiveness of management control, they do agree that managers are committed to the organisation and to ensuring that recalcitrant workers comply with policy instructions. However, their analyses play down the potential influence of another, professional, idea of discretion, its influence on what is understood as the basis and extent of (professional) discretion, and the possible influence of shared professional backgrounds on the relationship between practitioners and their managers. I argue that these factors are recognised by another perspective on discretion in contemporary managerialised Social Services, which I have called 'discursive managerialism'. This approach to discretion offers a complex analysis which, while recognising the growing influence of managers and management ideas within Social Services, also points to the continuing influence of a professional culture which interacts with the new management culture in various ways in various settings, creating different discretionary settlements in each setting.

Outline of the Book

The focus of this book is the extent of discretion experienced by professional social workers in adult Social Services, and the basis of this freedom. In using Lipsky's work to explore this area, I have concentrated on particular aspects of the street-level bureaucracy perspective. Lipsky's account both examines discretion's continuation in a managerialised organisation and seeks to evaluate and describe the ways in which street-level bureaucrats use their discretion in relation to users of street-level services. However, to engage in a study of both the extent of discretion and the way in which it is used would be beyond the scope of this book. This book restricts its focus to the extent and basis of discretion.

Chapter 1 considers Lipsky's account of the nature of discretion in street-level bureaucracies and his description of the relationship of managers and street-level bureaucrats. It also discusses the subsequent development of a street-level bureaucracy literature that has sought to test and develop Lipsky's ideas. The key issues arising from the examination of the street-level bureaucracy perspective focus on the characterisation of management within street-level bureaucracies; the limited recognition of professional claims and status on the extent of discretion exercised by street-level workers; and, related to this, their impact on the nature of the relationship between managers and the street-level workers they manage.

Work on street-level bureaucracy theory has largely been conducted in North America. In the UK, while the initial reaction to Lipsky's work was positive, it has been criticised as irrelevant in the face of the managerialisation of Social

Services and developing control of professional practice. In Chapter 2 I consider these positions and argue that the evidence suggests that Social Services continue to share the basis characteristics of street-level bureaucracies (persistent and pervasive street-level discretion even in the context of managerial reforms and modernisation); and I point to the revival of interest in the street-level bureaucracy perspective in Britain. In short, the street-level perspective, while accepting that managers have replaced the professional dimension with a system of controls, seeking to restrict and restrain workers, is sceptical of managers' ability to control practitioners, who have extensive discretion.

Chapter 3 considers the street-level bureaucracy perspective in relation to arguments about the impact of managerialism within public services, with particular reference to Social Services. It examines current debates about discretion, which have tended to polarise in terms of either management control and the elimination of discretion; or the continuation of workers' freedom and discretion within their role. In relation to these arguments I suggest that, while there is a broad consensus that management and a business culture-inspired approach have had a significant impact on policy and practice within social services, the nature and extent of this impact is not clear. I suggest that it is possible to distinguish two broad strands in the managerial analysis, which offer different perspectives on professional discretion. The *domination perspective* sees managers as breaking with the past and fully in control, committed to the organisation, managing practitioners as workers, and using budgets and procedures to minimise discretion. In contrast to this the *discursive perspective* sees managerialism as an increasingly important principle in the structuring of services, but does not see its impact as uniform. In many areas it operates alongside pre-existing bureaucratic and professional principles, which support practitioner discretion. Discretion is made up of a complex set of factors, which operate in different ways in different sites. The chapter concludes with a summary of the three models of discretion and management control considered in chapters one, two and three—street-level theory perspective, domination managerial analysis and discursive managerial analysis.

In the remainder of the book these models are examined in the context of a case study of social work discretion within an adults' social services department. This case study is outlined in Chapter 4. The case study considers the ways in which the extent and nature of discretion can vary within the same professional group (comparing and contrasting social work discretion in an Older Persons Team and a Mental Health Team); and it looks at ideas of 'professionalism' and 'professional discretion' in relation to social work managers as well as practitioners. The study involved qualitative research of the views of professional social workers—eight practitioners and four front-line managers (all of whom are professionally qualified social workers)—in two social work teams in an English local authority. The main form of research data is individual interviews, but this is supplemented by observational data and documentary sources. Interviews were tape-recorded with the participants' permission. Data analysis was based on an iterative process of critical reading and categorisation (Edwards and Talbot 1999). The confidentiality of interviewees was assured, and this is reflected in the use of anonymised quotes and the removal of names of third parties/institutions. The overwhelming majority of practitioners and managers interviewed were women (two of the eight practitioners and one of the managers were men). Gender did not emerge as a significant factor in the analysis of this data. Accordingly the findings are reported in terms of the practitioner and manager groups; where individual practitioners or managers are referred to by gender this has been randomised to further support confidentiality in a small interview group.

The remaining chapters consider the findings of the case study in relation to the nature of management control, the impact of managerialism on street-level professional discretion and the relation of professional workers and their managers at the local level. Chapter 5 considers the motivations of managers. The domination and street-level perspectives characterise managers as committed to organisational values and in conflict with the concerns of the staff they manage. Studies of the motivation of managers are limited but, contrary to this picture, what is known about their motivation is that it is complex, and that a significant number of managers share similar concerns to those of practitioners—a view suggested by the discursive perspective. The case study points to views of managers at different levels of the organisation being significant and different, and to the views of local managers coinciding in important respects with those of local practitioners. The data suggest that the motivations of managers should not simply be equated with the policies and ideas of managerialism, but that there is also a continuing professional dimension in their concerns.

Managerial reforms have been closely associated with extending budgetary control and the development of policies and procedures guiding practice. Chapter 6 considers these strategies as techniques of remote control of street-level practice by senior managers. Evidence from the case study, particularly the Older Persons Team, suggests that budgetary control is a powerful technique used by senior managers and, increasingly, by central government to direct street-level practice. However, procedures are identified as crude tools of control which are open to interpretation and, paradoxically, give rise to extensive local discretion. Proceduralisation was more evident in the Older Persons Team than in the Mental Health Team (where the organisation emphasised the professionalism of staff). The case study data offer some support for the view that budgetary techniques of control are effective, but the extent of proceduralisation is uneven and the effectiveness of control through procedures is severely limited. The reason for the continuing importance of proceduralisation within social services is considered and the conclusion drawn that procedures play an important role in a rhetoric of blame and responsibility—a strategy of risk management by senior managers.

Chapter 7 focuses on the relationship between local managers and practitioners. It examines the idea that managers' and practitioners' interests are at odds, and that their relationship is fundamentally based on conflict. This idea, put forward by the domination and street-level perspectives, is challenged by the discursive perspective, which suggests that managers and practitioners might continue to share professional values. The evidence from the case study across both teams points to shared commitment to professional ideas of practice, and suggests that they work collusively to challenge and subvert aspects of policy which they see as running counter to their professional commitments.

The concluding chapter considers the contribution of the three models of discretion to the analysis of management control and worker freedom with managerialised public services. It draws together the themes of analysis and considers these broadly in relation to the case study, considering the basis on which more general conclusions can be drawn. The study's key conclusions point to the need to approach discretion in a more nuanced way than is suggested by Street-Level Bureaucracy Theory or Domination Managerialism. Instead I suggest an approach which, employing conjunctural analysis, identifies a range of factors, configuring discretion in particular ways in particular settings. The equating of management with managerialism is questioned: local managers, particularly, are identified as occupying a complex territory, involving managerial and professional commitments. In enforcing procedures, local managers consider their own ideas of professional roles and collude with local practitioners in ensuring that policy reflects continuing commitment to professional values in its implementation.

Chapter 1

The Street-Level Bureaucracy Perspective and Discretion

Introduction

Lipsky's account of discretion in street-level bureaucracies is closely related to his understanding of the relationship of managers and street-level bureaucrats. This chapter will outline this aspect of Lipsky's theory and consider the subsequent development of a street-level bureaucracy literature. Lipsky's analysis was well, but not uncritically, received when it was published. The contemporary reactions to *Street-Level Bureaucracy* will be outlined, as well as the literature that has sought to demonstrate and develop the street-level bureaucracy perspective through empirical research. These studies initially focused on demonstrating the validity of Lipsky's account of discretion. However, recently a more critical strand has developed in this literature, which has started to raise questions about aspects of Lipsky's analysis. The discussion will identify the claims of proponents of the street-level bureaucracy perspective that it is sufficient for the understanding of the motivation and behaviour of street-level bureaucrats (and their managers). It will then point to the need to consider wider issues, particularly the influence of professionalism—and related ideas of discretion and supervision—which raise questions about how street-level bureaucracies operate. In an examination of Lipsky's theory, key areas for further investigation are: the way in which professional street-level bureaucrats and their managers operate; and how this conforms to and differs from the picture Lipsky presents. In the final section of the chapter I will address questions that have been raised about the continuing relevance of Lipsky's theory in the context of the growing influence of managerialism within public services.

Lipsky's Analysis of Discretion

Discretion—the freedom in exercising one's work role—is a central concern for Lipsky in *Street-Level Bureaucracy*. In the complex and chaotic world of public service, he argues, discretion is necessary to make policy work, but the need for discretion can give rise to street-level practices that undermine effective policy implementation and the organisational accountability of street-level workers. Central to his examination of discretion is the tension he identifies in the relationship between street-level workers and organisational managers.

Lipsky's analysis of discretion in *Street-Level Bureaucracy* focuses on the nature and conditions of street-level bureaucrats' work and hierarchical control over their work. His account of discretion is closely tied to his analysis of work undertaken by front-line staff delivering services to individuals and communities from large public organisations, and the particular characteristics of these types of organisation. Lipsky's analysis developed in the context of the study of American urban politics in the 1960s and 1970s (Lipsky 1971, 1976, 1980). In the 25 years following the Second World War there was a significant expansion of public services at federal and local level, particularly in the late 1960s, with the expansion of social programmes associated with the war on poverty (Eisinger 1998). In this context, Lipsky observes that:

> The public sector has absorbed responsibilities previously discharged by private organisations in such diverse and critical areas as policing, education and health. Moreover, in all these fields government not only has supplanted private organisations but also has expanded the scope of responsibility of public ones (Lipsky 1980: 6).

Within the expanded public sector professionals in health, welfare and education had become powerful groups able to achieve significant discretion in their work (Lipsky 1980). However, in the mid-70s state and city public services were facing substantial cuts in their budgets (Diner 1998). The context of constrained public services, an environment of pressing demand, concern about funding levels and programme efficiency, and political conflict (Hawley and Lipsky 1976, Kaufman 1998) gave rise to Lipsky's understanding of street-level bureaucrats and street-level bureaucracies.

Lipsky's aim is to move away from traditional approaches to the study of public administration, which emphasised formal structures, and to examine the day-to-day conditions of policy implementation (Bream and Gates 1999). His work builds on a strand in post-war analysis of public bureaucracies that examined the balance of control and discretion in public service work and suggested that the balance was tilted towards discretion. Prottas, a research assistant of Lipsky's in his work on street-level bureaucracy, summarises the impact of this literature on the formulation of Lipsky's key problem: 'Street-level bureaucrats make public policy as it emerges on the street level, and ... they do so despite the massive mechanisms designed to control and direct their behaviour' (Prottas 1978).

Lipsky's explanation for this apparent paradox focuses on a picture of complex and confusing policies which, at street level, have to be interpreted, prioritised and made to work. In this context, he argues that the issue of discretion is central in policy analysis because: '... the routines they [street-level bureaucrats] establish, and the devices they invent to cope with uncertainties and work pressures effectively *become* [*his emphasis*] the public policies they carry out' (*ibid.* xiii). In effect, he says, they become significant policy-making actors—the '... street ministers of education, dispute settlement, and health services' (Lipsky 1980: 12).

The nature of the organisations within which street-level bureaucrats work is central to his understanding of their discretion. Lipsky characterises bureaucracies as public rather than business organisations and defines street-level bureaucracies as public bodies whose services are predominantly provided or allocated by street-level bureaucrats. Street-level bureaucrats are not all public service employees, but those:

> ... who interact directly with citizens in the course of their jobs, and who have substantial discretion in the execution of their work ... typical street-level bureaucrats are teachers, police officers and other law enforcement personnel, social workers, judges, public lawyers and other court officials and many other public officials who grant access to government programs and provide services within them (*ibid.* 3).

Furthermore, Lipsky presents street-level bureaucracies as difficult organisations within which to work, characterised by the challenging working conditions they create for workers—conditions of resource shortages and policy confusion (Lipsky 1991). This environment of uncertainty and scarcity is placed at the centre of Lipsky's understanding of the dilemmas and tensions that impact on street-level bureaucrats' work and extend their discretion. According to his account, policy objectives tend to be ambitious, ambiguous, vague or conflicting, and have to be matched to resources. Working in the context of policy complexity and resource paucity that characterise street-level bureaucracies, street-level bureaucrats have to make sense of what their work involves and survive by prioritising policies, choosing between incompatible policies and ignoring impractical policies (Lipsky 1980). For Lipsky these conditions are not incidental but are fundamental to understanding street-level bureaucracy: 'The analysis presented here depends upon the presence of the aforementioned working conditions. If for some reason these characteristics are not present, the analysis is less likely to be appropriate ...' (*ibid.* 28).

According to Lipsky street-level bureaucrats, unlike similar workers in other bureaucracies, '... have considerable discretion in determining the nature, amount, and quality of benefits and sanctions provided by their agencies' (*ibid.* 13). Street-level bureaucrats are involved in dynamic work situations, where there is a need to respond to the human dimension of service. It is work made up of: '... complex tasks for which elaboration of rules, guidelines, or instructions cannot circumscribe the alternative' (*ibid.* 15). They need discretion to respond to the unexpected and to ensure that services are responsive to individual need. Lipsky does not claim this to be the case for every piece of work carried out, but argues that, within their role, there is a recognition that situations can arise that will call for them to think on their feet and produce appropriate responses. However: '... possible responses are often circumscribed, for example, by the prevailing statutory provisions of the law or the categories of services to which recipients can be assigned' (*ibid.* 161). The tension between the requirement to follow organisational guidelines and responsiveness to individual requirements is at the heart of Lipsky's analysis of discretion. For him, the organisational characteristics that delineate formal discretion paradoxically create both pressures and opportunities to act beyond the street-level worker's formal role.

In summary, Lipsky characterises street-level bureaucrats' conditions of work as 'the corrupted world of service' (*ibid.* xiii). He talks of: 'The ambiguity and unclarity of goals and the unavailability of appropriate performance measures in street-level bureaucracies' (*ibid.* 40). Street-level bureaucrats have to work with ill-defined organisational goals and unrealistically high public expectations of the agency and its staff. Policy objectives tend to be overblown, ambiguous, vague or conflicting. The problem of policy imprecision is compounded by insufficient resources for the job. They have fragmented contact with their clients, work with people from diverse backgrounds and need to make rapid decisions, typically under conditions of limited time and information. Simultaneously, the services that street-level bureaucracies provide are under-resourced to meet demand. In this context street-level bureaucrats have to exercise discretion; they have choices to make about services and how they are delivered. They have to decide how to make policy work through exercising discretion about whom to help, which needs to meet and which policies to follow.

For Lipsky this level of discretion is a problem because it threatens policy implementation. Managers find it difficult to control and direct discretion in line with organisational goals. He emphasises the problems that managers have in controlling street-level bureaucrats, whose goals are, he argues, fundamentally different from theirs and the organisation's. Lipsky's analysis of this problem of control is not just in terms of managers' ability to monitor and apply solutions but also in terms of the micro politics—the conflict and dependency that exist between street-level workers and their managers.

Street-Level Bureaucrats and their Managers

For Lipsky, street-level bureaucrats and their managers operate in significantly different ways. They have different job priorities and commitments and different values, and they use different strategies. Street-level bureaucrats want at least to make the conditions of their work as bearable as possible and, where they can, to take control of the direction of their work. In contrast, managers are concerned with implementing the policy that they are directed to put into effect, and with doing this as effectively as possible. Street-level bureaucrats are guided by their own preferences, including a desire to maintain as much discretion as possible, and tend only to follow those agency objectives to which sanctions are attached. Managers, however, have a clear commitment to carrying out policy. While managers are committed to equal treatment, workers' commitment to procedural fairness is more ambivalent: they want to treat people on an equal basis, but they also want to adapt the rules and they bring their own concerns into play.

Street-level bureaucrats and managers in Lipsky's account are, then, in separate, antagonistic camps:

> ... it is a relationship best conceived in large part as intrinsically conflictual. The role of the street-level bureaucrat is associated with client-processing goals and orientations directed toward maximizing goals. Managers' roles in this context are associated with worker–management goals directed toward aggregate achievement of the work unit and orientations directed toward minimizing autonomy (*ibid.* 25).

Lipsky also argues that, while they may well have different interests, street-level bureaucrats and managers work with one another, and often have to compromise to achieve their different goals as best they can. Managers have power, but it is limited in a number of ways. Surveillance and sanctions cost in terms of time and disruption. Regulation of the workforce to induce performance through the manipulation of benefits and sanctions tends to be limited by employment rights. Managers can also make work more or less interesting for individuals; but these opportunities tend to be on the margins. Managers, then, in Lipsky's view, are: '... ultimately constrained by law, labor agreements, political opposition and worker solidarity from dictating decisions or otherwise compromising the role of street-level workers in determinations about individual clients' (Lipsky 1991: 216–217). Significantly, managers also need workers to perform. If the job is not done, it reflects not only on workers but also on managers themselves. Their status as managers relies on being seen to get the job done, which in turn is largely in the gift of the workers: 'Workers can punish supervisors who do not behave properly toward them, either by refusing to perform work of certain kinds, by doing only minimal work, or by doing work rigidly so as to discredit supervisors' (Lipsky 1980: 25). Similarly, workers can bend and break rules, but they are also aware that managers wield power and that non-compliance, if pushed too far, could give rise to sanction: 'Formal sanctions, although costly for managers to invoke, are also costly to workers, who thus try to avoid receiving them' (*ibid.* 24).

The relationship between street-level bureaucrats and their managers is one of:

> ... mutual dependency. Thus managers typically attempt to honor workers' preferences if they are rewarded by reciprocity in job performance. To a degree reciprocity will characterize all working relations; in street-level bureaucracies, however, the resources of lower-level workers are greater than those often possessed by subordinates in other work contexts. Hence, the potential for reciprocity is greater (*ibid.* 25).

Management control and street-level discretion are, in part, an armistice between managers and workers. However, managers also have to accept their own limited ability to control and direct street-level bureaucrats (*ibid.* 164).

The 'corrupted world of service' described above affects managers as well as street-level workers: street-level bureaucracies are difficult organisations to run. Management strategies of control, such as performance measures, are difficult to put into effect in the conditions of street-level bureaucracies. It is problematic, for instance, to define what a 'good' service is; and there is the constant risk that imposing crude performance measures could distort service delivery: 'There is often a fine line between inducing workers to better conform to agency policies and inducing workers to be open to fewer options and opportunities for clients' (*ibid.* 164). Furthermore: '… street-level bureaucrats, in recognition of the importance performance measures have to limiting their autonomy, actively resist their development and application' (*ibid.* 53).

Another aspect of the tension in the relationship between managers and street-level bureaucrats is reciprocity in the operation of discretion: managers allow the letter of policy to slip, provided street-level bureaucrats respect its spirit. But for Lipsky this is a 'cold-war' reciprocity, based on a recognition of limited power and distrust. This becomes evident in his detailed analysis of the nature of discretion in street-level bureaucracies.

Professionals and Street-Level Bureaucracy

The everyday world of public service involves conflicting priorities, cost concerns and inadequate resources and street-level bureaucrats frequently find themselves having to make sense of rules and procedures that collapse complex goals with many, often conflicting or outright contradictory aspects, paradoxically creating further confusion. Human services can also throw up situations for which policy has not yet been developed, and street-level bureaucrats are left to decide policy for themselves. Within this broad framework of policies, discretion involves being practical and pragmatic; not letting the detail get in the way of the service; abiding by the spirit, if not the letter of policy:

> It is desirable to clarify objectives if they are needlessly and irrelevantly fuzzy or contradictory. However, while agency goals may be unclear or contradictory for reasons of neglect and historical inertia, they may also be unclear or contradictory because they reflect the contradictory impulses of the society the agency serves. The dilemma for accountability is to know when goal clarification is desirable, because continued ambivalence and contradiction are unproductive, and when it will result in a reduction in the scope and mission of public services (*ibid.* 165).

Lipsky argues that in response to this inevitable policy tension and confusion street-level bureaucrats either leave, buckle under the strain or stay, adapt and survive. The adaptations identified by Lipsky involve either a narrow idea of discretion or one that is very wide-ranging.

Some street-level bureaucrats, Lipsky argues, adopt a bureaucratic stance, following rules and using only a very limited idea of discretion in the sense of retaining a basic flexibility to respond to different human needs as fundamental to the provision of human services. He also identifies an extreme version of this approach, which involves workers hiding behind rules and regulations, as a defence against discretion; denying their freedom and flexibility to make policy work and operating strictly according to rules and regulations:

> Workers seek to deny that they have influence, are free to make decisions, or offer service alternatives. Strict adherence to rules, and refusals to make exceptions when exceptions might be made … "it's the law", and similar rationalisations not only protect workers from client pressures, but also protect them from confronting their own shortcomings (*ibid.* 149).

An opposite response is also identified by Lipsky. Because of the extent and need for discretion at street level, street-level bureaucrats can turn discretion against policy: 'They may assert discretionary dimensions of their job to a greater degree than called for in theory …' (*ibid.* 150). They have leeway not only to work in accordance with organisational goals, but also to operate in ways which contravene or subvert those goals, making it relatively easy for workers to tailor their behaviour to avoid accountability: 'Street-level bureaucrats resist organizational pressures with their own resources. Some of these resources are common to public service workers generally and some are inherent in their position as policy deliverers with broad discretion' (*ibid.* 25). The key tactics which street-level bureaucrats can use to circumvent interference from supervisors are: control of information upwards; playing on the essentially private nature of their work; and exploitation of management's reliance on their good will and initiative, on which continuing service provision depends.

Lipsky is critical of what he sees as this tendency of street-level bureaucrats to either minimise or maximise their discretion. He sees them as distorting public policy in ways which undermine managers' emphasis on using discretion pragmatically to best achieve policy-makers' intentions. Street-level bureaucrats become the key policy-makers, resulting in a democratic and accountability deficit: 'The political significance of routines is highlighted by the fact that the policies that result from routine treatment are often biased in ways unintended by agencies whose policies are being implemented or are antithetical to some of their objectives' (*ibid.* 84).

However, Lipsky does not give sufficient attention to the possibility that some street-level bureaucrats'—such as professional workers—may be required to exercise extensive discretion by the organisation because of their particular attributes. He also equates policy distortion with the freedom that street-level bureaucrats exercise and fails to acknowledge that policy outcomes are the aggregate of activity within the organisation, and may be the result of management discretion, as much as that of front-line workers.

Contemporary Reaction to *Street-Level Bureaucracy*

The general reaction to *Street-Level Bureaucracy* when it was published was positive (Anon 1981, Hasenfeld 1981, Joffe 1981, Magnusson 1981, Perlman 1981, Goldner 1982, Hill 1982, Yates 1982, Stone 1983). Goldner, for instance, described it as a rich compilation and summary of 'what we know about worker discretion' (Goldner 1982: 153), while Yates saw it as an important and original contribution to public administration scholarship (Yates 1982). Stone welcomed the work as a timely contribution to understanding a key problem in public policy around the gap between high expectations for services and problematic delivery (Stone 1983). However, within this generally positive picture reviewers were not uncritical, and it is possible to identify two key critical themes in their comments on *Street-Level Bureaucracy* which relate to discretion.

The first set of criticisms relates to the sweeping nature of Lipsky's account of street-level bureaucracy. Commentators point out the need to recognise that street-level bureaucrats and street-level bureaucracies, while they have some similar characteristics, may also be significantly different. An anonymous reviewer in the *Michigan Law Review* (Anon 1981) is critical of the absence of a nuanced account, pointing out that:

> [Lipsky's] analysis suffers from the inevitable difficulty of fitting into one mold such diverse services as police patrols, elementary school classes, and legal services interviews ... Lipsky's method emphasizes selected similarities but does not highlight differences that might have provided additional insight (*ibid.* 813–814).

Hasenfeld argues that Lipsky fails to take sufficient account of the impact of different political and economic contexts of practice. While he accepts that street-level bureaucracies are generally under-resourced, he points out that the level of under-resourcing and the nature of the policy context of practice can vary and that these variations can, in turn, affect the opportunities that street-level bureaucrats have to respond positively or negatively in the situations they encounter (Hasenfeld 1981).

The second theme concerns the implementation gap in policy, discretion and the role of managers. These critics suggest that the unanticipated policy outcomes from street-level bureaucracies that Lipsky ascribes to street-level bureaucrats are more likely to be the result of a complex, multi-layered and multi-actor process than the result of the actions of one group of workers. Several commentators are critical of Lipsky's focus on street-level bureaucrats as the key policy-makers. While they agree that street-level bureaucrats play a role in changing and implementing policy, they point out that the response of street-level bureaucrats to their situation—such as rationing contact time—may be a management strategy, as opposed to a worker response (Anon 1981) Hasenfeld states that: 'There simply is no evidence to support his argument that the service practice in the welfare departments or the school system are more a function of the discretion of lower-level workers than the deliberate policies of the organisational elites ...', and goes on to say that this is not to deny the importance of street-level discretion, 'but to suggest that its impact is far more limited than the author implies' (Hasenfeld 1981: 156).

Furthermore, the emphasis on the role of street-level bureaucrats to explain policy distortions does not acknowledge the part of managers and policy-makers throughout the organisational hierarchy, who themselves play a role in developing and changing policy, and who often use 'technical experts' to provide them with cover when problems arise in the implementation of their own, impractical strategic policies (Stone 1983).

Critical Examination of Lipsky's Analysis

Street-level bureaucrats and 'professionals'

Lipsky's account emphasises the generic characteristics of street-level bureaucracies, the nature of their discretion, its control and its use. However, I would argue that there is some confusion about the way street-level bureaucrats are conceptualised. This touches on how discretion might be approached by street-level bureaucrats and how the relationship with managers is negotiated. Professionalism, for instance, can influence the nature of discretion and the nature of the relationship between practitioners and managers (Freidson 1994). Lipsky's theory is so intent on emphasising similarities that it fails to take sufficient account of differences in occupational status and their potential impact on the elaboration of his perspective.

A central issue here is Lipsky's treatment of professional street-level bureaucrats (and bureaucracies). In his account of street-level bureaucracies Lipsky often talks of street-level bureaucrats as 'professionals' (Magnusson 1981: 213). As noted above he also characterises street-level bureaucrats as possessing substantial discretion in the exercise of their work (Lipsky 1980). The use of the term 'professional' can range from being synonymous with skilled, often white-collar, staff to a more restricted meaning of an occupational group that has certain attributes, status and power (Johnson 1972). However, while there is a wide range of skilled workers, professionals are generally thought of as different because of their particular skills, values and status, which afford them some degree of control and regulation over their work (Freidson 1994). Lipsky uses 'professional' in both ways. He tends to use it in the first broad sense throughout *Street-Level Bureaucracy* to cover the wide range of public employees he identifies as street-level bureaucrats. But he also talks about the professional norms and commitments of street-level bureaucrats, alluding to the narrower idea of professionals. Here he seems to be eliding 'street-level bureaucrat' with the more restricted term of 'professional'. He includes in his definition of street-level bureaucrats a number of occupations—lawyers, doctors, teachers, and social workers (Lipsky 1980)—that would be considered professional in the technical, restricted sense.

The significance of whether street-level bureaucrats are conceived of as white-collar employees or more narrowly as professional staff is threefold.

First, it influences the coverage of the perspective. The narrow sense of 'professional' would restrict its application to a limited range of public welfare bureaucracies which predominantly employ professionals at street level, whereas the first sense is more inclusive. In relation to the coverage of the theory, Lipsky clearly sees it as wide-ranging and inclusive: 'In developing the street-level framework, I identify the common elements of occupations as apparently disparate as, say, police officer and social worker' (*ibid.* xvi).

Secondly, the idea of a core of necessary discretion to do the job (see above) would involve very different claims depending on how street-level bureaucrats' professionalism is understood. The nature and extent of discretion is likely to be both more robust and more extensive if street-level bureaucrats are understood to be professionals in the narrow sense, rather than if they are understood as all white-collar staff. When Lipsky alludes to the street-level bureaucrat's attributes, he seems to be using this narrower sense of 'professionalism'. To the extent that street-level bureaucrats are professionals, the assertion that they exercise considerable discretion is fairly obvious. Professionals are expected to exercise discretionary judgement in their field. They are regularly deferred to in their specialised areas of work and are relatively free from supervision by superiors.

This fluid use of the notion of 'professional' is problematic, in that it fails to distinguish the level of discretion available to all street-level bureaucrats from that additionally available to street-level bureaucrats who are professionals in a narrow sense.

Finally, where street-level bureaucrats are seen as professionals in the narrow sense, it points to another perspective on their organisation and its managers' expectations of their use of discretion. This is the idea that professionals have a role not only in implementing policy but also in developing it. This notion is central, for instance, in understanding the role of professionals in the post-war British welfare state in translating general welfare rights into particular provision (Marshall and Rees 1985) and has also been noted in American public administration (Kadish and Kadish 1973). The emphasis here is on regarding obligations not in an unquestioning way but responsibly and thoughtfully. Discretion is necessary not only because of possible conflicts between means and ends, as Lipsky suggests, but also because policy is necessarily sketchy, requiring professional staff to create and develop a workable policy in practice.

For the most part, Lipsky is concerned with the common experience of street-level bureaucrats and their general responses as workers. While he acknowledges—almost as an afterthought—that there may be differences between workers, his emphasis is on their commonalities (Lipksy 1980). He is focused on his goal of developing a universal approach to street-level bureaucracy. Lipsky tends to emphasise the 'central tendencies' (*ibid.* xvi) in diverse public services—the (lowest) common denominators of discretion, difficult work conditions, challenges to central control and a discretionary response to these conditions that emphasises pragmatism over idealism.

Managers and Street-Level Bureaucracy

A similar comment could be made about Lipsky's account of managers in street-level bureaucracies. He presents managers in stark, undifferentiated terms as obedient organisational agents. The basis for this is unclear in the body of his argument. While in *Street-Level Bureaucracy* he recognises that: 'The focus on the divergence of objectives between the organization and lowest-level workers could with some modifications be applied to the relation between lowest-level supervisor and the roles to which this position is subordinate' (Lipsky 1980: 216), he does not develop this point; in fact he leaves it out of the main body of his argument, locating it in a footnote at the end of the book. This is surprising, because the implications of this observation for his argument are significant for understanding the role of managers and the relationships between layers of management within the organisation. The implication is that policy, the standard that Lipsky assumes can be used to assess the use of discretion, is not simply transmitted through layers of management in the organisation unaltered, but that, in the same way that street-level bureaucrats adapt the objectives of their managers, so their supervisors adapt the objectives they have been given by their supervisors, and so on. Managers, as well as street-level bureaucrats, exercise discretion.

Actors and motives

This discussion relates back to the micro-politics of the relationship between street-level bureaucrats and their managers. Lipsky characterises managers and street-level bureaucrats as having fundamentally different orientations. Managers, according to Lipsky, are the creatures of the organisation; workers seek to resist it. However, in line with the earlier argument, where street-level bureaucrats are professionals, the nature of their relationship with management may be very different from this: professionals working in organisations tend to be managed, at least at the level of their immediate supervision, by fellow professionals (Freidson 1994). Here Gouldner's distinction between cosmopolitans and locals is instructive. Looking at the orientation of workers within organisations, he distinguishes locals, who identify with and are loyal to the organisation, from cosmopolitans, who identify more with their peers, who have specialist skills and professional commitments (Gouldner 1957). Accordingly the concerns, priorities and commitments of the professional group may cut across the antagonism and conflict which Lipsky sees as inevitable in the relationship of street-level bureaucrats and their managers, and it may be the basis for shared commitments that are strikingly different from official policy. This suggests the need to analyse the practices of street-level bureaucrats and their managers in a way which can recognise additional professional responsibilities, commitments, and so on, that professional street-level bureaucrats and managers may have—and how these impact on their working relationship—as well as those they share with other street-level bureaucrats and other managers respectively.

Lipsky's perspective is seen as applicable to all street-level workers, including professional staff, through the adoption of a level of generalisation that denudes organisations and organisational actors of important characteristics. (This seems to reflect an assumption that these workers have been de-professionalised. However, this is an empirical question that requires empirical investigation and cannot simply be assumed.)

My argument here is that, in developing the street-level bureaucracy perspective, Lipsky has over emphasised central tendencies and, in the process of doing this, has ignored diversity and relegated differences to footnotes and passing comments. However, the observations above suggest that the street-level perspective is best approached as a tentative framework rather than as a fully developed model of how all street-level bureaucracies work. *Street-Level Bureaucracy* is a starting point for analysis—a picture of factors which helps us to understand these complex public organisations but which also requires critical adaptation and augmentation to take account of specific differences in particular settings. Lipsky, I would argue, recognises this when he points out that:

> Just as one of the most important contributions of the concept of 'professionalism' is to facilitate understanding of the difference between, say, doctors and nurses, in the same way the concept of street-level bureaucracy should encourage exploration of important differences in public service as well as contribute to an understanding of central tendencies that they share … it is to be expected that an elaboration of central tendencies such as the description of street-level bureaucracy cannot apply evenly to all the cases from which the generalizations are drawn (Lipsky 1980: xvi).

However, Lipsky fails to foreground this tentative dimension of his analysis in the analytical framework.

Street-Level Bureaucracy Theory and Empirical Research

As the body of research associated with the street-level bureaucracy perspective has developed (primarily in the USA), similar issues to those identified above have emerged. Initially, the empirical research focused on demonstrating the basic claims of street-level bureaucracy: that street-level bureaucrats exercised significant discretion in terms of their ability to select and adapt policy through implementation and practice. However, particularly in the past decade, a more critical literature has also developed which has questioned important assumptions of the street-level bureaucracy approach.

Street-level bureaucrats: Employees or professionals

A central theme in the research, especially in the initial stage, involves the validity of the street-level bureaucracy perspective, particularly through demonstrating the extent of discretion exercised by street-level bureaucrats. Lovrich *et al.* (1986) present the findings of a survey of the employees of Washington State, which, they argue, provide empirical validation of Lipsky's theory (Lovrich *et al.* 1986). The survey, which involves 781 state employees (75 per cent of the work force responded), looks at workers' perception of their work and the organisational context. Respondents are categorised as street-level bureaucrats or non-street-level bureaucrats. The researchers find that street-level bureaucrats are demonstrably more active than non-street-level bureaucrats in seeking opportunities to develop and use their discretionary power, and that there is a general perception amongst the interviewees that fellow street-level bureaucrats do not stick to the letter of agency rules.

Another study looks at how police patrol officers define their jobs in different ways from their supervisors (Gianakis 1994). Gianakis' survey of patrol officers in a city in Florida (206 out of 294 officers) is supplemented by interviews with a small number of officers and supervisors. He finds that, while there is a broad surface agreement about what the job involves—which could be specified in job appraisals etc.—this still leaves considerable room for operational individualism and job-customising by each officer. In Gianakis' view, this confirms Lipsky's claim that public servants function as *de facto* policy-makers in that they decide how to define and operate their particular role and so directly determine the quality and nature of the service they provide.

Brodkin (1997) and Meyers, Glaser and MacDonald (1998) look at the implementation of 'welfare to work' programmes in two US states (Illinois and California). Brodkin looks at the Job Opportunities and Basic Skills (JOBS) programme in Chicago and does supplementary research on Work Pays programmes in California. Meyers, Glaser and MacDonald look at the Work Pays programme in California. While these are separate studies, the authors of both acknowledge the other and make links between them, drawing similar conclusions (Brodkin 1997 and Meyers *et al.* 1998). In both the JOBS and Work Pays programmes, Brodkin and Meyers *et al.* are interested in the way workers respond to both a new policy and a new role—no longer just determining eligibility for benefits, but now required to encourage welfare beneficiaries to consider work as an alternative to benefits and provide advice and guidance on services to enable people to reintegrate in the work world where appropriate. Brodkin finds that street-level bureaucrats used their discretion to resist the new policy: '... case workers routinely failed to elicit this information [about special circumstances] or respond when clients indicated problems' (Brodkin 1997: 22). Meyers *et al.* also identify problems with programme implementation. They find that both workers and their office superiors explicitly disavow responsibility or even authority to discuss entry into work with clients (Meyers *et al.* 1998). Furthermore, workers frustrate the programme by failing to exercise positive discretion (that is, actively promote the Work Pays message) and relying heavily on routinised and scripted interviews.

Winter (2002) and May and Wood (2003) have also looked at discretion in relation to street-level bureaucrats who perform regulatory roles. These researchers tend to talk about discretion in terms of different regulatory styles, pointing out that while some street-level bureaucrats choose to adopt a literalist approach to the regulations they enforce, others operate within a more flexible understanding of the regulations, seeking to educate and persuade those they regulate into complying with regulations, and only enforcing them in extreme circumstances.

A common theme in these studies is the way in which they approach street-level bureaucrats as an homogenous group—as employees, as workers employed to implement policy—taking this as the basis upon which any exercise of discretion by them should be understood. In part, this view may reflect the fact that many of the empirical studies have focused on non-professional street-level bureaucrats: police patrol officers, welfare clerks etc. (Brodkin 1997, Gianakis 1994, Lovrich *et al.* 1986, Meyers *et al.* 1998, Jewell and Glasser 2006). However, it also seems to reflect a conscious decision to see street-level bureaucrats as non-professionals. In one study, for instance, professional staff are excluded from the street-level bureaucrat category: 'professional/technical job classifications were assigned to the management/specialist group' (Lovrich *et al.* 1986: 21); and the implication of adopting a street-level bureaucrat as employee perspective is exemplified by Brodkin (1997) and Meyers *et al.* (1998), as seen above. Meyers *et al.* and Brodkin are critical of the workers for not being responsive to their employers' changing requirements in implementing policies, and for not adapting and changing their practices to achieve this; they fail to consider the possibility that workers are not skilled in terms of the new role, or that they may see it as inappropriate to jettison their established role and take on a new role. Similarly Jewell and Glaser (2006) build on this work to develop a framework for the analysis of organisational factors that influence street-level behaviour. While they see their work as generalisable to street-level bureaucracies, it is exclusively based on studies of non-professional staff in primarily programme administration roles. They also fail to take account of the particular attributes and claims of professional staff that can arise in such areas as knowledge and skills and role expectation.

While the conceptualisation of the street-level bureaucrat as including professionals is not a prevalent reading, it is the focus of one empirical study. Kelly (1994) distinguishes between professional and non-professional street bureaucrats in order to explore their approach to discretion. She looks at street-level bureaucrats, their work context and their ability to exercise discretion. Her research involves open-ended interviews with 28 professionally qualified school teachers and 15 unqualified welfare workers, and she analyses their stories of justice and injustice. She finds that different groups of workers report significantly different organisational cultures, allowing them greater or lesser freedom to put their beliefs into effect in their work. The teachers she interviews are encouraged to be innovative and have significant freedom to achieve what they see as fair outcomes—e.g. in grades (Kelly 1994: 122–131); while, in contrast, the welfare workers constantly reiterate their lack of freedom and the rule-centred nature of their work.

Kelly's findings are also interesting because, in contrast to the major strand of empirical research, they suggest that there is a difference in the degrees of discretion available to different groups of street-level bureaucrats, such as professional workers, who, because of the contexts within which they work and different evaluations of their role, have different levels of discretion.

Managers and discretion

As mentioned above, Lipsky's account of the role of managers is both ambivalent and emphatic. While he acknowledges, *en passant*, that managers may themselves adapt and change policy in the process of implementation, as well as acting as straightforward policy implementers, he emphasises their role as obedient and committed implementers of policy.

An assumption of the street-level bureaucracy perspective that is directly questioned in the empirical research is that managers act only to put policy into practice, even if it sometimes involves recognising the limitations of their ability to direct street-level workers and make strategic compromises with street-level practices. The perspective accepts that managers tweak policies, or compromise with street-level discretion, but asserts that they do this only: '… to increase the probability that outcomes on the whole will be more favourable to the preferred policy direction' (Lipsky 1991: 216). However, research looking at the influence on policy implementation of senior officers in the local variations found in highly centralised systems of welfare provision suggests that these managers are themselves significant policy actors.

Keiser (1999) looks at the variations in the level of disability benefit payments between American states. (The disability benefits programme at the time of the study was funded by the federal government but administered by states.) Keiser considers local economic and political factors to identify influences on variations in funding. He looks at policy outcomes—the *de facto* policy of the bureaucracy— which, in terms of the logic of the street-level bureaucracy perspective, are the products of street-level bureaucrat behaviour. However, he points out that a factor in the variation between states is the influence of senior state officials in the policy implementation process.

An earlier study, by Weissert (1994), also points to the role of senior officials using their discretion to influence and change policy. Weissert looks at variations in spending between local welfare offices on Medicaid within Michigan, a state renowned for its highly centralised and proceduralised system. Despite strict policies of eligibility and monitoring of caseworkers, he finds that there is still a good deal of room for local discretion. Weissert contrasts generous offices, characterised by a 'culture of service giving', with non-generous offices, characterised by a 'culture of poverty' (*ibid.* 229). Seeking to account for this difference, he finds that: '… while supply, demand and political factors are important in predicting intrastate Medicaid spending patterns in Michigan, recipient behaviour—shaped in large part by the behaviour of the social service office leadership and the environment of the county—matters as well' (*ibid.* 225). The style of local directors differs in terms of the importance of following rules and guidelines, and reflects different managerial goals and work styles: '… the office manager's discretion, attitude, and activism in the community differed substantially … equated with the generosity of the office in Medicaid spending and participation' (*ibid.* 251). In contrast to the influence of local managers, Weissert does not identify caseworkers as playing a significant role in local policy variations. However, he points out that this may be a result of his method of data collection—caseworkers were surveyed using close-ended questions—and that the: '… professionalism and discretion of caseworkers and political party association were difficult to assess even in the more detailed analyses of six counties, and they need further attention as well as future studies' (*ibid.* 251).

In another study, looking at the role played by local police departments in the implementation of legislation, Grattet and Jenness (2005) found that local policy departments took an active role in interpreting state law. They found that:

> … police administrators possess considerable authority to "set the tone" for how their department will do its work as personnel discharge their duty to enforce criminal law. One way they do this is through agency policy, which is designed to reduce officer discretion and signal the agency's philosophical commitments. Understanding how local law enforcement agencies exercise discretion at the organizational level by creating agency policy requires orienting to police and sheriff's departments as sites of legal meaning-making (*ibid.* 935).

Furthermore, at the level of line management, Meyers *et al.*, in their study of the Work Pays Programme (mentioned above), also find that managers play as significant a policy-making role as the street-level bureaucrats they manage. Contrary to the picture of the obedient manager and recalcitrant street-level bureaucrat, they identify first-tier managers as actively resisting policy, pointing out that managers as well as workers block policy implementation and seek to disavow responsibility for reorientation the service that they manage (Meyers *et al.* 1998).

Conclusion

Lipsky presents street-level bureaucracy not simply as bureaucratic public administration but as a context within which managers seek to control, as well as coordinate staff with extensive discretion. However, he argues, the nature of the organisation—particularly its wide-ranging and imprecise goals and the mismatch between resources and policy—and the limited ability of managers to control street-level staff give rise to extensive street-level discretion. Discretion is a result of street-level staff's ability to circumvent control and managers' need to collude with them in order to get the job done. This is a picture supported by the empirical research. Nevertheless, a close reading of Lipsky's analysis raises questions about the nature of discretion that is available to different street-level bureaucrats and points to professional status as a significant factor in enhanced levels of discretion. While most of the research within a street-level bureaucracy perspective has not explored this question, one study by Kelly points to important differences in discretion between a professional and non-professional staff group. This is an area of the theory that requires further investigation. In addition, Lipsky's account of the role of managers—and the empirical research—raise questions about his portrayal of managers as simply compliant policy implementers. This area has not been extensively researched, and again highlights the need for further exploration. The relationship between managers and street-level bureaucrats is rather starkly drawn, in terms of opposed interests and concerns. When professionalism is introduced into understanding the organisation of street-level bureaucracies, it suggests the need to consider the role of managers and their relationship with the professional street-level bureaucrats whom they manage. Shared professional concerns may break down the barrier which, Lipsky suggests, divides managers and street-level bureaucrats. Where managers and street-level bureaucrats share professional concerns, this may lead to cooperation and collusion—not necessarily, as Lipsky suggests, on the basis of purely pragmatic concerns, but perhaps also in the pursuit of shared professional commitments.

These issues will be now be explored through the examination of social work discretion within British Social Services, as an example of street-level bureaucrats and their operation in street-level bureaucracies.

Chapter 2
Social Services—Street-Level Bureaucracies?

Introduction

The preceding chapter looked at Lipsky's examination of discretion and management control in street-level bureaucracies and considered the research literature that developed in response to this work. The issues arising from the examination of the perspective in relation to the operation of discretion focus on its characterisation of management within street-level bureaucracies; the impact of professional claims and status on the extent of discretion exercised by street-level workers; and, related to this, their impact on the nature of the relationship between managers and the street-level workers they manage. These issues will be explored through the examination of the management and practice of social work discretion within British Social Services.

When *Street-Level Bureaucracy* was first published in Britain it was greeted as a cogent and credible account of the extensive discretionary practices of employees of public bodies such as Social Services: '... too much rings true ... for it to be dismissed as a recital of American problems ...' (Hill 1982: 78–80). In the decade following the publication of *Street-Level Bureaucracy* in Britain, Hudson has observed that it was a valuable but little-used research perspective in the study of public services (Hudson 1993). However, in the past decade there has been a resurgence of interest in Lipsky's work in Britain, where it has been employed in the analysis of Social Services (Baldwin 1998, 2000, 2004 and Ellis *et al.* 1999 Ellis 2007), social circumstances reports in the criminal justice system (Halliday *et al.* 2008), the administration of housing benefit (Blackmore 2001), GP services (Checkland 2004), and discharge from hospital care (Allen *et al.* 2004).

A Redundant or a Relevant Perspective?

Welfare services in Britain up until the early 1980s have been characterised by observers as dominated by professionals and discretion. This was a golden age of professionalism—a period in which: '... Doctors, teachers and social workers were granted a major role in policy-making, power to define needs and problems, power in resource allocation, power over people, and substantial control over their own area of work' (Foster and Wilding 2000: 144). *Street-Level Bureaucracy* was published in this context; critics associate its arguments about discretion with this context, and argue that, in the wake of public sector reforms, which have increased the power of managers and management ideas in welfare organisations, the theory is increasingly irrelevant (Howe 1991, Cheetham 1993). These critics point to the strategies of Conservative governments in the 1980s and early 1990s, which sought to challenge what they saw as professional domination of welfare services, and to control this through the promotion of managerialism—the idea that managers should be in control of public organisations and that they should run these organisations in line with business principles and concerns.

Across welfare organisations these strategies were reflected in increased scrutiny and inspection; and attempts to insert a business culture and ethic through performance measurement and regimes of competition. Administrators were transformed into, or replaced by, managers. These managers were explicitly required to pay attention to the bottom lines of efficiency and financial probity. Throughout the public sector there was an increase both in the number of managers and in their intrusion into the regulation of day-to-day practice (Foster and Wilding 2000). In social services, these processes came together in the major reform of community care associated with the NHS Community Care Act 1990.

Community care reforms were driven by government's concern to control public expenditure (particularly, to limit spending on residential care); and to shift the role of public welfare from direct provision to purchasing services in a mixed economy of care (Lewis and Glennerster 1996). In practical terms, these goals were achieved by promoting care management as the primary function of adult care social workers. Practitioners were to assess needs and identify appropriate services in the community; and also to make decisions about which needs should be met at public expense (Department of Health 1991).

Care management entailed a process of assessment, planning and arranging for services which were then subject to regular review. Practitioners were required to decide whether a person's needs, identified in the assessment process, should be met by the local authority in the light of eligibility criteria, which described the type and level of need that the authority considered itself liable to meet. The reforms shifted social work into a role more liable to management supervision, identifying steps and processes that could be monitored, and were also accompanied by the development of procedures which specified how the role should be carried out; and eligibility criteria, which specified entitlement. Commentators argued, social workers within local authorities had lost their discretion.

Howe's argument is interesting here because of the challenge it makes to a core proposition of the street-level bureaucracy perspective: that is, the extensive nature of discretion at street level within street-level bureaucracies. He fundamentally disagrees with this view in relation to social work and Social Services: 'Most of the writing by social workers about social work is still discussed by its practitioners as if they are a group capable of determining all that they do' (Howe 1991a: 203). He characterises Lipsky's argument as an 'interesting and clever boost for the advocates of professional discretion, through its emphasis on the active role of street-level bureaucrats, including social workers, in the implementation and interpretation of public policy' (*ibid.* 203–204). However, he is sceptical about the applicability of Lipsky's framework in the changed context of state social work, which has resulted in a decisive shift in power away from practitioner discretion and towards practice defined and driven by managers (Howe 1986, 1991a, 1991b, 1996).

Howe's argument draws on a study he undertook in the early 1980s examining the role of social workers within Social Services (Howe 1986). He concluded from this study that managers have now displaced professionals as the key players in Social Services, and now control practice: '... the basic design of services, including the routes to them and the gateways met on the way, is constructed by managers interpreting legislation' (*ibid.* 130). Within the organisation managers, he argues, are now the only people with discretion, and they use this to create procedures and routines to control practice: 'Managers extract whatever uncertainty there is in the process so that their "act" of devising the system of practice, surveillance and resource allocation which determines the work of subordinates remains the major free act in the whole business' (*ibid.* 151). Howe's contention is that Lipsky's analysis is no longer relevant: practitioners no longer have discretion (Howe 1991a) because managers have created a coherent system of management that is able to control practice through the mechanisms of procedures, budgets and surveillance (Howe 1986, Howe 1991a).

Baldwin takes the opposite view of Lipsky's work to Howe. He sees it as a perspective that continues to have contemporary relevance in the understanding of street-level practitioners' discretion (Baldwin 2000, 2004). In his study of the implementation of the community care reforms in two local authorities, he examines the street-level bureaucracy perspective to '... see to what extent ... [it] helps explain the findings from the research interviews' (Baldwin 2000: 79). Baldwin recognises that there have been significant changes in the British context of Social Services since the publication of *Street-Level Bureaucracy*, particularly in terms of an increasingly managerial environment and increasingly inadequate resources. However, unlike Howe, he argues that the essential characteristics of street-level bureaucracy persist in Social Services in Britain: 'The context of practice that Lipsky describes—resource shortfall, indeterminate objectives and a dearth in controls on the use of discretion—describes an organisational environment that has changed little since his book was published in 1980, apart from a worsening of the resource position because of demographic changes and political decisions' (*ibid.* 83).

Baldwin, like Howe, is interested in examining the influences on professional practice, but contrary to the picture of management control of practice through procedures presented by Howe, he concludes that: '... it was apparent that of the many influences on practice in assessment, not all related either specifically or even incidentally to policy guidelines. There was evidence of [practitioners'] unconsidered reliance on intuitive approaches to practice—[quoting one of his interviewees] "a lot of gut feeling, a lot of intuition, you've just jolly well got the vibes"' (*ibid.* 40). While he finds some commitment to procedures amongst a small number of care managers (practitioners—not necessarily qualified social workers—who assess and develop packages of care), his general finding is that most care managers are suspicious of influences such as bureaucracy, resource control and the techniques of managerialism. In fact, Baldwin finds not only resentment of managerial requirements but also many examples of resistance to control; for instance: 'There was one example of workers in a team running two systems side by side—the old and the new—because they found the new system inimical to their preferred method of practice ...' (*ibid.* 44). Baldwin considers his research as providing support for Lipsky's view that street-level bureaucrats such as social workers are able to exercise wide discretion and resist management control. He concludes that his research casts '... a useful light upon the extent to which intentions [of policy-makers] are undermined through the unreflective use of discretion by implementers such as care managers in the way that Lipsky describes' (*ibid.* 183).

These two different evaluations of the continuing relevance of Lipsky's work are instructive because of their similarity as well as their difference. The similarity relates to their shared recognition of the increasing attempts by managers to control and direct street-level practice. However, while Howe sees this as undermining Lipsky's relevance, this is not the case for Baldwin. I would argue that this difference arises, in part, from a misreading by Howe of Lipsky's argument, and that Lipsky's street-level bureaucracies are, in fact, the sort of organisation in which managers play a significant role.

It is important—particularly for British readers—to draw out implicit elements of Lipsky's analysis in *Street-Level Bureaucracy*, which the title of the book itself might obscure. Welfare bureaucracy is often contrasted with more managerial and business-focused organisations in the social policy literature in Britain (Butcher 1995). However, Lipsky's street-level bureaucracies are quite unlike this British notion of public administration bureaucracies. These are organisations with managers, not administrators, where there is concern for what is produced, not the process. His account of these organisations is permeated with the language of management (Lipksy 1980). They employ performance indicators to measure outputs and use eligibility criteria to ration access. Workers are resource units to be applied to achieve the organisation's goals. Managers are concerned with achieving agency objectives and are distrustful of the motives of the workers they supervise. Furthermore, 'managers' are not limited to the higher echelons of the organisations: they make up the hierarchy of supervision, including '... someone in an immediate supervisory position vis-à-vis street-level bureaucrats' (*ibid.* 216). In a comment on the objectives managers seek to implement through supervision of subordinates, Lipsky notes that: '"Objectives" refers to the goals that the supervisor is charged with realizing. It is necessary to put it this way because the role of supervisor is itself subordinate to other roles in a complex bureaucracy' (*ibid.* 216).

Lipsky's characterisation of street-level bureaucracies is, then, more in tune with the contemporary Social Services that Howe acknowledges, in the sense that they are characterised by the presence of a significant management dimension within the organisation. The interesting issue, however, is the different ways in which Howe and the street-level perspective approach the analysis of discretion.

Discretion: De jure *and* de facto

Discretion is freedom within the work role: 'A public officer has discretion whenever the effective limits on his [*sic*] power leave him free to make a choice among possible courses of action or inaction' (Davis 1971: 4). Within the idea of discretion as freedom to act, it is important to ask how this freedom to act is acquired. A distinction is often made between freedom that arises in the circumstance and freedom that is formally given by authority such as a hierarchical superior within a bureaucracy. These two different bases of discretion are usually referred to as *de facto* discretion—having the power to act, though not necessarily officially recognised; and *de jure* discretion—having the power to decide as an officially recognised entitlement. The first, *de facto*, sense of discretion can be associated with a capacity to act because of the absence of effective control. In the second sense it is about the authority to act, the official recognition of a right or entitlement to decide, such as professional discretion.

When we recognise these different dimensions of discretion we can see that Howe and Baldwin are at cross-purposes in their argument about discretion in Social Services. Howe tends to focus on formal systems of control and responsibility and points to the increasing reduction in the formal discretion of professional workers (the curtailment of their *de jure* discretion). He is concerned with what practitioners are allowed to do and the growing level of formal controls managers exercise over them—the: 'documents, devices and drilled people [that] allow those at the centre to control those at the boundaries of an organisation's activities' (Law quoted in Howe 1991a: 218). Baldwin, on the other hand, acknowledges that managerial strategies seek to control social workers, but points out that, despite the increasing level of formal management controls, practitioners still have the capacity to exercise significant *de facto* discretion in their work—freedom beyond that which is officially recognised. He is less concerned with formal discretion than with the ways in which practitioners can undermine and circumvent structures and processes to retain a significant degree of freedom to act, confirming: '… Lipsky's contention that coercive forms of management will result in covert … forms of discretion which are likely to be destructive of policy intentions' (Baldwin 2000: 86). The nature of the organisational context of social work discretion raised by Howe and Baldwin can be explored by examining the policy context of Social Services; and the nature and effectiveness of managerial control.

Howe's position is that: '… managers interpret welfare legislation, determine the resources to meet legal needs, design the systems which allow statutory matters to be handled' (Howe 1986: 161), and he clearly anticipates the contemporary political accounts of the policy process as a mechanical process by which '… governments translate their political vision into programmes and actions to deliver "outcomes"—desired changes in the real world' (Cabinet Office 1999: Chpt. 2, para 1). Howe (1996) points to the growth of check lists and procedures governing practice and their impact on day-to-day practice in support of his view. And he is not alone in his view that managers are in control, implementing the clear direction and policy given to them from the centre. His observation about increasing management control of practice and the concomitant decline of discretion (Howe 1986, 1991a, b and 1996) resonates with the views of contemporary social work commentators. (This perspective will be further discussed below.) The idea that managers can organise conflicting policies and better match resources to policies is also expressed by Macdonald (1990), who argues that managers should use their power in Social Services the better to clarify and delineate social workers' roles. Cheetham, considering the impact of the implementation of the new community care legislation, argues that the picture presented by Howe, in contrast to Lipsky's portrayal of extensive discretion, offers '… a much more sober account and one which is probably nearer the day to day experience of contemporary local authority workers, particularly as they deal with the progress charts, tick lists and performance indicators which are now so central to managerial practice' (Cheetham 1993: 171).

Howe and Cheetham are making two points here: first, that the *de jure* discretion social workers have taken for granted has been superseded by management control; and second, that management control is so effective that it has limited the ability to exercise choice in day-to-day practice. The latter point—the effective limitation on *de facto* discretion in social work practice—will be considered first.

There are good reasons and a growing body of evidence to call into question an unqualified picture of managers' ability to implement a policy as a blueprint, and closely control and direct the work of their subordinates in line with this goal. The evidence challenges this top–down ideal that the centre can direct and implement predetermined policy through its formal control of the hierarchy of the organisation (Hogwood and Gunn 1984). It offers support for the more qualified view of the street-level bureaucracy perspective that, while managers may seek to control the freedom of street-level bureaucrats such as social workers, they are more limited in their ability to do this than may at first appear to be the case.

Lewis and Glennerster, reviewing the literature on public policy implementation, observe that this view assumes: '… that, if not the local detail, then at least the broad intellectual rationale for the policy is tightly conceived by the centre' (Lewis and Glennerster 1996: 20). However, they point out: 'This is frequently not the case or is at least questionable' (*ibid.* 20). Rather, policy-making and policy implementation can be a messy business. More often than not policy-making is a process of compromise, imprecision and managing tensions (Rhodes 1999, 2008). Evidence from the implementation of the community care reforms suggests that policy is a complex of goals, different priorities, and public and private agendas (Lewis and Glennerster 1996). For the Conservative governments of the late-1980s/early-1990s, for instance, the development of community care policy involved concerns about controlling spending; fraught relationships with local government; a belief in market models of provision, and public rhetoric of choice and consumer responsiveness (Alaszewski and Manthorpe 1990). While there was a clear concern with managing the Social Security budget, they had to do this in a politically acceptable way (Lewis and Glennerster 1996).

Research examining the application of changing guidelines for community care services illustrates the impact of policy tensions on street-level practice. Bradley identifies '... insufficient clarity or openness in local procedures ... coupled with local political and economic expediency ... as significant factors in creating extensive discretion in application of charges for services amongst practitioners and managers' (Bradley 2003: 653).

Another problem with the top-down approach is that it assumes that the authors of a policy can determine the way their statements are interpreted (Evans and Harris 2004a). However, policy, like any text, is not fully under the control of its authors. The intended content of any document (what the authors mean) is not necessarily the same as its received content (what the document's readers understand) (Scott 1990). The author takes for granted a certain context of interpretation that the audience(s) does not necessarily share. Implementation studies often note local confusion and misunderstanding—'puzzlement'—about what the centre is asking them to do (Harrison *et al.* 1992: 3–4). In relation to the implementation of the community care reforms, researchers have noted that local authorities sought to make sense of the policy, giving rise to a range of interpretations which often tended to fit their existing commitments—for instance, in terms of responsiveness to users or willingness to use market mechanisms (Lewis and Glennerster 1996). The role of local interpretation was also made more complex by the way in which politically sensitive policies, such as reducing expenditure, had to be 'sugar-coated', as noted above.

Preston-Shoot and Wigley (2002), who look at the implementation of government guidance on vulnerable adults, also point to local puzzlement about and misunderstanding of policy: in implementing policy, managers and practitioners have to make sense of the guidance, but it is unclear what is directive and what is permissive. Policy also has to be interpreted in order to apply it to concrete situations, a constant problem for managers and practitioners because the policy cannot really deal with 'grey areas' (*ibid.* 317).

In addition to 'honest' misinterpretation of the centre's requirements, the process of policy clarification by the centre can itself complicate and confuse more than it clarifies. As tensions and unexpected problems in policy emerge, the centre has to deal with these in addition to the implementation of the policy itself. For example, Gostick *et al.* (1997) find that the work of the Social Services Inspectorate, given the task of implementing community care, grew as it responded to an emergent combination of anxieties arising in central government and in feedback from reviews identifying particular problems. In emphasising certain areas of practice, guidance produced by the SSI focuses attention on some aspects of the policy agenda and shifted attention away from others. Lewis and Glennerster (1996), for instance, talk of 'clouds of guidance' being issued by the SSI, which tried to reconcile growing tension between financial restraint and increasing user choice (*ibid.* 13–15).

Researchers also point to the problem of policy and resource incongruity: the mismatch between rhetoric and resources. Lewis and Glennerster find in their study that while, at first, funding was less of an issue than their research authorities anticipated, as the study progressed it became more significant. Towards the end of the research period some of the research authorities were starting to feel severe financial pressure, a situation reflected in the experience of many authorities outside the study.

A Local Government Association (LGA) survey of Social Services budgets (LGA 2002) finds local authorities spending over their predicted budgets in the financial year 2001–2, despite the imposition of increasingly restrictive eligibility criteria on access to services. The problem of the mismatch of resources and policy rhetoric was also acknowledged by the Chief Executive of the Commission for Social Care Inspection (CSCI), who has pointed to the need for additional funding for Social Services to meet the demands being put on them by the government (*The Guardian*, 1 December 2005). The continuing nature of this problem is reflected in a recent survey of local authorities with Social Services responsibilities in which 55 per cent of the authorities forecast an overspend of their budget for adult social care in 2008–9 (LGA 2009).

The impact of these tensions on practice is noted by Postle (2002) and Newton and Brown (2008). Postle looks at the experiences of care managers implementing community care, and finds them caught between 'the idea and the reality' of community care policy, in the sense of trying to match the generous rhetoric of community care with increasingly restricted resources; seeking to achieve needs-led assessments, in the knowledge that resources are insufficient to meet the needs they identify. Newton and Brown (*op. cit.*) undertake a review of studies into the operation of eligibility criteria and identify variations in the application of standardised eligibility criteria within and between authorities, and explain this, in part, in terms of care managers: '… acting, as Lipsky suggests, as "street level bureaucrats" making the best sense they can of the conflicting priorities …' (*ibid.* 245).

This problem is not confined to the implementation of community care. A study of the implementation of management reforms in children's residential services in the late 1990s (Kirkpatrick 2002) echoes Lewis and Glennester's description of policy implementation. Kirkpatrick also finds policy confusion and contradiction in terms of competing goals that emerge from core legislation (the Children Act 1989) and wider policy requirements in Social Services to contract out services (Kirkpatrick 2002). One of the main conclusions he draws from his study is that:

> … it is far from clear that demands for management reform necessarily represented clear and internally consistent archetypes or templates for how to organise … local organisations were presented with a multiplicity of competing goals and policy expectations all of which had potential implications for how they should re-structure services. In this case and perhaps more generally it seems

inappropriate to conceive of management restructuring initiatives in terms of a clear, well-designed project for change. Rather ... these initiatives often have more in common with a loosely formulated "bright idea" than a clearly defined "blue print" (Kirkpatrick 2002: 43).

The evidence suggests, then, that Social Services continue to share the basic characteristics of street-level bureaucracy central to the persistence of street level discretion identified by Lipsky: that is, the conditions of policy uncertainty and inadequate resources that create conditions within which actors have to make choices and exercise discretion, even when this discretion is not officially acknowledged or sanctioned. Baldwin agrees with Howe that managers are playing an increasingly significant role within Social Services; but disagrees with Howe's view that they have clarified policy and resolved problems of policy resource mismatch to the point where there is no longer any significant *de facto* street-level discretion.

These different conclusions about the continuation of street-level discretion also reflect different readings of Lipsky's analysis—perhaps a result of Lipsky's ambivalent treatment of professionalism and discretion within *Street-Level Bureaucracy*. Howe's argument against Lipsky is that managers have now replaced professionals as key players in public service bureaucracies; and that managers run these organisations like well-oiled machines, where policies and resources are all marshalled effectively to achieve the desired objectives—a system of control that has effectively eliminated professional discretion. In contrast, Baldwin's reading of Lipsky is as an analysis of employee discretion: workers' ability to avoid control. He sees managerial attempts to proceduralise practice as limited by conflict, confusion and resource inadequacy. This is a setting in which practitioners retain discretion, but often informally, in their capacity to adapt and alter policy, which echoes Lipsky's account of street-level bureaucracies.

Howe criticises Lipsky as an advocate of professional discretion. In so doing he suggests two interrelated areas for the analysis of discretion in organisations such as Social Services that require further attention: the assumptions that management can control all aspects of organisational activity—the point of dispute with the street-level bureaucracy perspective; and that professionalism, as an organising principle in understanding discretion, is no longer significant. In the next chapter the question of the nature of the impact of managerialism and the continuing influence of professionalism in understanding discretion will be considered.

Chapter 3
Management and Professionals: Arguments and Perspectives on Discretion

Introduction

The preceding chapter considered a view within the British social work literature that the street-level bureaucracy perspective is no longer useful in the analysis of modern Social Services, where practitioner discretion is effectively eliminated. My argument was that, contrary to this view, Lipsky's perspective does directly address itself to managed public service organisations; furthermore, rather than asking whether street-level bureaucracy is relevant, a more fruitful question involves exploring its analyses of discretion with that adopted by different critics and their assessments of the ability of managers to control and direct street-level practice. In this chapter the impact of managerialism on Social Services and its significance for the application of the street-level bureaucracy perspective will be considered, and the argument made that it is possible to distinguish two broad views of the impact of managerialism: domination managerialism, which sees managerialism replacing the previous organising principle of Social Services, which emphasised professionalism; and discursive managerialism, which sees it as another influence alongside professionalism in the organisation of Social Services.

Following on from this analysis, the role of managers in controlling (and supporting) street-level discretion will be considered. A distinction will be drawn between senior, strategic managers and local managers within the teams. Senior managers largely rely on remote control strategies—control of resources and procedures—to direct practice. The effectiveness of these strategies, and local management and practitioner resistance to them, will be examined. Finally, the relationship between local managers and street-level practitioners will be considered, to identify how this relationship influences street-level discretion.

In summary, in the preceding chapter I argued that Lipsky's work was developed in the context of nascent managerialism and that it is a prescient challenge to ideas of managerial omnipotence. In this chapter I will argue that the street-level bureaucracy perspective can be criticised for not giving sufficient attention to the impact of professionalism on manager–worker relations and on the practices of discretion within some street-level bureaucracies.

Managerialised Social Services: The End of Professionalism?

Historically, Social Services Departments have been strongly influenced by the ethos of professional social work (Hadley and Clough 1996, Lewis and Glennerster 1996, Payne 2005), recruiting senior officers from the social work ranks and recognising the professional status and discretion of social work staff within the organisation (Brown 1975, Harris 1998a, b, Payne 2005). For adult client groups, as well as the provision of professional social work as a service, these departments also fund broader social care services (understood as practical, day-to-day assistance and support) such as daycare services, help in the home to adults in need and residential accommodation for vulnerable adults. The persisting influence of professional social work in Social Services is evident in the continuing role of social work as the dominant professional group within social care. In the decade from 1999-2008 the local authority social care workforce has contracted by nearly 10 per cent. However, within this workforce social work has expanded by 24 per cent, increasing from just over 36,000 in 1999 to 45,300 (whole time equivalent) in 2008; and senior professional support staff at centre and strategic levels have increased by 46 per cent to over 5000, whole time equivalent (w.t.e). (Department of Health 2009).

State social workers have always been subject to management control, in the sense of a mode of organisational coordination (Clarke 1996). Historically, in departments such as Social Services in local government, management was professional-led, rather than drawn from separate management cadres, as in the NHS (Brown 1975, Laffin and Young 1990, Harris 1998a, b, Evans 2009). In this context managers were seen as committed to the idea of professional social work and advancement in the organisation was based as much on professional standing as on managerial authority (Harris 1998a). However, in the past 20 years managers are widely seen as having become increasingly powerful *vis-à-vis* the practitioners they manage, and increasingly distanced from professional commitments and concerns. Managers in Social Services, as in other parts of the public sector, have had to shift from the role of adequate administrator to one of the proactive, effective manager (Hugman 1991, Pollitt 1993, Flynn 1999). The increasing focus on management as control, rather than coordination, in Social Services has, it has been argued, led to a significant weakening of the professional links between managers and professional street-level staff, to the point where they are now distinct, antagonistic groups with very different concerns (Carey 2006, Hadley and Clough 1996, Howe 1986, 1991a, b, 1996, Jones 1999, 2001).

This argument draws on a broader literature, which points to the growing power of managerialism in the public sector: that is, the introduction from the commercial, private sector of business approaches to the management and organisation of services. Managerialism is associated with the focus on output, control of costs (often summarised as efficiency, effectiveness and economy), responsiveness to the business environment (especially consumers) and innovation and risk-taking. These attributes are seen to be central to the idea of a manager who is free to make the decisions necessary to get the job done (Pollitt 1993, James 1994, Clarke and Newman 1997). Managerialism took on its current significance in Britain following the election of the Conservative government in 1979, which promoted it as a 'natural solution' to the ills of the welfare bureaucracy:

> … "better management" sounds sober, neutral, as unopposable as virtue itself. Given the recent history of public-service expansion the productivity logic has a power of its own which stands independently of the political programme of the new right. Yet simultaneously, for new right believers, better management provides a label under which private-sector disciplines can be introduced into the public sector, political control strengthened, budgets trimmed, professional autonomy reduced, public sector unions weakened and a quasi-competitive framework erected to flush out the 'natural' inefficiencies of bureaucracy (Pollitt 1993: 49).

Two Views of the Impact of Managerialism

While the phenomenon of managerialism is widely recognised, it is possible to identify two strands of analysis within the literature examining the impact of managerialism on public services such as Social Services (Evans 2006, 2009). The 'domination' analysis focuses on the increased power of managers within Social Services, and characterises managers as committed to the organisation for which they work (rather than to the profession from which they come) and as motivated by a concern to implement and enforce hierarchically directed policy. In contrast, the 'discursive' strand of analysis suggests the potential continuation, alongside an increasingly powerful managerialist discourse, of professional concerns and practices—a bureau-professional discourse—in which, for instance, management may be consultative and concerned with support and accountability, as opposed to just punitive. The 'domination' perspective of managerialism presents managers and professionals as distinct occupational groups: practitioners as workers doing the bidding of managers, managers as creatures of the organisation, with corporate authority and identity.

These two approaches to understanding the impact of managerialism on public services are underpinned by two different conceptualisations of power. From the domination perspective, managers now have power, and practitioners do not; managers are in control and can command and direct powerless practitioners, who are bound to comply because of their powerlessness. This is power as something that is exercised over others: it is domination, radically asymmetrical and irrevocable. Authors adopting this position draw on a range of analytic frameworks. Howe (1991a: 218), for instance, drawing on Law (1986), adopts a Foucauldian analysis, in which managers discipline workers as drilled and reliable automata (*ibid.* 256), while Jones's position emphasises a Marxist analysis that characterises managers operating power as the clients of the New Right (Jones 1999). The result for both, however, is the same: practitioners are controlled by managers through surveillance and threat (Howe 1986, 1991a, Jones 1999) and by procedures: 'Rules, resources, and routines can define what a social worker might do in a situation without a manager looking over her shoulder' (Howe 1991a: 218).

The discursive managerialist approach to power is different, emphasising power's fragmentary and dispersed nature and seeing it everywhere and at all levels in the organisation. This analysis of power and discursive subjection is critical of approaches which 'treat such strategies [of control] as though they worked rather than as attempts to achieve their desired results' (Clarke and Newman 1997: 31). This notion of power characterises the organisation quite differently: as networks of ideas, practices and relations which are supported by particular interests but which are also subject to challenge and subversion (Leonard 1997: 90–92). Harris (2009), for instance, points out that in contemporary social services social workers: '... may be subjected to the modernisation discourse but not subjected by it. The intentions of modernising social work should not be mistaken for unequivocal accomplishments' (*ibid.* 170).

Discursive managerialism, like Howe's version of domination managerialism, has been influenced by Foucault's analysis of power, but it draws more on Foucault's later analysis of power than on his earlier works (Clarke and Newman 1997). Foucault's earlier work approaches power as a 'juridico-discursive' force that can be seen as external, top-down, law-like domination (Foucault 1981: 82). However, in his later work Foucault comes to accept the criticism that this approach is problematic, particularly in that his analysis is based on the contradiction of dismissing the idea of freedom and agency while at the same time relying on the idea of freedom for the critical force of his position (Foucault 1981, McNay 1994). In his *History of Sexuality*, Foucault explicitly reformulates the notion of power in line with this self-critical analysis of his work, and puts forward a view of power that, he argues, better fits his analytic method. This account of power contrasts the earlier, top–down view of power with the reformulated view of power as complex and multi-dimensional:

> By power, I do not mean "Power" as a group of institutions and mechanisms that insure the subservience of the citizens of a given state. By power, I do not mean, either, a mode of subjugation which, in contrast to violence, has the form of rule. Finally, I do not have in mind a general system of domination exerted by one group over another, a system whose effects, through successive derivations, pervade the entire social body ... It seems to me that power must be understood in the first instance as the multiplicity of force relations immanent in the sphere in which they operate and which constitute their own organisation; as a process which, through ceaseless struggles and confrontations, transforms, strengthens and reverses them; as the support which these forces find in one another, thus forming a chain or a system, or on the contrary, the disjunctions and contradictions which isolate them from one another; and lastly, whose general

design or institutional crystallization is embodied in the state apparatus, in the formulation of law, in the various social hegemonies (Foucault 1981: 92–93).

In this later account, power and freedom are intertwined: power relations are understood as contingent, fluid and reversible (McNay 1994).

In contrast to the first (domination) strand of managerial analysis, this discursive approach identifies tensions around the aim of managers to control practitioners, while also seeking to engage professional expertise and commitment (Newman and Clarke 1994, Harris 2003). These tensions create ground for: '… struggle between regimes. They produce new focal points of resistance, compromise and accommodation … managerialism has shifted the terms of reference on which conflicts and tensions around social welfare are fought out both within and beyond organisations' (Clarke and Newman 1997: 76–77).

From the domination perspective, Jones and Howe, for instance, identify the establishment of the new Social Services departments in the 1970s as the key point in the rise of management and its separation from professional concerns. Professionals and managers were no longer employed in small departments where they shared similar concerns and outlooks, as they were in the pre-Seebohm mental welfare, children's and welfare departments. Instead managers became part of large bureaucracies, where they focused on developing the skills to run these organisations. Howe talks about managers becoming more businesslike, going on high-powered training courses and becoming saturated with business wisdom (Howe 1991a). Jones points to the presence of an increasingly careerist management cadre in Social Services and this group's growing concern with personal advancement and embrace of the New Right agenda, in terms of accepting the reduced role of the local state, moving away from direct provision and supporting the imposition of market principles in Social Services (Jones 1999).

By contrast, the 'discursive' perspective locates managers at the intersection of discourses of power which define their role and their relationships with the street-level staff they supervise in very different ways: managers may or may not subscribe to managerialism; they are likely to be struggling with and operating within discourses of professionalism as well as managerialism (Clarke and Newman 1997, Evans 2009).

These two accounts of managerialism and its relations with professionalism bring out different issues in terms of understanding the application of street-level bureaucracy to the analysis of discretion. Paradoxically, in the light of Howe's critique, the domination perspective bears strong similarities to the way in which Lipsky characterises the nature and role of management in street-level bureaucracies. They both present welfare organisation as employing management strategies to control and direct services. However, they differ in so far as Howe, and the domination perspective, take the rhetoric of management control as reflecting the reality, whereas Lipksy is sceptical about the uncritical claims about the effectiveness of management strategies (as is the discursive perspective). However, the discursive perspective moves beyond the street-level bureaucracy perspective in calling for a more nuanced analysis of the role that managers play, their motivation and the nature of the relationships that they develop with staff in their teams. This account, while seeing an increasing focus on management concerns, locates it within a context of a weakened but continuing culture of professionalism in Social Services and points to the tension and contradictions that this creates for understanding the operation of discretion.

The Nature(s) of Management: Reviewing the Evidence

The foregoing discussion emphasises the need to analyse the nature of management in order to understand practitioner discretion. Discretion is located within the relationship between managers and practitioners, rather than being an attribute of one or the other. Management within Social Services is a relatively under-researched area. Many of the empirical studies that do consider managers presume a unity of management. The National Institute of Social Work (NISW) study of Social Services work undertaken in the mid-1990s, for instance, distinguishes between different areas of work within Social Services—fieldwork, residential care and domiciliary—but treats management within these different areas as a distinct and unified category (Balloch *et al.* 1999b). However, other studies of Social Services suggest that it is, in fact, a segmented category. A consistent distinction emerging from research studies is that between local operational management and central strategic management (Parsloe and Stevenson 1978, Satyamurti 1981, Pithouse 1998, Harris 1998a, b, 2003). This distinction is useful in examining the evidence, as it will allow us to identify any differences between the two levels of management and also assess how well this distinction still holds in the context of contemporary Social Services.

The domination perspective account of managers focuses on senior managers as the powerful organisational actors, and tends to equate 'manager' with free and powerful senior Social Services managers (Howe 1986, 1991b, Nixon 1993). There is a paucity of research into senior management in Social Services, but in the broader body of empirical evidence on policy implementation and Social Services organisation, there is some support for the view which domination managerialism (and Lipsky) puts forward: that senior managers' primary identification is with the organisation rather than with social work as a profession. A persistent theme in the research literature is that, historically, there is a gulf between local teams—field-level workers and their managers (Satyamurti 1981, Parsloe and Stevenson 1978, Pithouse 1998, Harris 1998a, b)—and senior managers, certainly from the point of view of the local teams, with senior managers often viewed as alien: 'Social workers did not view the organization outside the area teams as an object of loyalty or identification. They viewed it as a source of frustration or, at best, as devoid of meaning' (Satyamurti 1981: 35). However, according to research into the views of senior managers in local government, including Social Services directors, they may also see themselves as professional advocates for their department within the organisation (Laffin and Young 1990).

Kirkpatrick, who looks at management reforms in Social Services in the late 1990s (Kirkpatrick 2002), finds that, in all seven of the authorities examined, managers often have to struggle with ambiguous and conflicting policy demands (*ibid.* 34), and that they respond to these in different ways for different reasons. While he finds some examples of senior managers taking a clear managerial stance—calling for 'corporacy' and '... one view, one aim, one statement ...' (an assistant director quoted in *ibid.* 35)—he also finds numerous examples of managers responsive to professional concerns about how to provide the best service.

In another major implementation study, Lewis and Glennerster (1996) question the suggestion (made by Nixon 1993) that '... managers who have wanted to shed their professional association with social work have had reason to welcome the changes' (*ibid.* 205). Their findings suggest a range of attitudes to the professional culture of social work within Social Services. Some managers express impatience with this professional culture, while others—including some who were not themselves social workers—remain committed to it. Furthermore, while many managers see managerial approaches as a way of realising the goals of community care, standardisation of organisational procedures are used as much to promote good professional practice as to constrain it. This view, that procedures and policies propagated by managers can promote shared professional concerns and legitimate good practice, is also identified by Robinson (2003).

Kirkpatrick and Lewis and Glennerster's studies also call into question the view that senior managers approach their instructions from policy-makers with an unproblematic, literal reading and seek to implement them within their commitment to a management approach. Kirkpatrick, for instance, points out that they have to negotiate conflicting demands and local political, organisational and professional structures in formulating policy (Kirkpatrick 2002: 41–43). Murray (2006), in a study of home supervision in Scotland, has also noted the discretionary role of senior managers who, together with practitioners, subverted '... the intent of policy makers as specified in primary and secondary legislation' (*ibid.* 218).

The admittedly fragmentary picture that emerges of senior managers from these studies calls into question the image presented by Lipsky and domination managerialism of autonomous management cadres within Social Services, acting as loyal implementers of a clear policy direction, distanced from professional concerns. Some managers may see themselves and seek to act in the way suggested by the domination perspective, but the evidence suggests that this stance is neither so extensive nor so consistent as to justify the street-level bureaucracy perspective and the domination managerialism flat, one-dimensional portrayal of (senior) organisational managers.

The presentation of managers as a distinct group—managers, not professionals—does not reflect the more complex picture of the nature of senior management in Social Services suggested in the research evidence. Another problematic aspect of this binary approach is the picture of (senior) managers and practitioners with middle managers and supervisors as ciphers between fieldworkers and the 'strong but remote managers' (Howe 1986: 162). This fails to recognise that management in Social Services departments is multi-layered; and that, within Social Services 'management', there are not only senior managers but also middle managers and supervisors, who are significant actors. It also neglects the fact that conflict can exist between management layers, and that there may also be alliances between managers and street-level practitioners (Harris 1998a and b, Evans 2009, White 2009). Hugman, for instance, notes that within the complex environment of professional concerns and organisational priorities: '… the team leaders are regarded by more senior managers as well as by practitioners as occupying the borders between the two worlds, a position imbued with ambiguities' (Hugman 1991: 77). The significance of this is that the focus on managers at senior level ignores what is, for most practitioners, their main experience of management— day-to-day supervision at team level (Seden and Reynolds 2003)—and does not engage with the possibility that these subordinate managerial actors may not just carry out the work of surveillance and policy policing in compliance with the goals of 'the managers', but are themselves 'active shapers of the way initiatives develop', making sense of policies and procedures in terms of their own understanding of the organisation (Balogun and Johnson 2005: 1596).

Freidson points out that, at first and second management level, professionalism has a strong influence in organisations that employ professionals (Freidson 1994). Unlike the health service, where management is a distinct organisational group, in Social Services Departments social workers have tended to be managed by fellow professionals (Pahl 1994, Evans 2009). While official statistics tend not to give information on the professional background of front-line managers, reviews of job advertisements in the press suggest that this continues to be the case. For instance, Henderson and Seden (2003) examines 40 job descriptions and personal specifications for front-line managers in Social Services, finding that employers mostly seek professional qualifications and that: 'There was little evidence of employers prioritising management expertise rather than professionally defined skills, abilities and experience' (*ibid.* 87). The line between managers and workers is more blurred than the domination and street-level bureaucracy perspectives suggest and many front-line managers occupy hybrid roles that cross the manager/professional divide (Causer and Exworthy 1999). Part of the domination managerialism argument, however, is that, on becoming managers, qualified professionals jettison their backgrounds, suggesting that we need to look beyond those backgrounds in order to gain a sense of their commitments (Howe 1986, 1991a, Nixon 1993).

Many local social work managers are professionals and this raises interesting questions about the way they see themselves as managers and how they view practitioner discretion. In a current text book for front-line managers, they are characterised as being guided by '… the values and ethics of social care, while at the same time meeting the requirements of government, employers and policy makers' (Seden and Reynolds 2003: xiv). Reynolds also emphasises the need to recognise the professional dimension of management: '… there are links between practising and managing, and … new managers should not only be able to build on some of their practice skills but also have responsibility to maintain a commitment to practice in managing other people's practice' (Reynolds 2003: 32).

Evidence from a number of studies suggests that some local managers can conform to the domination view of managers as a separate cadre hostile to professional discretion. Since the mid-1980s, and with increasing emphasis, researchers have identified significant changes in the behaviour and orientation of local managers, reflected in a tendency for managers to exercise increasing control of professional practice and to focus on the enforcement of corporate concerns, usually rationing resources (Howe 1986, Nixon 1993, Pahl 1994, Carey 2008). Within Social Services the community care reforms in the early 1990s, which now form the basis of state social care for adults, were widely seen as a sea change in the role of Social Services managers:

> As well as a more prescribed and rigid role for front-line workers, a more prominent part was expected of their superiors. It has been recognised that front line managers offered an opportunity to complete such roles as regulating the duties of subordinates, survey the stricter eligibility (for services) criteria applied to clients during assessment, and also guard finite resources against claims for assistance from outside (Carey 2003: 122).

In an influential analysis of 'the social work business', Harris observes that operational managers have developed a 'business orientation' with close scrutiny of practice, particularly focusing the use of resources and worker productivity, using procedures and information technology. He also points to the changing basis of recruitment of practitioners into management, having changed from professional qualities as a practitioner to an ability to manage budgets and information systems (Harris 2003). Pithouse, in the mid-1990s, finds a changing focus to work and its supervision: 'care' and 'relationship' work within the team is now largely the responsibility of unqualified staff. For qualified staff and managers the priority is child protection work—legal, technical and focused on risk—and this is the focus of supervisory oversight (Pithouse 1998).

Hadley and Clough also report an increasingly tense relationship between practitioners and managers. They find that managers and professional workers seem to inhabit different worlds—the former a world of efficiency, value for money, objectives achieved; the latter a world of crises in services, impossible pressures and inability to deliver (Hadley and Clough 1996: 195). 'The result is that the majority of the workers in our sample find the behaviour of their organisations increasingly confusing and difficult to understand or predict, and become suspicious and cynical about the motives, pronouncements and actions of managers' (Hadley and Clough 1996: 187).

Carey also finds that managers are generally unpopular with the practitioners who have day-to-day contact with them, who describe them as strict or incompetent

(Carey 2003: 127–128), and Pahl observes that there is now a chasm between social workers and their managers (Pahl 1994). While social workers tend to gain most satisfaction from their direct work with clients, the managers tend to gain satisfaction from organising well (Balloch *et al.* 1995).

However, alongside evidence of conflict between local managers and local practitioners, studies suggest, in line with the discursive perspective, that local managers can also be critical and question the priorities of the organisation for which they work, and retain a professional commitment (Evans 2009, White 2009). Carey, for instance, finds that managers express frustration with the policies of their organisation and sympathy for the difficulties staff experience in a context of resource constraint (Carey 2003). Pithouse also finds that team leaders are sensitive to the pressure on their staff and seek to lessen the impact of supervision on staff, protecting their supervisees from 'the intrusive gaze' of senior managers (Pithouse 1998).

A striking finding of the NISW study of the social care workforce (Balloch *et al.* 1995, 1999a) is the ambivalence amongst many managers about the organisation for which they work. Managers feel as disempowered as social workers in their work—with only about a third of each group feeling satisfied with the amount of influence they have in the organisation (Balloch *et al.* 1999c), and with two-thirds of both groups equally frustrated by a failure to meet the service users' needs (McLean 1999). Over a third of managers feel that their values are different from those of the organisation—only a slightly lower percentage than for field social workers (Balloch *et al.* 1995).

The NISW study also calls into question the idea of the transformation of practitioners when they become managers. It finds that preparation for the management role and commitment to the organisation's values is patchy amongst managers, who feel insufficiently trained and ill-prepared for their role (Balloch *et al.* 1995). Fewer than 50 per cent of the managers interviewed say they received any support from experienced managers when they first started in their role, and only a third have received any initial training; only a quarter of the managers interviewed have or are studying for a management qualification (Balloch 1999).

Another body of evidence claimed by the domination point of view is the increasing proceduralisation of practice. However, if management continues to have a significant professional element within it, then increasing numbers of procedures may include a strong professional element. Procedures and guidance, viewed from this perspective, are not necessarily alien to professional social work practice, but can, in fact, support it, while still exerting a form of control. Procedures can be professional tools, embodying good practice, legitimating professional expertise, and promoting professional commitments to the rights of service users (Baldwin 2000, Kirkpatrick 2002, Robinson 2003, Evans and Hardy 2010).

The empirical evidence paints a complex picture. Management concerns have become increasingly prevalent within social services, but there is also conflict between local managers and local practitioners. However, managers and practitioners also collude to subvert policy objectives (Murray 2006). The idea of managers shedding their professional concerns and becoming exclusively organisational creatures is also called into question. Treating management as an homogenous category fails to recognise the different experiences and perspectives of different levels of management (Harris 1998a, b); dilutes issues associated with the management of particular work groups such as professionals; and—related to this point—obscures the different quality and nature of relationship between management and workers in different settings.

The discussion up to this point has considered the broad issues of the nature of social services organisation, specifically the impact of managerialism and the continuing influence of professionalism in the structuring of discretion and the relationship between street-level workers and managers. The literature points to managerialism having had a significant impact on social services organisations. However, this has not invalidated the relevance of Lipsky's analysis, because Lipsky's view of street-level bureaucracies entails seeing bureaucracy as a managerial organisation. A debate exists, nevertheless, about the nature of managerialism, which raises questions about the application of the street-level bureaucracy perspective to social services, but in quite a different way from the criticism of Howe and domination managerialism—namely, citing the continuing influence of professionalism, and challenging the idea of management as a separate occupational cadre. This argument, put forward by proponents of the discursive perspective, highlights the continuing potential of professionalism to influence discretion and management oversight.

Professionalism in Managerialised Social Services: Still Going or Gone?

The preceding analysis identifies different characterisations of the nature of managers and management with social services. In the course of this discussion, alongside the street-level bureaucracy perspective (outlined in the preceding chapter), two other analyses have emerged: domination managerialism and discursive managerialism. The distinction between the two arises from the way in which the encroachment of managerialism is understood against the backdrop of the idea of bureau-professionalism. Bureau-professionalism refers to the combination of organising principles of bureaucracy and professionalism in Social Services Departments during the first decades following their establishment in the wake of the Seebohm report. Social Services, while located within the bureaucratic structure of local authorities, were strongly influenced by professional principles of organisation, emphasising professional supervisors as supportive colleagues rather than directive managers, and professional staff operating with a significant degree of discretion, trusted by fellow professionals who occupied the significant hierarchical posts within Social Services as an organisation (Stevenson 1978, Parry and Parry 1979, Clarke 1996, Harris 1998a, b, Payne 2005). The difference between the domination and discursive approaches to managerialism focuses on whether or not they see it as a clear break with this mode of organisation within Social Services organisations.

The domination approach characterises managerialism as a conclusion (e.g. Howe 1986, 1991a, b, 1996, Pahl 1994, Jones 1999 and 2001, Carey 2003, 2008). Managers are the winners in a zero-sum game: managers have now displaced professionals as the key actors in Social Services because: 'Except in matters of style, all the substantive elements of their [social workers'] work are determined by others ...' (Howe 1991a: 204).

In contrast, the discursive perspective casts managerialism as a continuing, but not complete, process. This more tentative analysis characterises managerialism as an 'emergent culture of control' which is changing, overlaying and altering existing professionalised structures, rather than replacing them; but within which actors are not seen as simply passive; they are also able to resist and challenge and subvert managerialism (Leonard 1997).

These different approaches to managerialism give rise to different analyses of the extent to which discretion has been removed from professionals. The domination strand of this literature argues that social work is no longer a profession because it is no longer autonomous, due to both the extent and effectiveness of external controls and the way in which managerial ideas are now embedded and taken for granted. Here, professionalism is presented in 'either/or' terms: either social work is autonomous—a profession—or it has no real freedom of decision-making and is not a professional occupation. The other strand—discursive—adopts a more nuanced view and recognises that, while practitioners may be subject to increasing controls—external and ideological—this does not exclude the possibility of professional discretion in their work, or of subverting the control of managers, albeit to a different degree than in the past.

Key authors in the domination literature, such as Howe, Jones and Carey, focus on the growing strategies and techniques of managers to control practitioners and the profession (such as procedures, guidance and tick charts) as real limitations on social workers' traditional discretion. Jones points to evidence of increasing regulation of practice by central government and local managers, and emphasises the feeling amongst practitioners that their work is now governed by paperwork and procedures, and a frustration arising from the sense that they are no longer respected and trusted within the organisation (Jones 1999, 2001).

This perspective characterises managerialism as managers in control: managers have power and have used it to disempower and control professional staff; power is understood as domination through direct and ideological control (Howe 1986, 1991a, 1996, Pahl 1994 and Jones 1999, 2001, Carey 2008). Managers, sponsored by the New Right (Jones 1999), have played and won the occupational power game: 'The recent spate of legislation related to Social Services has created heavy work loads for managers, but it has also given them power in a way which many have found quite exhilarating' (Pahl 1994). In contrast, according to this perspective, social workers as an occupational group have now failed in their professional project (Lymbery 1998a). Social workers have failed to gain status and discretion, and are now subject to management control, to the point of being no more than drones (Howe 1986). 'Less and less', in Howe's view, '... is the social worker expected, or indeed allowed, to make an independent, on the spot judgement or diagnosis of what is the matter. Less and less is the social worker likely to respond with a tailor-made, professional intervention based on his or her own knowledge and skills. There is a move from reason to rote' (Howe 1996: 93–94).

Discursive managerialism does not see managerialism as being the conclusion of a strategy of domination that has wiped away professional discretion. Rather, it sees managerialism as a dynamic process affecting all occupational groups within Social Services—managers as much as social workers—and identifies professionalism as a site of resistance to and possible adaptation of managerialism (Clarke *et al.* 2000). It is another stratum in the geology of the organisation, which, rather than replacing what has gone before, is laid upon it, with the two interpenetrating each other to different degrees, in different ways, and in different settings (Clarke and Newman 1997). There is a range of management styles, such as: the neo-Taylorist control; crude, market-driven strategies; the processes and relationships through empowering partnership models; and New Labour's turbo-driven modernisation (Pollitt 1993, Fergurson 2008, Harris and White 2009). Behind these differences in style, however, is a shared discourse: the commitment to the goal of the intensification of labour, seeing work identified and measured in terms of commitment to organisational performance, which '... foregrounds the calculus of "efficiency" and "performance" as the frame of reference for organisational action' (Clarke and Newman 1997: 64). These managerial ideas are not hegemonic, sweeping all other perspectives aside. Rather, managerialism is seen as seeking to reconstruct social work in various ways, through processes that are not uniform but are dynamic, interactive and shifting according to specific conditions. Managerialism has not swept away every residue of professional power, but is seeking to contain and channel the discretion that has been an historic feature of field social work in Social Services (Harris 1998a).

These two approaches to the analysis of managerialism share a sense of an historical shift. However, they differ in terms of how they characterise the nature of this shift and its impact on professionalism. They also differ in their characterisation of the idea of professional freedom.

The Nature of Professional Freedom

The idea of 'professional' is difficult to pin down but tends to involve an occupational group that has a degree of recognition and status—often based on its knowledge claims, organisation and norms of practice—giving it a greater ability than non-professional groups to guide and direct its own work (Freidson 1994, Noon and Blyton 2002). Within this definition, analysts disagree on the level of control over work and freedom—discretion—that constitutes a defining characteristic of a profession (Noon and Blyton 2002, Noordegraaf 2007). What is clear is that professionals are widely understood as workers who are authorised to act with a degree of freedom from external control in their work (Evetts 2002):

> In Anglo-American social systems, the occupational control of work has been a defining characteristic of that special category of occupations called professions. Professional workers have been characterized as having autonomy both in respect of their professional judgments and decision-making, and in respect of their immunity from regulation or evaluation by others (*ibid.* 341).

However, discretion and autonomy are very different ideas: autonomy suggests a complete freedom of action while discretion suggests a more restricted freedom to act within a framework (Dworkin 1978, Evetts 2002: 345). Dworkin points out that even when we think of discretion as extensive: 'We must avoid one tempting confusion. The strong sense of discretion is not tantamount to license, and does not exclude criticism. Almost any situation in which a person acts ... makes relevant certain standards of rationality, fairness, and effectiveness' (Dworkin 1978: 33).

The domination managerialism perspective equates professionalism with autonomy and presents the shift in control to managers within Social Services as seismic, wiping away professionalism. Jones exemplifies this position and also illustrates its central problem: the idea of an historical golden age (Harris 1998b). He contrasts the current imposition of managerialism with the 1980s, when social workers had freedom to act, and management regulation was focused on the constraint of radical practice (Jones 2001). However, in 1983 Jones was arguing that the organisation of Social Services undermined professional discretion as such (Jones 1983), in contrast to earlier times, when managers were only concerned with restraining discretion where there was a risk that social workers would go 'native' [*sic*] (Jones 1983: 131).

In contrast, the discursive managerialism account focuses on professionalism as discretion, the continuation of a degree of freedom; it sees managerialism seeking to reshape the historical bureau-professional culture of Social Services (Harris, 1998a). This culture emphasises a parochial professional loyalty at fieldwork team level, and the distrust of senior managers (Parsloe and Stevenson 1978, Satyamurti 1981, Pithouse 1998, Harris 1998a, b). Local management control of staff is noticeably light, with a wide-ranging acceptance of discretion and autonomy amongst professional staff (Harris 1998a). Local managers in this context tend to characterise themselves in professional terms—for instance, in their approach to supervision, which is seen as a consultation between equals (Harris 1998a). In a similar vein, Pithouse concludes that local managers see their role as nurturing and protecting practitioners and their service ideals against central interference, keeping a safe distance between the team and senior managers (Pithouse 1998). This is not to say that practitioners are totally free to act as they choose. Newman and Clarke, for instance, identify: '... three ways in which managerialism has reshaped the place and power of bureau-professionalism: displacement, subordination and co-option' (Clarke and Newman 1997: 76). Displacement—the total control of professionals (as suggested by the domination perspective)—is rare. More often, managerial influence can be seen in professional subordination: 'This takes the form of framing the exercise of professional judgement by the requirement that it takes account of the "realities and responsibilities" of budgetary management— need is now disciplined by managerial calculus' (*ibid.* 76); or co-option: 'This refers to managerial attempts to colonise the terrain of professional discourse, constructing articulations between professional concerns and languages and those of management' (*ibid.* 76).

Managerialism, then, in the discourse perspective, is seen as reconstructing professional discretion rather than abolishing it. While these processes are widespread, they do not operate in a uniform way (Clarke and Newman 1997), but are varying in different situations, interacting with particular contexts and shifting according to specific conditions. The following section will consider the evidence from research studies about the nature of social work discretion within Social Services.

Social Work Discretion in Social Services: The Evidence

Lipsky describes the common basis of street-level bureaucrats' discretion as their work in street-level bureaucracies, where freedom arises from policy confusion and resource inadequacy. Managers in this context are both limited in their ability to control this freedom and, to some extent, in collusion with it, in order to get work done (Lipsky 1980). The two strands in managerialist analysis indicate two other different ways of understanding social work discretion within Social Services. The domination strand is less sceptical of managers' claims to control in the street-level bureaucracy perspective. On the other hand, the discursive perspective alerts us to the continuing influence of professional social work discretion within Social Services, suggesting more caution in applying the street-level bureaucracy framework without some adaptation to local circumstances.

Over the past decade a wide-ranging literature has developed which has detailed the increasingly significant role and power of managers in Social Services and its impact on professional social work. This literature, covering the curtailment of discretion, offers support for the domination view of the demise of professional discretion in social work (Pahl 1994, Simic 1995, Hadley and Clough 1996, Harris 1998a, b, La Valle and Lyons 1998a, 1998b, Lymbery 1998b, 2000, Irving and Gertig 1999, Jones 1999, 2001, Postle 2001, 2002, Carey 2003, 2008, Harris 2003). Within this literature there is a growing body of empirical research which substantiates and illustrates the significant impact of managerial control of professional practice, particularly in terms of the curtailment of social workers' professional discretion (Hadley and Clough 1996, Harris 1998a, Jones 2001, Carey 2003).

Researchers have identified a significant shift in the role of social workers, who have become care managers, and this is seen as having undermined professional discretion. Jones (2001), for instance, who surveys 50 practitioners working in local authorities in the North of England, argues that the traditional role of social worker, focusing on the needs of clients, has been distorted by managers, who have sought to control practice and have transformed social work, imposing 'hard-nosed commercial logic' (*ibid.* 560), a process in which:

> ... the contact [with service users] is more fleeting, more regulated and governed by demands of the forms which shape much of their interaction ... I was told [by his interviewees] that social workers were pressured to be speedy in their assessments, limit the contact with the potential client and get in and out quickly ... (*ibid.* 533).

Hadley and Clough (1996), who, in a study of the implementation of the NHS and Community Care Act (1990), interviewed community care practitioners in settings including social work, find that: 'In the Social Services, the split between purchasing and providing imposed an immediate reduction in both discretion and autonomy by splitting the role of the social worker' (*ibid.* 186).

A consistent theme arising from these studies is that professionals are now facing greater scrutiny and control of their activities by managers who emphasise social workers' accountability to the organisation: '... our interviewees are also aware of the influence of the development of a new form of scientific management that sees detailed information on workers' activities as an essential prerequisite for controlling the organisation' (*ibid.* 186–187). This theme, that social workers are now being subject to close monitoring through information systems and close supervisory control to ensure financial and productivity expectations, is also identified by Harris in a small-scale study of the impact of community care reforms on social workers (Harris 1998a).

Jones (2001), encapsulating these themes, paints a picture of a work environment that is no longer professional—that is less trusting, more highly regulated and more mundane (*ibid.* 552); one of his interviewees claims that: '... now everything is controlled and other people make the key decisions and feed it back to you to implement. It all seems to be about covering people's backs and saving money' (*ibid.* 555–556).

Finally, Carey, in a study of care managers, also finds that routines and procedures have been imposed on practitioners which have bureaucratised their practice to the point where they are almost brainwashed (2008). Managerial routines, he finds, not only structure work and discretion but facilitate monitoring and surveillance of practitioners by managers. He points out that, within this developing system of control, practitioners have been encouraged to recognise their corporate responsibility to organisational goals of efficiency and economy, and that the world of practice is increasingly dominated by budget restrictions (Carey 2003, 2008).

The picture painted by the research so far reviewed appears to confirm the domination perspective, in that managers are increasingly assertive in seeking to control practice and have succeeded in doing so. However, another body of literature presents a different picture of professional practice in Social Services, indicating some continuation of social work discretion within the context of managerial progress (Lewis and Glennerster 1996, Lapsley and Llewellyn 1998, Pithouse 1998, Ellis *et al.* 1999, Kirkpatrick 2002, Robinson 2003, Bradley 2003, Dunkerley *et al.* 2005, Ellis 2007, Halliday *et al.* 2008, Evans 2009).

Ellis *et al.* (1999) present a complex picture of local responses to the community care reforms. Their study of two authorities, which includes observing practice, looks at the implementation of the NHS and Community Care Act (1990) in a range of adult social work teams. While they find that the community care reforms have had an impact on social work practice, this is not consistent; and they point to continuing street-level discretion in significant areas of practice. A fundamental issue they identify is that practitioners feel engaged in a struggle between maintaining their professionalism and conforming to managerial procedures. While in some teams practitioners talk of their continuing autonomy, the researchers also observe conformity and identification with managerial objectives. Generally they find that operational guidance is inconsistently carried out: 'Contrary to the rationalizing thrust of both central and local authority guidance ... no common approach to the task of determining access to assessment existed amongst teams included in this study' (*ibid.* 277). In addition to continuing discretion in terms of interpretation and adaptation of guidance to local circumstances, they also find that some teams disregard procedures. Teams also vary in terms of the level of their resources and the impact this has on their level of discretion. Specialist teams, in particular, tend to have more time and greater access to resources (including non-Social Services funding), which give team members greater professional freedom in terms of their approach to practice and the range and level of services they can provide. Paradoxically, though, within these teams better resources also enable them to conform to procedures on recording unmet need, which the generic and hospital teams fail to do.

In a more recent study Ellis (2007) comments on the continuing significance of professional discretion. In a study looking at the implementation of direct payments she concludes that: '... social workers in this study appeared to enjoy considerable discretion at each stage of assessment and care management to manage access to direct payments. They managed information from point of referral, exercising choice about the way the option was presented or even whether it was made known to prospective recipients' (*ibid.* 417).

While identifying the continuing extent of social work discretion, Ellis *et al.* are also critical of its use by some practitioners, contrasting those using discretion to advance professional norms with others who use it to '... reinforce rather than challenge dominant rationing imperatives' (*ibid.* 277). What is interesting here is that Ellis *et al.* identify continuing professional (*de jure*), as well as *de facto* discretion. In another study, conducted by Lapsley and Llewellyn (1998), the researchers examine professional commitment in discretionary practice and are interested in the extent to which the new community care and its ethos of managerial concerns about resources influence professional practice. They find that social workers, on the whole, continue to demonstrate a commitment to professionalism in their use of discretion, while noting that there is some concern for the more economic values of efficiency and effectiveness.

Lewis and Glennerster's (1996) study of the implementation of the community care reforms involves a mixture of observational, documentary and interview-based research in four local authorities in the south of England. While they focus on the strategic process of local implementation, they also look at the experience of practitioners of the new system and conclude that, while: 'Managerialism has had an effect on the exercise of professional discretion' (*ibid.* 205), this should not be exaggerated. Despite practitioners' fears that their work would become routine and mechanistic, 'On the whole these extreme fears have not been realised. But the transparency of the new transactions, for example the visibility of assessment and the resulting service decisions, and the need to achieve consistency, for example in respect of eligibility criteria and response times, have inevitably required more standardisation of professional practice' (*ibid.* 205).

In another major study of community care reforms (Bauld *et al.* 2000) a similar picture of increased but limited managerial intrusion into practice is presented. An area examined by the research is the autonomy of care managers. The researchers find that the least qualified staff tend to have the least constraints on their practice—because they tend to work in the most routine, low-spending areas of care management. Qualified staff, predominantly social workers, tend to work with complex and resource-intensive cases, and are more subject to management surveillance and budgetary controls. Using the experience of amendment to assessment or care plans as an indicator of autonomy (non-amendment equalling greater freedom), they find that, while 10 per cent of all care managers have had work amended, this rises to 20 per cent for those working with complex cases—predominantly social work staff. They see this as a reflection of managers' concerns with control of expenditure. However, this still means that 80 per cent of workers in these complex, resource-intensive areas of work have not been subject to the curtailment of discretion suggested by the domination perspective. The general picture of discretion as it emerges in the study is of a patchwork, both in the nature of discretion and in its extent, but with most staff in all areas identifying continuing significant freedom in their work.

Furthermore, in settings that are particularly characterised by prescriptive and intrusive procedures, such as work with asylum-seeking young people (Dunkerley *et al.* 2005) and preparation of social enquiry reports for courts (Halliday *et al.* 2008), discretion has been found to be a continuing aspect of professional practice and suggests the '… continuing pertinence of Lipksy's concept of "street-level bureaucracy" for the study of social work' (Haliday *et al.* 2008: 202).

Guidance, as mentioned above, is frequently portrayed in the literature as a sign of increasing managerial control and reduced professional discretion. Robinson (2003) challenges this view, however. She looks at the impact of a structured assessment instrument in a probation setting. The instrument was a four page detailed questionnaire predicting risk of reoffending. Reaction to the instrument is mixed—it is seen as having the potential to limit freedom but is also seen as enhancing professional practice and status, promoting quality and backing up judgement. Rather than replacing 'clinical judgment', Robinson argues, initiatives such as the assessment tool operate within a context of complexity that continues to require discretion and freedom in professional practice.

The evidence reviewed here points to a complex topography of choice, constraint, freedom and control, offering support for aspects of arguments suggesting the curtailment and the continuation of discretion. As well as evidence of continuing *de facto* discretion, there is also recognition of *de jure* professional discretion: freedom to act within the organisation based on the acceptance of professional claims to expertise. This complex picture is captured by Pithouse (1998). He returns after 10 years to the site of his ethnographic study of childcare field social work teams. The original 1980s study found that professional discretion was taken for granted in the team. While practitioners had little control over services or resources, they expected to have a considerable degree of self-regulation of their practice. The relationship between professional discretion and management control was characterised by loyalty to the team, trust and a commitment to care. When Pithouse returns he finds changes but also continuities. The relationship between supervisors and practitioners seems more strained. Team leaders, while trying to ameliorate the pressures of increased departmental supervision of casework, also have to monitor the conduct of cases more closely; at the same time team leaders feel over-stretched in coping with the demands on them to supervise practitioners. Practitioners seek to tread '... a careful line between seeking advice from a manager and retaining some autonomy around a preferred plan of action, while at the same time not exposing herself to risks that might accrue by withholding some aspect or other about a case' (*ibid.* 121).

Pithouse finds that, while for some practitioners, the increased involvement of managers in day-to-day issues is difficult, others see their involvement as helpful, an acceptable process of scrutiny in which they can share responsibility for difficult decisions and complex work (*ibid.* 34). Related to these developments in practice is the changing focus of work. 'Care' and 'relationship' work within the team is now largely the responsibility of unqualified staff. For qualified staff and managers the priority is child protection work—legal, technical and focused on risk—and this is the focus of supervisory oversight.

Interpreting the Evidence

The argument about the curtailment of discretion is not only concerned with the existence of freedom to make decisions. It also entails an evaluation of the character of this freedom. This is particularly the case in relation to the domination and discursive managerialism analyses of discretion.

Domination managerialism arguments about the curtailment of discretion weave together claims that practitioners are not professionals because they are not autonomous with the view that practitioners are effectively and closely controlled by managers. Jones puts forward a picture of the occupational dominance of managers in a context in which: '… what is required is a managed workforce with no illusions about professional autonomy … focused on ensuring the "right" conduct on the job' (Jones 1999: 47). The analysis presents a stark choice between autonomy and subjugation—there is no middle ground.

Howe's argument about the dominance of management locates social work within one of the three categories of 'professional' developed by Johnson (1972). Howe places state social work in a category that he calls 'third party control'—where a third party defines both the nature of needs and the manner in which they are to be met (Howe 1986: 118)—in contrast to Johnson's other two categories of 'colleague or collegiate' (closely associated with the ideal type of professionals as autonomous) and 'client-controlled' profession.

This characterisation of Johnson's schema is problematic. It replaces Johnson's original title of 'mediated' with the label of 'third party control'—suggesting there is no room for argument from the outset. However, this account of Johnson's categories does not acknowledge the capacity for professional freedom as well as the bureaucratic control he sees experienced by 'mediated' professional groups.

For Johnson this 'mediated' category is where a third party (usually the state) intervenes in the relationship between client and professional: 'Mediation arises where the state attempts to remove from the producer or the consumer the authority to determine the content and subjects of practice' (Johnson 1972: 77). Here professionals have increasingly been incorporated into the framework of the state, with a professional hierarchy reflecting the organisation's bureaucratic structure. But, Johnson points out, differences in organisational structure and location can influence the occupation's own self-identification and influence their commitment to their bureaucratic role and ability to operate in their professional role. Johnson identifies social work in local authorities as a prime example of a mediated profession.

An ideal standard of professional freedom in terms of autonomy permeates the domination managerialist analysis. It creates a dramatic, but false, choice between free-autonomous-professional and unfree-controlled-bureaucrat. However, there is good reason for seeing the idea of a profession as an occupational group able to control its own work as a myth: '… no occupations manifest professional autonomy of this ideal typical type. It is also questionable whether historically any ever did, although autonomy is retained and persists as a "golden age" image of what professional work might entail' (Evetts 2002: 341–342).

Setting up the choice between autonomy and control is too crude. It ignores the experience of the vast majority of professionals who are employed by organisations (Freidson 1994: 130). While professionals are incorporated into the bureaucracy of the organisation, they continue to operate with some freedom, even though they are controlled in some aspects of their work, in settings where they are often 'loosely coupled' to the organisation (*ibid.* 138). Like other street-level bureaucrats, social workers are able to practice *de facto* discretion in their work—as Lipsky argues. However, as professionals they are also different from other street-level bureaucrats in the degree of freedom that they are able to exercise and the extent to which it is formally recognised.

Howe (1991a) concedes that practitioners retain some freedom in their work, but in areas that, in his view, are not significant. First, there are areas of work not open to standardisation that call for '*in situ* judgement', such as counselling, where the practitioner is the only resource available to meet the need. Secondly, in areas of work that are not a managerial or political priority, the style and manner of work is left to the worker until service users begin to exhibit behaviours that are of direct relevance to organisational operation—for example, involving resource costs, anti-social conduct or threats to physical or developmental well-being. However, Howe argues, the freedom that workers have is not significant because it does not relate to the use of resources and key practice areas such as the definition of need.

Here Howe seems to be saying that social workers do have some freedom, but that, because this freedom is not important, they are not autonomous and cannot really be seen as having professional discretion. However, the areas of freedom he identifies in his own account are significant when we look at evidence about areas of recognised and officially sanctioned discretion, and are significant in organisational terms. Resources, procedures and need are central to community care, and from the beginning practitioners are given a significant discretionary role in the implementation of the policy and translating it into practice. Professional judgement fleshes out community care policy. According to the Department of Health's guidance for practitioners on the implementation of community care, for instance: '... having weighed the views of all parties, including his/her own observation, the assessing practitioner is responsible for defining the user's need' (Department of Health 1991: 3.35). The guidance goes beyond seeing this as just interpreting rules: the assessment of need requires expert knowledge, which the professional brings to the assessment, filling an intended gap in the procedures: 'The same apparent need may have many different causes ... The proper identification of the cause is the basis for selecting the appropriate service response' (*ibid.* 3.32).

The continuing and central role of professional judgement in the assessment and the determination eligibility for services is reiterated in the policy guidance issued with the implementation of Fair Access to Care Services. The guidance emphasises the role of professionals in gathering information, evaluating this to identify needs and risks, and then making decisions on eligibility for services (e.g. Department of Health a, 2003: para 42). The practice guidance develops this point and notes that:

> ... needs assessment and risk evaluation rely for their quality on person-centred conversations with individuals seeking help carried out by competent

professionals prepared to exercise their judgement. Frameworks, case examples and the like can only support the exercise of person-centred, competent judgement. … identification of eligible needs will depend on competent professionals exercising their judgement. In some situations, professionals will deem it appropriate to address all or most needs. In other situations, professionals will consider it appropriate only to address certain needs (Department of Health b, 2003: 6–7).

While Howe says that until the central interests of the organisation are at stake the style and manner of work are left to the worker, he does not acknowledge the significance of this concession. Who, for instance, decides when the point has been reached at which the circumstances require a shift from the practitioner's discretionary judgement to procedures? This is in large part a question of how the practitioner understands and interprets the facts of the situation and whether the practitioner is recognised by the supervisor as the decision-maker. Rule-saturated practice does not entail rule-bound practice (Maynard-Moody and Musheno 2003). Policy implementation is not simply applying rules; it is also about deciding whether the rule applies in the given situation. Policy-makers and managers often assume that procedures will not be followed to the letter, but that practitioners will use their judgement to make them work. This is clearly the message from the Chief Social Services Inspector in her exhortation to practitioners to use their discretion in terms of: 'A culture of care, which knows that consistency is important but it has to be implemented with intelligence and enterprise, not dogma; a culture of care, which puts an end to checklists that replace thinking and judgment' (Social Services Inspectorate 2001: 8).

A possible reason for not recognising social workers' professional discretionary role is the emphasis in domination managerialism on the proliferation of rules and procedures and the equation of this with control and deprofessionalisation (Howe 1986, 1991a, Jones 1999, 2001). Jones offers an historical explanation, portraying the entry of social work into Social Services Departments as the beginning of the end of 'vocationalism' (Jones 1999: 45), with social workers becoming workers, drawn into local state bureaucracy and required to follow instructions, procedures and directions (Jones 1999). Howe makes a similar point, drawing on the work of Jamous and Peloille to support this view (Howe 1991a). Jamous and Peloille (1970) argue that the achievement of professional freedom relates to the relationship of the level of indeterminacy (work characterised by uncertainty and unpredictability of outcome) and the amount of technicality (capacity to formulate and proceduralise responses) in work content (the I/T ratio). The greater the indeterminacy, the greater the chance of achieving professional status. Groups claiming professional status are caught on the horns of a dilemma. Their claim to discretion relates to their ability to deliver the goods in areas of work that have the uncertainty and unpredictability (indeterminacy) necessitating their intervention. However, in order to intervene effectively, they need a body of knowledge that explains and makes predictable the problems with which they are dealing. Insofar as this body of knowledge is formulated, it has the potential to be codified and proceduralised and hence to undermine their claims to special qualities and skills. The higher the level of indeterminacy, the more potential there is for the operation of discretion. Howe uses this argument to challenge the idea that there is discretion in social work: '... to the extent that the occupation can systematically formulate its knowledge, practice, and outcomes, the work is prey to routinisation, de-skilling, and organisational regulation, and these are the strategies of managers' (Howe 1991a: 216).

There are three difficulties with this argument: two theoretical, the other empirical.

First, there is a problem in the assumption that the presence of rules equates with determinacy. The idea of 'essentially contested concepts' (Gallie 1955, Weitz 1977, Freeden 1996) provides a useful set of ideas to help understand why the presence of a body of rules may give rise to indeterminacy. Different but equally valid interpretations of procedures could be made by drawing on elements in the same body of rules, with these elements being outlined, emphasised or downplayed in different ways by different interpreters. The idea of evaluative and internally complex knowledge characterises much, if not all, policy and procedure that pertains to social work practice, allowing procedure to be prioritised and described in significantly different ways by different actors. Paradoxically, more rules may create more discretion; the complex nature of rules and their interaction and the problems of applying rules to concrete situations is, after all, the basis of the legal professions' I/T ratio claim to discretion (Evans and Harris 2004a).

Second, the idea that rules and protocols developed to guide professional practice are necessarily instruments of management control is problematic. It is not just that rules themselves can build up into a complex, interrelated body of knowledge; it is also that rules of practice entail a context of interpretation and background knowledge (Evans and Hardy 2010). Tick charts, by themselves, are meaningless: they require expert knowledge to make them usable (Munro 1998). For managers to control practitioners they have to recruit professional knowledge and expertise. That this is often the case is suggested by the continuing reliance, at least in relation to first-level management, on professionals being managed by fellow professionals (Freidson 1994), and by the observation of managerialism's attempts to colonise professional supervision (Clarke and Newman 1997)—which shows both the power and the weakness of managers and managerialism. Colonisation surely is not a one-way process. Through the proceduralisation of professional practice, management itself has to change. It has to adopt that professional knowledge and, in doing so, change its identity and subject itself to the standards and concerns permeating that knowledge.

Third, Robinson (2003) is critical of the assumption that increased technicality in work—that is, prescribed practices expressed in procedures—should be uncritically read as undermining professional claims. As mentioned above, her study of the implementation of a risk assessment instrument in a probation service finds that, despite trepidation about its introduction in terms of undermining professional discretion, the instrument is welcomed by many practitioners and managers as a useful tool in helping them to assess and manage complex situations and a spur to greater consistency, transparency and equity in assessment practice. The impact of procedures on professionalism cannot be prejudged; it needs to be evaluated in each setting.

The presence of rules does not mean the absence of freedom. However, the opposite of this may also be the case. The absence of rules does not necessarily mean freedom. Carey (2008), for instance, has developed the position associated here with Jones to argue that managerialism, as an ideology, now dominates practice:

> Whether unambiguous and frank, or subtle and implicit, the language games offered by most care managers suggest that the impact of a predominately essentialist and increasingly universal ideological turn have been experienced as potent, compelling, effective and belligerent … [at] … both a conscious and subconscious level, to the point where it can become the only type or form of "social work" from which to choose or identify with and understand … there was only limited evidence discovered of any unified and coherent counter-ideology being articulated, even at group level (other than within the neoliberal framework already discussed) (Carey 2008: 357–8).

Here I want to consider three aspects of this account of managerial ideology. The first is that there seems to be an assumption that, in some way, language is fixed and corresponds to some external reality, eliminating the requirement for actors to understand and interpret instructions or procedures. This 'correspondence' idea of language fails to recognise its contextual and dynamic nature, located in the flow of social identity and social action. Using language is not a passive activity: we may be subject to its rules, but at the same time we use those rules to play games with language and to develop and change the rules themselves (Wittgenstein 2001).

The account also gives the impression that the managerialist discourse has wiped the slate clean. The suggestion is that re-education is complete; that it is not feasible to think of a past before this discourse or a future without it. There may be murmurings at the margins, but according to this approach, there's now only one real game in town. This, however, is implausible. Rather than having ripped up the foundations, managerial discourses have been laid down upon previous ways of working. In some settings, they penetrate further than in others; but people can remember the way things were done before and use this as a source of critical judgement.

There is a plurality of discourses. Some may be more compelling or more obvious than others. Actors are confronted with choices, not inevitabilities (Williams 1993). They may be faced with situations where a powerful discourse simply doesn't correspond with their experience or commitments, and they have to choose what to do. This is not to say it is an easy choice—the choices made may be uncomfortable; they may be inarticulate, in the sense that they try to push a discourse in a way that makes more sense than the situation they're in. Choices may also be painful, where the position taken by the actor contradicts powerful interests. But the struggle and discomfort do not remove the choice. This, perhaps, explains the discomfiture of discretion.

Professional knowledge structures and can constrain professional practice, and still leave room for discretion. These arguments emphasise the value of assessing professional social work's status against the standard of discretion, rather than autonomy—freedom which is not absolute but set about with limits (Evetts 2002). By this measure, social workers within Social Services continue to be a professional group.

Another possible argument against this view is that it ignores the role of sponsorship and support for professional status (Jamous and Peloille 1970)— something which many social work commentators identify as having been lacking for professional social work over the past two decades (Hopkins 1996, Bradley 2005, Payne 2005). However, while there is reason to believe that support for social work as a professional group has been reduced, it has not disappeared. Professional discretion continues to have its supporters and its uses in a managerialised service. Harrison, for instance, points out that professionalism in the welfare state is still supported by consumers, who often value an independent professional rather than a state bureaucrat being involved in their care (Harrison 1999).

There are other reasons, too, why powerful actors may continue to see a role for social work discretion. While discretion may give freedom, it also ascribes responsibility. As Ellis *et al.* observe: 'Front-line staff had ultimate responsibility for managing inflated and conflicting policy objectives with inadequate levels of resources relative to demand, yet were subject to low managerial scrutiny' (Ellis *et al.* 1999: 276). There is an assumption in much of the discussion about managers that they are happy to take both responsibility and control in their organisation. However, responsibility is a risky business. Modern society is widely characterised as concerned about the management of risk (Malin *et al.* 2002). Beck, for instance, has pointed to the impact of science in demystifying nature and giving the impression that risk can now be calculated and is susceptible to technical interventions (Beck 1992, Lupton 1999). Government has been seen as taking on a protective responsibility to control and reduce the risks to which its citizens are exposed (Hood *et al.* 2001). In this context, Hood *et al.* argue that organisations not only manage risks but also manage the organisation's exposure to blame when things go wrong: risk regimes. They identify a number of elements in risk regimes, including the management of information release; but they also identify more fundamental changes to the basic structure of the organisation. Here they identify two key strategies. One is proceduralisation, which involves the increasingly detailed specification of procedures and guidelines, setting out the right way to do things, so that when something goes wrong the organisation can point to the procedures as a defence against criticism. Another strategy is 'service abandonment'. The risk, for the organisation, of proceduralisation is that it implies an acceptance of responsibility. In many situations this is unavoidable, but in others the organisation can reduce its exposure to blame by clouding its responsibility for a service area. At its most extreme service abandonment involves withdrawing from providing a service, but more often it can mean not '… issuing advice or information for fear of blame, legal liability or other adverse risks' (*ibid.* 2001: 166). An example of this process can be seen in the use of retaining some idea of professional discretion and decision-making within social care organisations to distance managers and the organisation from responsibility for problems. Wells (1997), for instance, argues that managers are as much involved in a strategy of shifting responsibility as they are in seeking control, and that continuing professional discretion can be seen as an element in this process. He identifies a chain of blame-shifting in mental health policy from the top down, and points out that while government policy calls for the targeting of specialist mental health services on people with a 'severe and enduring mental illness', it has failed to provide a clear definition of the term. The definition provided by the government is a framework within which precise definitions are to be agreed locally: 'The government requires managers to strike a balance between demands, needs and resources but it avoids direct responsibility for what can and cannot be met' (*ibid.* 336). In turn, professionals are put in the position of managing individual demands for resources from service users, thus 'distancing management and policy makers from the reality of the "felt" experience of policy, which is ultimately left to practitioners to interpret' (*ibid.* 340). Marchant (1993) and Bradley (2003) point to a similar process in Social Services organisations generally, where practitioners are faced with vague and imprecise criteria and regulations, which distance senior officers and politicians from difficult rationing decisions.

The continuation of a professional element in the organisation of social work within Social Services organisations can, therefore, be seen, in part, as a managerial strategy to redistribute blame. (The significance of this practice is suggested by Laming's criticisms in the Climbié report [Lord Laming 2003], which highlights the way in which senior managers distanced themselves from professional decision-making.) However, there may also be more positive reasons within the culture of Social Services for the continuation of an element of professional discretion associated with the continuing culture of bureau-professionalism, not only amongst practitioners but also amongst their managers.

Conclusion

Lipsky's analysis of discretion in street-level bureaucracies has been considered in relation to contemporary debates about the impact of managerialism within Social Services, particularly the nature of management and the extent of professional influence on discretion. Lipsky's work has been identified as directly relevant to the analysis of practitioner discretion within social work by authors such as Baldwin and Ellis *et al.* However, other commentators such as Howe and Cheetham argue that Lipsky's work no longer provides a convincing analysis because of the increasing influence of managerialism.

The argument in this chapter develops from the recognition that, contrary to this criticism, Lipsky's street-level bureaucracies are organisations in which managers and management concerns and techniques play a significant role. In contrasting these two analyses of discretion, Howe's argument is related to a broader literature on managerialism, which presents managers as dominant forces in organisations. Contrary to the perspective suggested by Howe, it has been mooted that street-level bureaucracy theory and domination managerialism are similar in their characterisation of the orientation of managers as committed to organisational goals, and in their portrayal of workers as deprofessionalised employees. They also share the view that there is a fundamental conflict between management and these workers, although within this conflict the street-level bureaucracy perspective portrays managers engaging in pragmatic compromises with workers. This relates to the significant difference between these points of view. Domination managerialism's account of discretion emphasises the effectiveness of management control and the minimal nature of street-level practitioners' resources for resistance to this control. The street-level perspective, in contrast, sees managerialist techniques as flawed, in a context of necessarily vague policy and uncertain resources, giving rise to extensive means at street level to resist management control. The result is that, while domination managerialism underlines the minimal and residual nature of discretion, the street-level bureaucracy perspective points to extensive, day-to-day and practical discretion, exercised by street-level bureaucrats. Alongside the domination managerial perspective, I have argued that it is possible to identify another strand of managerial analysis, here called discursive managerialism, differing from the street-level perspective in questioning the assumption that managers' orientation is necessarily and exclusively organisational, and that their relationship with practitioners is necessarily conflictual. While it recognises that practitioners are part of an organisation and are, as such, employees, this perspective also points to the continuing influence of professionalism as a factor in managers' understanding of their role and as a resource used by practitioners to claim discretion in their work. It shares with street-level bureaucracy a recognition of the limited effectiveness of managerial techniques of control, but also highlights the influence of professional discourse as an additional resource for resistance to managerial control. The picture of discretion put forward by this position is variegated, focusing on local constructions of discretion that draw in various ways on *de facto* conditions and professional claims.

These interrelated but different analyses of discretion are summarised in the table below. The key areas they identify for further exploration about discretion and the value and limitations of Lipsky's theory focus on: the organisational context of discretion; the orientation and concerns of management; the nature and effectiveness of management control of practice; and the nature of the relationship between street-level practitioners and their managers.

Regimes of Discretion within Managerialised Social Services

Table 3.1 Regimes of discretion within managerialised social services

	Domination managerialism	Street-level bureaucracy	Discursive managerialism
Orientation of managers	Organisational	Organisational	Organisational and professional
Organisational view of practitioners	Employees	Employees	Professional employees
Relationship between managers and practitioners	Hierarchical	Hierarchical	Collegiate/ Hierarchical
Strategies of management control	Effective/ Extensive	Limited effectiveness	Limited effectiveness and legitimacy
Practitioner resistance	Limited: Managers dominate and control	*de facto* opportunities widespread.	*de facto* and *de jure* resources widespread
Characterisation of discretion	Undesirable/ Severely constrained	Widespread, necessary but also problematic	Extensive, local variation and requires evaluation

This range of analyses suggests different ways of understanding social work discretion within Social Services Departments. Lipsky's perspective is, contrary to the arguments of some critics, directly relevant to British Social Services Departments and underlines the need to consider the effectiveness of management control. This organisational context of Social Services also points to the need to critically examine the street-level bureaucracy analysis of discretion in the light of the influence of managerialism and professionalism on social work practice. The interaction of these factors will be considered through the examination of discretion in relation to a particular organisational context by asking the question: is this setting characterised by the conditions of street-level bureaucracy?

Furthermore, the fact that a site shares the basic conditions of a street-level bureaucracy should not exclude the possibility that other factors may also have a significant impact on street-level discretion within the organisation. Accordingly, it is also necessary to consider: *what additional contextual factors contribute to the extent and nature of discretion within a particular site?*

Managers have been identified as playing an increasingly significant role within Social Services organisations. This development, I have argued, rather than making the street-level bureaucracy perspective less relevant, in fact increases its relevance. However, the idea of management, which is central to Lipsky's analysis of street-level discretion—he characterises management as an homogenous entity which is committed to organisational values and restricts the freedom of street-level practitioners—is called into question by the literature, which points to management as internally stratified and motivated by a range of concerns, not just organisational commitment. This analysis suggests the need to investigate *the nature of management within Social Services as a street-level bureaucracy, particularly at the interface between street-level and front-line management, and between front-line managers and senior managers in terms of its structure and the range of motivations of managers.*

Lipsky's analysis of discretion at street-level emphasises a dual process of control and resistance—managers striving to control, and street-level practitioners seeking to resist. He also points out that, within this context of conflict, managers and street-level bureaucrats collude in accepting limited discretionary behaviour in order to get the job done (managers) and to ensure that the job continues to be there (street-level practitioners). The literature which has been considered above is inconclusive about the capacity of management to control and the ability of street-level to resist, thus creating discretionary space. The literature also questions Lipsky's basic assumption that managers and street-level bureaucrats are motivated by different concerns—and particularly in the context of an historically professionalised bureaucracy such as Social Services. What Lipsky identifies as a collusion to keep things ticking over between managers and street-level practitioners may be motivated not only by pragmatic concerns but also by shared professional commitments. In light of the suggestion in the literature that there is a fundamental distinction to be drawn between senior strategic managers and local managers, I propose to explore two further issues about the relationship between managers and the control of professional street-level bureaucrats.

Senior managers rely largely on 'remote control' strategies, such as control of resources and procedures to direct street-level practice. *Is control through resources and procedures exercised uniformly across all areas of social work or only in certain areas? How effectively do these strategies control local discretion? To what extent can street-level practitioners resist? What role do local managers play in enforcing resource and procedural controls?* The relationship between local managers and street-level practitioners appears to be central in understanding management control of discretion, both in terms of the enforcement of procedures and in terms of the possible recognition of professional commitments. In terms of understanding street-level discretion, the nature of the relations between local managers and street-level practitioners requires closer examination. *What is the nature of relations between local managers and street-level practitioners? To what extent is it structured by the idea of conflicting interests of managers and street-level bureaucrats? To what extent is it influenced by shared commitments and concerns, particularly around professionalism?*

Chapter 4
Researching Discretion:
The Case Study Outlined

Introduction

The discussion of Lipsky's analysis of discretion in *Street-Level Bureaucracy* and the consideration of its subsequent development and application to the examination of professional discretion in Social Services have raised a number of questions. Critics have argued that the conditions of British Social Services Departments are quite unlike Lipsky's characterisation of street-level bureaucracy, and that the theory does not apply in the contemporary British context. I have argued that the street-level bureaucracy perspective is, in fact, directly relevant to the more managerialised nature of contemporary social work and raises important questions about the effectiveness and nature of management control portrayed by domination managerialist analysts. However, some proponents of the street-level bureaucracy perspective present it as a sufficient account of discretion. This is a disputable claim. Discursive managerialist analysts point to the way in which professionalism continues to influence the nature of discretion, both through the impact it might have on assumptions within the organisation about the freedom afforded to certain occupational groups, and through the relationship between managers and practitioners (and between managers at various levels in the organisation). While Lipsky provides a perspective on discretion within large, public organisations, its insights appear to be limited where professionalism is a significant factor in the structure of Social Services Departments.

In the preceding chapter I set out a range of key questions that arose from the review and critical examination of the street-level bureaucracy literature and its application to contemporary state social work. In this chapter I will outline the research approach—a case study—and outline the case study itself.

The Case Study Approach

Case studies are particularly useful in examining people's experience and relating them to their context, and for developing theoretical analysis that engages with '… the realities which conflict with [the researcher's] expectations' (Hartley 2004: 325). The complex and interrelated nature of the research questions reflects recognition of the actors' interaction and their context in public organisations and points to the appropriateness of adopting a case study approach. Case study research is suited to these interrelated questions because it involves examining the experience of actors in a specific context and seeking to understand the complexity and interconnectedness of their practices and the situation (Yin 2003: 13, Hartley 2004: 323). It also captures complexities of social life in a situation that enables us to develop a more nuanced and '... fine tuned exploration of complex sets of interrelationships' (Edwards and Talbot 1999: 50). Additionally, the case study approach combines the opportunity not only to explore these questions in a particular setting but also to use the lessons from this setting to elucidate and develop the theory further (Hartley 2004: 331).

Generalising from case studies: The theoretical case

Walton proposes an instrumental approach to case studies, emphasising the importance of theory in identifying cases. He rejects an intrinsic conception of cases—the idea that the case is a natural entity, 'out there' and predefined—and instead argues that the properties of events, actions, institutions etc. are constructed as a case in a relationship with theory (Walton 1992). Theoretical concerns define the case and identify significant dimensions and where its boundaries are. The same range of circumstances might be constructed as different cases from different theoretical perspectives—for instance, the same hospital could be a case of street-level bureaucracy (Lipsky 1980) and of negotiated order (Strauss *et al.* 1963), depending on the concerns of the researcher. However, his claim is not simply that theory can be imposed on any situation. For Walton (1992), there is a process of matching and adapting between theory and circumstances. The case study is in a dynamic relationship with theory; theory clarifies the focus of the case study, while the concrete circumstance of the case study is used to develop, adapt and challenge theory.

Walton sees this process operating in two ways. Theory is developed through analogy: it works in one case; another is seen as analogous, and the case study tests this analogy and demonstrates it (or not). Alternatively, cases are studied which, while similar, are also different: they are problematic, and require the theory to be adapted or changed to take account of the circumstances. A similar emphasis on the role of theory in case study work is made by Burawoy (1991), who argues that case studies provide the opportunity to look at theories of general structures and examine how these structures operate and interact in particular, often anomalous, cases.

A possible criticism of this emphasis on theory is that the facts are forced to fit the theory. Theory acts like a paradigm in normal science, where the goal is to confirm and elaborate the exemplar case (Khun 1970). The challenge is how to maintain a balance between extending theory from one situation to another, and still challenge and adapt that theory—and here, as mentioned above, the case study approach provides a powerful approach to unlocking assumptions and opening up thinking (Hartley 2004).

Walton's characterisation of theory as hypothesis held tentatively and continually open to change, development and adaptation, is an important notion in protecting against imposing theory on reality. Ragin (1987) also provides some pointers to how this can be achieved in practice. His view is that inductive theory-generation brings up points for consideration. These points are not hard and fast truths; they establish a dialogue between the investigator's ideas and the evidence, taking the initial hypothesis, developing and changing it, the better to explain complexity. In the context of case studies, the value of this questioning approach is that it looks behind apparent similarities and differences and acknowledges the interaction of individual factors and the broader context: '... to determine how different combinations of conditions have the same causal significance and how similar causal factors can operate in different directions' (*ibid.* 49).

Identifying the case

The first step in case study research involves choosing the case study, by asking what sort of study is needed to answer the questions being posed (Hartley 2004: 327). This raises the question: how does the researcher know when a case and a theory relate to one another? In answer to this, Schofield points out that:

> A consensus appears to be emerging that for qualitative researchers generalizability is best thought of as a matter of "fit" between the situation studied and others to which one might be interested in applying the concepts and conclusions of that study. This conceptualisation makes thick descriptions crucial, since without them one does not have the information necessary for informed judgement about the issue of fit (Schofield 2000: 92–93).

'Thick descriptions' do not have to be voluminous accounts of 'the case'. What is important is that the description provides sufficient background information, the context, to allow a reader to understand the findings (Lincoln and Guba 2000). A thick description gives a sense of the circumstances from which the findings emerge and within which the theory belongs. Its purpose is to clarify the background assumptions that make sense of the theory and help identify similarities and differences in the context of the original study and the new situations in which the theory can then be applied and developed.

The concern of this chapter is the critical examination of Lipsky's street-level bureaucracy perspective in relation to professional discretion in managerialised Social Services. The context of this perspective, without which '... the analysis is less likely to be appropriate ...' (Lipsky 1980: 28), is the conditions of work which characterise these organisations. This is what constitutes the thick description and the basis of establishing fit between the theory and particular cases. Street-level bureaucracies are organisations characterised by problems of scarce resources that are compounded by ill-defined organisational goals and unrealistically high expectations of public agencies and their staff. They are also organisations in which 'performance oriented toward goal achievement tends to be difficult if not impossible to measure' (*ibid.* 28). They are difficult organisations to work in and to manage. Transferability, though, is not about establishing an identical match; it is often more like a family resemblance, and as well as recognising similarities is concerned with understanding possible differences (Guba and Lincoln 1989). In relation to the examination of issues raised in the preceding chapter, an important dimension of difference is the presence of professional staff at street level and in management roles.

This study is designed as a single case study of social work in adult services in a local authority Social Services Department, which focuses on two embedded units of analysis: an older persons social work team; and a mental health social work team (see below). The rationale for adopting this design is that a single case study provides the opportunity to undertake the critical examination of theory—street-level bureaucracy theory—and, within this, the use of two units of analysis to compare and contrast the influence of professionalism and managerialism on discretion and the relationship between practitioners and managers within this street-level bureaucracy setting. To this end I have compared social workers in an older persons' team and in a Mental Health Team. Social workers are the predominant professional group in social care (Department of Health 2009), and increasingly so as social care is focused on the assessment and management of the most vulnerable in society. Social work is also a profession that has been closely associated with the ethos and management of Social services (Hill 2003: 197–199). Social work within the new Social Services Departments was primarily seen as a generic role, but subsequent developments gave rise to the increasing specialisation of social work along client group lines (Hill 2000b). The Mental Health Act 1983 and its establishment of the role of Approved Social Worker (ASW)[1] reinforced the historical separateness of psychiatric social work and enhanced the training and professional status of mental health social work (Shaw 2000, Payne 2005). The community care reforms of the early 1990s, which are closely associated with the insinuation of managerialism within Social Services, were primarily concerned with the control of expenditure on older persons services (Challis and Hugman 1993, Lewis and Glennerster 1996). In examining the impact of care management on older persons and mental health services, a distinction has been made between 'brokerage care management', which is largely administrative and concerns coordinating services, and 'clinical care management', which emphasises the central role of care managers as professional providers of services (Huxley 1993, Burns 1997). Using this distinction, Huxley has argued that the brokerage approach is more relevant in understanding adult community care, while in mental

---

1　Under the Metal Health Act 1993 the process for making a decision about whether someone with mental health problems required detention against their will in hospital involved medical recommendation and an assessment by a specially trained social work (an Approved Social Worker). On the basis of the recommendations and assessment, the Approved Social Worker would then make a decision about whether the person needed to be detained or not. (The role of ASW was abolished in 2007 and replaced by the role of Approved Mental Health Practitioner, a role no longer exclusively open to social workers.)

health the clinical approach is more appropriate (Huxley 1993). Burns also points out that in mental health, clinical care management has been more influential in the operation of the Care Programme Approach—the mental health version of care management (Burns 1997). The contrasting nature of these two different services points to their value as sites for examining the influence of professionalism and managerialism on discretion.

The remainder of this chapter is a description of the local authority in which the research was conducted, and the two adult social work teams studied. Characteristics of participants in the case study will then be outlined, and their possible effect on perceptions of the world of practice which participants inhabit will be considered. This will lead to consideration of the authority's recent history and its legacies in the current organisation and practice.

The Department and the Two Teams

The study authority, here called 'Newunit', is an English unitary[2] local authority which has a population of around 150,000 and is primarily rural, though dominated by its market town. The main call on Social Services, as measured by expenditure, is older people's services. The council has a long history of Conservative control, but in the past decade control passed to the Liberal Democrats. Newunit is a relatively new Social Services authority and inherited this responsibility from the former county council authority, which ceased to exist in April 1998, and which is here referred to as 'Oldshire'.

Oldshire was a large authority with a population of around three quarters of a million in a mixture of rural and urban communities. During the 1980s Oldshire was controlled by the Conservative party, but in the early 1990s the county moved to no overall control. The authority saw itself as businesslike, with the Social Services Department, for instance, welcoming the White Paper *Caring for People* (Department of Health 1989) in terms of creating a mixed economy of care with greater private provision, and pointing out that: '... we are ahead of the White Paper ... in ... the work which has been set in hand to establish Quality Assurance in the

---

2   Local authorities in England and Wales had been reorganised in the early 1970s, and outside the large urban areas they are organised according to a two-level system. Shire authorities were the top-level authorities, with large budgets funding major services such as education and social services. Within shire authorities there was a lower level of authority—the district authority—which provided more local services such as housing. This system was criticised as being complicated and creating large shire authorities which had little connection with local population; and during the mid-1990s the Conservative government decided to review these arrangements on a piecemeal basis and, in some areas, chose to abolish shires and moved responsibility for providing their services down to local level, combined with the district council services. These sing-level local authorities are referred to as unitary authorities.

Department, the developed management initiatives which will give our providers a head start …' (Oldshire Social services Committee Paper March 1990).

Within Newunit the research looks at two different social work teams: an Older Persons Team (OPT), and a Community Mental Health Team (CMHT). These teams are made up of a number of staff; my interest is in the professionally qualified social workers, who enabled me to look at street-level bureaucracy as mediated by professionalism. Two different adult teams also provide an opportunity to compare and contrast the impact of managerialism and professionalism on discretion within different working contexts.

The council recently reorganised its structure, with Social Services now split between children's and adults' services. Adult community care services, which include services for older people and people with mental health problems, were recently amalgamated with housing. The corporate director (Community Care and Housing) was also the Director of Social Services.

Within the elderly and physical disabilities service (EPDS) there is a clear split between commissioning, such as care management, and service provision, such as home care. There are two, geographically organised Older Persons Teams (OPTs); both are care management teams responsible for assessment, care planning and commissioning. The teams are made up of social workers and occupational therapists (all employed by the authority) and take direct referrals and referrals from individual and other agencies. I looked at one of these teams. The OPT structure is summarised in Figure 4.1.

The Community Mental Health Team (CMHT) covers the whole area and is a joint Health and Social Services team made up of social workers, community psychiatric nurses, psychiatrists and a day service, with social workers employed by Social Services and other staff employed by Health (the CMHT structure is summarised in Figure 4.2).

In the OPT the team manager and two assistant managers are all women who are qualified social workers. The assistant managers manage both occupational therapists and social workers. They also carry a small caseload. Newunit's publicity material about the service does not mention professional titles, only referring to the generic 'care manager' role.

In the CMHT both the team manager (male) and the assistant manager (female) running the social work service are social workers. The manager is a joint Health and Social Services appointment, and is employed by the local NHS trust. The assistant manager is employed by Social Services, manages the social work team and runs the Approved Social Worker (ASW) service, and is also a practising ASW. The CMHT is a specialist mental health service combining commissioning and provider services, and takes referrals only from other agencies, mainly general practitioners (GPs). 'Core services' provided by Social Services to the CMHT are described in the official documents in broad terms, including: '… ongoing intervention and interaction with clients and carers' (Newunit Community Care Plan 1999–2000).

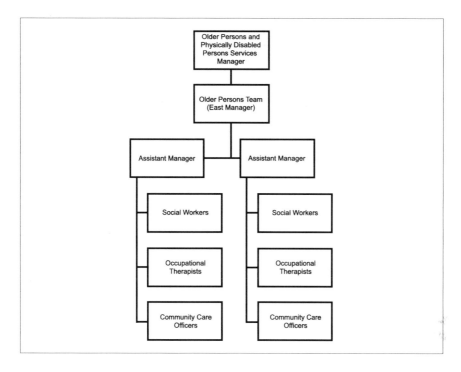

Figure 4.1 Older Persons Team organisational structure

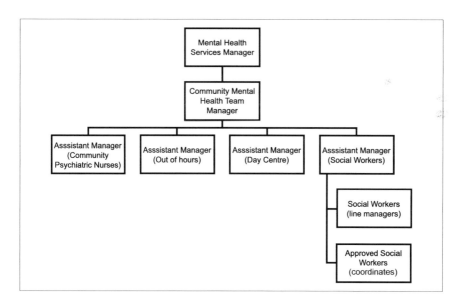

Figure 4.2 Mental Health Team organisational structure

My focus in both teams is on social workers and their line managers. All the social workers and managers interviewed are qualified. There are six social workers in the OPT and in the CMHT. In each team one social worker declined to participate in the research. The social worker in the OPT sought me out to tell me that her decision stemmed from her anger about the authority's cuts in older people's services. The CMHT social worker's reasons for declining are not known.

In the OPT three of the social workers interviewed are full-time and two are part-time; all the CMHT social workers are full-time, as are all managers in both teams. Most managers and workers are women: of the five managers one is a man; eight of the ten social workers are women. All but one of the people interviewed are White British.

In the CMHT both managers have been managers for over 10 years. In the OPT only the team manager has extensive management experience (11 years). The other two managers have two years' and one year's management experience respectively.

While there is a range of experience both as social workers and as employees of the authority in both teams, there is a significant difference in the pattern of worker experience in terms of the number of years each interviewee has been qualified and the amount of time worked for Newunit or its predecessor authority. The two groups of social workers and managers in each team are quite different in relation to their career histories. Most workers in the OPT have worked in the authority since they were qualified (one social worker appears to have extensive experience outside the authority, but this is mainly the result of a career break; another person worked for the authority for some time before being sponsored to undertake social work training). The exception to this pattern is the team manager, who has worked in social work teams elsewhere. By contrast, in the CMHT all the workers and managers have been employed as social workers by other authorities than Newunit or Oldshire.

(See appendix for explanation of interview data codes.)

In order to understand the current organisation and issues in Newunit, it is necessary to review the recent history of the teams and the department. Despite recent changes at the senior level of Social Services, the day-to-day organisation—care management and Social Services policies and systems—was largely developed in Oldshire, then taken over and continued by Newunit. Recent policy initiatives, such as the control of financial overspend, can be understood only in the context of Oldshire's legacy, which is outlined below.

The implementation of care management

A pivotal point for adult Social Services in England and Wales was the implementation of the NHS and Community Care Act in 1993 (Hill 2000a), which was central to the intrusion of managerialism into adult Social Services (Harris 2003). Oldshire embraced the reforms of adult Social Services in the early 1990s. In implementing care management, local authorities had to consider the context within which it was to be put into effect, particularly the idea of Social Services as an enabling authority, and the idea of a market of care, which distinguished the roles of purchasers and providers of services within social care (Hill 2000d, Harris 2003).

Oldshire took a proactive approach to implementation of the new community care. The form of care management adopted in the county was strongly administrative and based on a clear purchaser/provider split. The authority saw itself as blazing a trail for care management and a more market-based approach to care provision. In a Social Services Committee Paper, senior officers comment that: 'Many of the ideas contained in the White Paper are already to be seen in the way in which we work in [Oldshire]', and that the consultation primarily sets the scene and asks questions about how, precisely, the authority should go forward. For instance, in its role as enabling authority, it predicts that: '... a clear distinction will need to be made between the purchasing and providing functions within the local authority' and emphasises the need for a training and personnel strategy focusing on new skills for 'case managers' [*sic*] in negotiating and designing care packages and financial management for managers (Oldshire Social Services Committee Paper March 1990).

Alongside organisational changes within Oldshire, the community care reforms were accompanied by important changes, closely associated with the purchaser/ provider split, in the authority's view of professionals such as social workers. Social workers became care managers:

> ... social workers as care managers or whatever, they were put in commissioning. You were buyers or you were sellers. Social workers were buyers, and what they bought were services from providers. So the sense that social workers could be providers as well—it was still acknowledged verbally, as, oh yeah, well of course, we might be providing a service as well. But we were situated on that kind of a divide (OM1).

While these changes had a significant influence on adult community care services, a range of other factors seemed to reduce their impact on social workers in the CMHT. In relation to the community care reforms, national policy reinforced the separateness of mental health. In putting forward its community care policy, central government went against Griffiths' proposal and split lead responsibility for community care. While local authorities were responsible for most community care, it gave responsibility for mental health planning to the NHS (Shaw 2000). As care management was being implemented in Social Services, a different but parallel form of care management, the Care Programme Approach, was implemented in mental health.

In Oldshire, mental health services were not a priority. Before these reforms there was a third lower investment of Social Services resources in mental health services locally when compared with the national average for Social Services (2 per cent of annual revenue expenditure, as opposed to 3 per cent) (Social Services Inspectorate Report 1989). There was an emphasis on joint Health and Social Services provision and CMHTs were developed in Oldshire, one of the first of which was in what would become the Newunit area (Oldshire Three Year Plan 1990). Social workers within the team felt that mental health was increasingly marginal to the local authority:

> I remember going up to Shire Hall, a group of us here, because we were feeling so frustrated that there didn't seem to be any policy, there didn't seem to be any overall views ... mental health seemed the poor cousin. There was more emphasis on elderly and children and families, and we just felt there wasn't any strategy (MS2).

Team work and professional social work

Both the CMHT and the OPT were and are, in Ovretveit's terms: 'Formal multidisciplinary community team[s]: a working group with a defined membership of different professions, governed by an agreed and explicit team policy, which is upheld by a team leader' (Ovretveit 1993: 64). Under the umbrella of formal teams, Ovretveit distinguishes different forms of organisation and, using his typology, helps clarify the differing ways in which these two teams were organised, and how this organisation has changed over time.

At the time of the introduction of community care, Oldshire was organising its teams in terms of client groups. In the older people's services, this involved teams of both social workers and occupational therapists. In Oldshire, the OPT was a 'fully managed multidisciplinary team[s]: team members from different professions, fully managed by the team manager' (*ibid.* 75). The team was made up of social workers, occupational therapists and unqualified staff, who were employed by Social Services and jointly managed by the same managers. The CMHT, on the other hand, corresponded to another type of formal team identified by Ovretveit: the 'managed-core and coordinated-associate team'. Here, some team members are line-managed by the team leader, while others come under another organisational structure; their contribution to the team is negotiated and coordinated (*ibid.* 68). At team level the leadership role was taken by the consultant psychiatrist, although, as the following comment from a practitioner suggests, this leadership was not accepted uncritically by all:

> The Mental Health Team was set up 15 years ago; it's been looked after by two consultants up to last year—white, English middle class and paternalistic. They were keen to educate up the social work staff in the medical model. They left last year. It's been a big change, it's been a steep learning curve (field note: CMHT, comment by social worker).

When Social Services were transferred to Newunit, the CMHT remained unchanged: it was already geographically based in the district. The OPT was reconstituted with some geographical changes to its boundaries and with social work staff previously based in hospitals brought into the team.

The internal organisation of the OPT as a single agency (Social Services) multi-disciplinary team has, then, remained the same, although the particular geographical areas to which the team relates changed slightly over recent years.

In 2000 the CMHT was reorganised into a jointly managed, multi-agency, multi-disciplinary team with a team manager (from a social work background) appointed by Health and Social Services. Amongst other things, the team manager oversaw community psychiatric (CPN) nurses and social workers. However, unlike the OPT, where occupational therapists and social workers are managed by the same managers and share the same room, in the CMHT there are separate CPN and social work teams, each led by a member of its own profession; and the social workers, who are still employed by Social Services, work within both Social Services and local trust policies. Social workers and CPNs as professional groups occupy different rooms.

The picture that emerges from the CMHT is of social work in the context of entrenched and strong professional identities, central to the defining of role. One practitioner who worked in adult services in the early 1990s (and subsequently moved to the CMHT to be the assistant manager) contrasts the impact of community care reforms in both teams in terms of a continuing professional identity:

> The adult and disability team embraced care management full fold; we took on joint working very readily. I learnt a lot about OT, and understood buying and selling services between each other. In the Mental Health Team they had their profession, they were not going to be care managers. From the outside they were seen as isolated, peculiar (field note: CMHT, comment by assistant manager).

All interviewees in the CMHT make a point of drawing a clear line between their roles— which they characterise as continuing to have a 'clinical' dimension— and that of workers in the OPT, which is more administrative. This point is echoed in the authority's Community Care Plan, which, in contrast to other adult client groups, talks of care managers in mental health providing '… ongoing intervention and interaction with clients and carers' (Newunit Community Care Plan 1999–2000: 28).

The structure of Social Services budgets for the OPT and the CMHT reflects these different roles. Forty-four per cent of the current mental health services budget is spent on 'assessment and care management' (even after allowance is made for ASW assessment time), whereas in the OPT the percentage of budget covering the cost of professional staff is much lower, at 13.2 per cent (Newunit Community Care Plans 1999–2000 and 2000–2001). The proportion of professional time, as compared with the rest of the budget, may be higher in the CMHT because there are fewer funds for the purchase of services and lower in the OPT because of economies of scale. Nevertheless, even taking this into account, there remains a significant discrepancy between the two teams' budgets for professional staff— a point underlined in a recent SSI inspection report, which points out the low proportion of professional social work staff in the OPT compared with other authorities.

Impact of local reorganisations

The picture so far in adult services has emphasised the impact of care management reforms, and therefore of managerialism, particularly in older persons services. However, a number of limiting factors within the organisation, particularly the effect of the reorganisation of Social Services in 1998, have curtailed management influence within Newunit.

Newunit became a Social Services Authority following the abolition of Oldshire. In a national study of the partial reorganisation of local government in England, Craig and Manthorpe (1999) find Social Services Departments expressing concern about reorganisation because of loss of central expertise, having to refocus existing service provision in line with new local priorities and losing economies of scale.

Senior managers within Social Services criticised the local government commission proposal to abolish Oldshire and shift Social Services to six district authorities. They questioned the capacity of the unitaries to provide Social services and support professional staff, and argued that the change would result in increased management costs (Oldshire Social Services Committee Paper, July 1994). A report by the Director of Social Services also points out problems with budgets: '[Oldshire] spends significantly above its Standard Spending Assessment on social services—a seamless transition of services will only be achieved if this level of funding is matched' (Oldshire Social Services Committee Paper October 1994). A year later the Director of Social Services reiterated her concerns that the reorganisation was likely to lead to an increase in costs, disruption and loss of momentum in the implementation of community care (Oldshire Social services Committee Paper March 1995).

The new unitary authority was able to attract senior figures from Oldshire's Social Services: the Deputy Director of Social Services, for instance, became Newunit's Director of Social Services, and a previous senior planner is the current director of Social Services. However, Social Services' move from the shire to the unitary disrupted central management control in a number of ways.

As part of the management reforms associated with community care, Oldshire introduced a 'client record and information system' (CRIS), designed to computerise records and manage and monitor case management. The computer system was countywide, and with the reorganisation it had to be disaggregated to operate at district levels. Within Newunit this resulted in its largely becoming a basic case-recording system, a situation reflected in the SSI's observation that: '... it was unable to meet modern management information needs' (Inspection Report 2002: para 9.9).

Another significant issue for management and control within Newunit was its ability to support a strategic management and control function. This largely seems to have been related to funding problems inherited from Oldshire, which will be discussed further below.

In relation to older people's services, a recent SSI inspection report highlights the problem of insufficient strategic management capacity to develop the service (*ibid.*).

The impact of the move also resulted in a loss of expertise at the centre. Newunit carried over and continued to operate policies developed within Oldshire, but the senior staff who developed them were distributed amongst the six unitaries. For instance, one practitioner, who moved from Oldshire to Newunit, comments that in terms of local procedures relating to the operation of the Mental Health Act:

> We used to have a county-wide legal team, who had a lot of confidence …
> who had a lot of knowledge of mental health law, and we then had to use our
> own lawyers in [Newunit] and basically had to help train them up, because
> they actually came in completely naïve on mental health … a lot of mental
> health legislation is not just going to the books: it's people's knowledge of such
> situations (MS2).

Alongside changes in Social Services, both teams have had to cope with changes in the organisation of local Health services and central government emphasis on partnerships across Health and Social Services (Hill 2000c) involving the pooling of budgets and integration of services (Mitchell 2000). Cross-agency work with Health has been problematic because of continuing changes in local NHS organisation—a point noted at national level by the Chief Inspector of Social Services (Social Services Inspectorate 2001). In this context, the OPT has set up working relationships with the two primary care trusts (PCTs) to which it relates, and with them has agreed a joint assessment document and eligibility criteria. The situation in mental health is slightly more complicated and was described by one manager as 'planning blight' (MM2). While the OPT is a primary care service, the CMHT is a specialist secondary service, with working relationships between Social Services and Health and a provider trust. The Local Priority Needs Trust (co-terminus with the unitary authority) was abolished and replaced with a Mental Health Trust, which was co-terminus with the old county. There are plans for a new trust to be developed which corresponds to the two PCTs, covering and extending just beyond the unitary authority.

Pressures on resources

Fundamental concerns about reorganisation are also voiced in terms of the resourcing of Social Services and the ethos of the new authority. Several practitioners in the OPT contrast the current resource problems in Newunit with their experience of the resource situation in Oldshire: 'All I know is that all the time we were a big authority, there just was not that restriction on resources' (OS4).

A recent Audit Commission/SSI joint review notes that:

> In 1998/9, the new Authority inherited a level of expenditure significantly above its Standard Spending Assessment (SSA) and increased Council Tax by 22% in order to cover planned commitments and avoid any disruption to services for users. There was a further 6% increase in 1999/2000. ... This higher level of contribution from local revenue, however, is more due to a relatively low central government grant settlement than because the Authority is a high spender (Inspection Report 2001: para 1.3.1).

The report criticises Social Services' incremental budget-setting and calls for the development of budget-setting based on 'year zero' needs. (Incremental budgeting involves using the previous period's budget as the basis for the next period's budget, with additions for new items. In contrast, a zero-base budget is where '... a manager responsible for its presentation is required to prepare and justify the budget expenditure from zero base i.e. assuming there is no commitment to spend on any activity' [Hussey 1999].) The report emphasises the need for politicians to make decisions about the levels of services they are willing to provide.

As a consequence, Newunit Social Services have seen attempts to reduce spending. The Director of Social Services, for instance, points out that: '[Newunit] is facing severe budget problems this year, and Social Services has to take its share. This means we are looking to make significant savings in the budget of adult services' (Newunit Community Care Plan 2000–2001).

However, within this overall picture funding for different teams within adult services has been uneven. In 1999–2000 older people's services were funded at 3 per cent over national average provision, while mental health services are 40 per cent below national funding levels (Inspection Report 2001). The focus for cuts has been on older people's services. Mental health services during the research period have been receiving increased funding in the form of specific grants from central government associated with the modernisation programme in mental health; but alongside this practitioners and managers describe core funding for care management in mental health as insufficient. In the older people's services, cuts are not just to bring expenditure in line with other authorities, but are also used more aggressively to reduce the level of Social Services funding:

> I asked when the savings would be achieved. Apparently the elderly team needed to save a quarter of a million, but so far they've saved nearly half a million. They're still being asked to make savings, because other adult services haven't managed to make savings. In part it's because the elderly services are easier to cut, because there's a high throughput and high volume—this will bring down costs quicker! (field note: OPT, conversation with manager).

The department has used two techniques to deal with its financial problems in the older persons service. Eligibility thresholds for service provision have been raised (this threshold was higher in the OPT area than in CMHT). There have also been active moves to reduce spending through the imposition on the OPT from the centre of a policy of 'two out, one in': for every new hour of home care allocated, two hours of the existing service have to be cut, for both domiciliary and residential care. This process of budget-cutting, however, seems to have gone beyond what is required to reduce the OPT budget.

Risk

Another factor that appears to differ between the OPT and the CMHT is the role of the idea of risk. Contemporary society is centrally concerned with the identification and management of risk (Lupton 1999). It has been argued that the presence of risk, insofar as it entails uncertainty, can contribute to a professional orientation within work contexts (Jamous and Peloille 1970). Within the mental health services, concern with risk has been central since the early 1990s, reflecting a shift in national policy to concern with risk, dangerousness and community (Department of Health 1995, Muijen 1996 and Reith 1998). This concern is, according to one of the mental health managers, echoed in the culture of the mental health service:

> I think we probably encompass risk in mental health in [*sic*] a greater extent. I suspect policy has pushed that along over the last 10 years. You'll be aware that most of the press going back 8, 10 years was about risk-taking and disasters happening in the community (MM2).

While risk, as uncertainty, can contribute to indeterminacy in that it reduces the capability of managers to predict and control practice (Jamous and Peloille 1970), it also gives rise to concerns that can result in increased monitoring of practice (Hood *et al.* 2001, Munro 2004). For instance, practitioners in the CMHT see increased discussion of risk at policy level and the introduction of risk polices as a means of checking up on practitioners, as much as a means of improving practice:

> There's much more conscious consideration of risk, on the risk assessment forms, which are helpful, because they help you focus a bit more ... [but] there is a little bit of a situation where, unless you've filled in the form, people are assuming you've not weighed up the risks (MS2).

While in mental health the focus of concern has been on violent or aggressive behaviour and suicide (Shaw 2000), concern in older persons services, locally and nationally, has been slower to develop, and has focused on vulnerable adults' risk of victimisation—particularly abuse and exploitation in residential care (Newunit Community Care Plan 1999–2000). Newunit acknowledged national concerns in this area and identified it as a high priority locally, pointing out that: 'On average there has been one incident [in adult services] requiring investigation over the past year' (*ibid.* 43). Local multi-agency procedures were developed which the authority felt raised public and professional awareness (*ibid.*). The Community Care Plan noted the intention to launch new procedures and develop a training programme (*ibid.*). Vulnerable adults procedures were introduced in line with central government guidance on the introduction of a framework for multi-agency assessment and coordination (Department of Health and Home Office 2000).

However, one social worker in the OPT points out that in the implementation of the plan, planned funding for staff training did not materialise (OS1), and another practitioner voices concern about the way risk is understood and used in local policies: '... there is a perception that if something does go wrong there's some sort of culpability there ... although you're sharing it with your line manager' (OS2).

Modernisation:
Intensification, Change, Focus and Performance Management

At the same time that Newunit acquired a responsibility for Social Services, the New Labour government came to power, promising to modernise public services. In relation to Social Services, this process involved building on the community care reforms, with an intensification of market and managerialist approaches (Mitchell 2000, Harris 2003).

The preceding account of the policy and financial context of social work practice in Oldshire and Newunit mentions the increasingly problematic financial context of service delivery, with expenditure subject to increasing scrutiny concerning Newunit's ability to fund the continuing level of Social Services (a classic situation in street-level bureaucracies).

Modernisation reforms have exacerbated this situation. The programme of modernisation is wide-ranging and complex (Mitchell 2000). Key elements which are relevant here are the emphasis on a performance management culture, which involves both a strategic framework and a mechanism for monitoring and achieving that framework and the use of ring-fenced budgets to drive forward specific modernisation projects. In adult Social Services, these moves have been clear in the government's development of National Service Frameworks for mental health (Department of Health 1999) and for older people's services (Department of Health 2001). The National Service Frameworks are part of a process Hudson has described as the nationalisation of Social Services: the increased control and direction of local services by central government (Hudson 2000: 224). They: '... lay down models of treatment and care which people are entitled to expect in every part of the country ... [and] spell[s] out national standards ... [of] what they aim to achieve, how they should be developed and delivered and how to measure performance ...' (Department of Health 1999: 1). The Performance

Assessment Framework (PAF), '... a set of indicators for adult services intended to reflect "effectiveness of service delivery and outcomes"' (Netten 2005: 97), is integral to this process. The PAF was first published in the form of league tables in 2001. Increasing central government funding for personal Social Services has increasingly taken the form of special and specific grants tied to satisfactory performance and outcomes (SSI 2001)—completing the performance management circle that underpins the modernisation agenda.

The local implementation of modernisation initiatives has exacerbated the tensions of management control, policy clarity and resources that already characterised the context for social work practice in Newunit. Under modernisation, the policy context of practice has been characterised by continuing change. This is particularly evident in reorganisations within Social Services and in relation to other organisations. Modernisation has emphasised the need for multi-agency and multi-disciplinary work to provide 'joined-up', seamless services. Social Services have been reorganised at a corporate level. When the department transferred from Oldshire, it retained the full range of responsibilities across children and family services and services for adults. However, more recently the authority split Social Services in line with anticipated moves in government policy towards the establishment of corporate children's services (Department of Education and Skills 2003), with children and families going to Education and adult services joining up with Housing under the former Acting Director of Social Services. At CMHT and OPT level, however, this split does not seem to have had a significant impact. It is unclear how far this reflects the division between adult and children's services that developed over the past 10 years (Hill 2000c) or whether the impact of this sort of change takes time to work its way through.

One of the key elements of national frameworks is the reiteration of the need for cooperation across care agencies. This includes the development of pooled budgets and possibly the development of joint Health/Social Care agencies (Health Act 1999, Health and Social Care Act 2001). In Newunit, the impact of this push has reflected national policy, with more explicit and shared frameworks for funding community care—for instance, in the older people's services, a joint framework for assessment and eligibility criteria for provision has been agreed between Social Services and the area's two PCTs.

Within the CMHT, the team has moved from joint but separate management to joint management under Health leadership. During this period there were also a number of reorganisations in the health service, and more are planned. These have contributed to what the CMHT manager characterises as 'a policy vacuum' (MM2).

The impact of demands for change and implementation has highlighted problems of management capacity within Newunit. Alongside policy developments, there has also been an increasing emphasis on regulation and review—a situation which, Power (1997) has argued, reflects a general tendency in modern government to require the demonstration of compliance and performance through the exercise of audit, which he calls the 'audit society'. The OPT and the CMHT were subject to a number of audits prior to my period of fieldwork. The continuing impact of this programme is perhaps captured in the following quote from a practitioner:

> Because we went into unitaries it's been absolutely relentless, the change, or it feels like it has. Shortly after going into unitaries there were various reviews. Again, that's just ongoing, from different areas, from different departments, internally and externally (OS1).

Performance monitoring has also become more prominent with the development of the PAF. The performance of all Social Services in England is monitored against common standards and recently Newunit was identified as a poorly performing authority. There have been two immediate consequences of poor PAF performance: management energies have been redirected to develop systems for the capture of performance data, in order to improve the authority's star rating; and it has fed into the local debate about Social Services funding in the council and in the press.

At management level, the poor PAF performance of the adult services has resulted in significant activity to review systems for recording; failure to routinely capture data is seen as the main problem, rather than actual performance. At the same time, PAF status is seen by managers as crucial to securing funds and retaining their freedom to manage. As one OPT manager puts it:

> ... it's mostly a data entry problem ... But it still does matter, actually, because if we're performing badly on that, or appearing to, and on other things, that affects the amount of money we get. It affects the fact that we may get told that we're put under somebody else's control ... So those things that seem bureaucratic are actually important (OM1).

Local press reports have focused on the underfunding of Social Services, especially in terms of service cuts and the authority's poor performance against the PAF targets. Headlines such as: 'One star council needs more cash to twinkle' and 'Council act over funding crisis' have raised the political profile of older people's services.

Another element of modernisation generally has been funding to support service development. In both services, managers and practitioners comment on the inadequacy of core funding and set this next to new money coming in to Health and Social Services, which is ring-fenced for specific services. They point to the value of many new services, but criticise the assumption that existing provision is sufficient. In the CMHT new monies are seen as bringing in necessary services and bringing the national framework into effect. In the OPT new monies are welcomed, but at the same time they highlight core funding problems and cuts experienced in core services and also create inequities, with people in certain hospitals having access to monies that are not available to those in other hospitals (funding to facilitate discharge is tied to only one of the hospital trusts used in this area).

Conclusion

Newunit, I have sought to demonstrate, is an appropriate site within which to explore the ideas of discretion discussed in the preceding chapters. Historically, Newunit and its predecessor authority, Oldshire, have been proactive in their implementation of managerialist reforms in Social Services. However, within this environment the key conditions associated with discretion in street-level bureaucracies—policy uncertainty and resource and policy mismatch—have also been identified. Practitioners and managers talk of relentless policy change and the tension between focusing resources on those in greatest need and, at the same time, undertaking preventative work, within the broader context of a budget crisis identified by the Director of Social Services. Alongside the significant influence of managerialism within Newunit, continuing elements of professionalism have also been noted in both teams, though in different ways, with more official recognition for the professional role in the CMHT and acknowledgement of professional status by local managers and practitioners in the OPT.

In the foregoing account I have sought to demonstrate the basis for my assumption that Newunit provides a valuable research site to explore street-level bureaucracy in the context of professionalism and managerialism. Additionally, the picture that I have presented of Newunit provides a backdrop against which to understand and consider the findings that will be presented in the following chapter.

Chapter 5
'Managers'—Are They All the Same?

This chapter considers the findings of the case study in relation to the nature of management within Social Services as a street-level bureaucracy, particularly at the interface between front-line managers and senior managers, in terms of its structure and the range of managers' motivations.

Managers are presented by Lipsky and the domination perspective as an homogenous and unified group: they implement policy, and they seek to control the discretion of street-level practitioners. Despite the differences in these two perspectives about the effectiveness of managerial control (which will be discussed below), they both assume that managers accept and seek to implement the policy required by senior managers. (On this basis, for instance, Lipsky assumes that discretion is located at street level: managers implement policy, and any deviation from policy is due to street-level discretion.) However, the idea that managers are simply ciphers implanting strategic policy makers' wishes is problematic (Murray 2006, Evans 2009).

Managers' Views of the Organisation

The first area examined here is the views of managers about the organisation within which they work, particularly of the policies and procedures that structure their work. In contrast to the view that managers accept organisational priorities and policies, the evidence from local managers interviewed in this study is that they are far from uncritical about the policy they have to implement, and most have major misgivings about the policy context within which they work.

The managers and assistant managers were interviewed in each team studied. The preceding chapter indicates that these two contexts involved organisational structures sufficiently different to require separate examination of the two sets of managers. The primary organisational difference is that, while the Older Persons Team (OPT) largely operates within the organisational context of the local authority, the Community Mental Health Team (CMHT) operates in the overlapping context of Social Services and Health.

Older Persons Team

Local managers in the Older Persons Team have strong misgivings about the authority's policy in relation to older people's services. They feel that the council and senior officers devalue their client group and lack commitment to professional social work with older people:

> We had to reduce our qualified staff numbers, so that only half of our field staff were qualified staff, and the other half were, I won't say were untrained, but were an unqualified community care outfit … it's a financial move. It's cheaper. … and that's not been a view that's been taken with any other service … my feeling is, it's a lot to do with the way elderly people are viewed in society, as being in a way people who only need practical services (OM1).

This local manager—the team manager—goes on to identify the authority's approach as ageist, and sees this as a wider discriminatory approach in society to older people:

> … you know, the rhetoric about bed-blockers … all hides the fact that what you're talking about is people. They are an institutional nuisance … There would be a national outcry if people starting calling people of any other age bed-blockers (OM1).

Local managers feel that the real importance of older people's services to the council and senior officers lies in their cost and in the need to reduce the general Social Services overspend. They feel that older people's services are used by the council as an easy way of cutting costs, through tightening eligibility criteria and through an additional rationing filter, where resources are not released to new eligible cases until twice the equivalent resource is saved: the 'two out, one in' policy. Local managers are highly critical of this policy, to the point where they describe it as illegal, but they also see it as difficult to challenge because of the compromises and corner-cutting they and practitioners sometimes employ to get the work done:

> We've had this … confirmed again by the solicitors this week … if somebody ultimately does go to a judicial review about it [Newunit] will almost certainly lose the case. So I suppose there are calculations about avoiding situations where people are most likely to go for that .. I think most of us [local managers] would be quite comfortable for something to go to a judicial review—but we want to be sure that it's a case where we haven't compounded errors with other things … you want to be sure that the policy issue isn't going to get lost in a whole load of stuff about someone didn't do this, or they didn't fill in that form properly (OM1).

In this setting of resource cuts, care management, which is seen by the council as the primary role of social workers, becomes increasingly difficult. Managers express frustration about a failure to recognise the resultant pressure on care managers and on them—that not having the resources to care manage creates more work, not less: 'How do they [care managers] find time? They find it at the expense of our waiting list getting longer, really. That's the only leeway there is' (OM1).

However, alongside this sense of conflict between local and senior managers, there is also an area of collaboration over achieving targets set for the authority by central government, particularly in terms of the performance assessment framework (PAF). Adult services, which were 'named and shamed', seek an acceptable star rating in order to access 'pots' of central government money and supplement insufficient core Social Services funding. Local managers express concern that the equity of services offered is compromised in this process:

> The Bed Clearance Programme (BCP) money is tied up to performance indicators, and this distorts services. It's only discharges from the [town] hospitals that the money can be used for … The team know the targets are distorted, and that people in other hospitals, e.g. [list], are not getting the service they should be getting, and that there are inequities. But unless they meet the performance indicators to discharge from the [town] hospitals, they won't get the money next year (field note: OPT, information from manager).

For local OPT managers, meeting performance targets is necessary not only to gain access to central government funding, but also to avoid being subject to special measures and replaced by other managers. Concern about the impact of poor performance ratings can be seen in local managers' reaction to an SSI inspection:

> It's the consequences. I mean, nobody likes to be seen as failing when you think you're doing good work, but it's also the practical things. We don't want outsiders scrutinising us even more closely over a longer period. We don't want to be put under special measures (OM3).

Mental Health Team

The CMHT combines Health and Social Services teams. However, local managers do not see the two services within the team as integrated to any significant degree. While the team manager—who has a social work background—manages both Health and Social Services staff, below this level the management structure reflects the Health/Social Services divide, with different assistant managers for the day service and social work team (Social Services) and for the community psychiatric nurses (Health). The team manager and the assistant managers responsible for supervising the social workers both see mental health as marginal to Social Services concerns. One manager's frustration is evident in this summary of the organisation of the team:

> I still manage Health staff and local authority staff, who still see themselves, there's still a divergence of what they do … I mean, the idea of integrated

teams is to have one set of procedures, but we're still responsible to different [organisations]—well, three—a PCT [primary care trust], health trust and Social Services (MM2).

For different reasons, local managers feel that the team operates in a policy vacuum in relation to the local Health service. The team manager emphasises the problem of 'planning blight' on the Health side because of continuing structural reorganisation, and subsequent problems in the development and implementation of policy:

> The other thing ... that sort of kaiboshes us a little bit is, if you like, the [new] trust is probably going to have a very limited life anyway ... we've gone from two trusts, one big trust for a limited period of time, and then we'll move back into probably six PCT-based Community Mental Health Teams (MM2).

The assistant manager acknowledges the connection between Health and Social Services, but for her this is less of a problem; her concern is that the social workers in the CMHT are 'semi-detached' from Social Services: that mental health is not seen as one of Social Services' priorities, and that Social Services policies do not often fit the particular needs and issues of mental health:

> I think that we're often forgotten about, because they're [senior Social Services managers] talking about children's services, adult services, and they just forget that mental health does actually need that little bit of a different approach (MM1).

She is also highly critical of what she sees as Social Services' active neglect of mental health, pointing to inadequate Social Services resources for mental health, and to the shifting of costs to local Health providers:

> We're going pre-Seebohm; we're going to be swamped over by Health, because Social Services is strapped with the poll tax and that; people will go into Health more and we'll be squeezed down and we'll have nothing to play with, social work-wise (MM1).

Local managers' views of their role as policy implementers

Managers in Lipsky's *Street-Level Bureaucracy* and in domination managerialism are portrayed as committed to policy implementation. Broadly speaking, it is possible to distinguish two approaches to the understanding of policy implementation: a top–down approach, where policy is specified by senior officers and implemented according to their instruction in a chain of command running down the hierarchy (Hogwood and Gunn 1984); and a bottom-up approach which emphasises the problems of translating centrally formulated policy into local practices, giving local actors a key role in interpreting, adapting and choosing policy according to local conditions and concerns (Barret and Fudge 1981). Lipsky's account, for instance, employs both these views of policy implementation but locates them in two different occupational groups within street-level bureaucracies: managers are characterised as top–down policy implementers, who have to struggle to control and curtail the bottom–up policy-making instincts of street-level bureaucrats.

Older Persons Team

In the Older Persons Team, managers describe a change in their role in the organisation, arising from their changing relationship with more senior managers in the organisational hierarchy over the past decade. They talk of a diminution in the professional element of the relationship, which is now better understood in terms of the interface between the two different worlds of business plans and professional practice. This change, the team manager feels, has to some extent been liberating:

> It's a business plan approach to the Social Services department. I think in the old days it used to be the people at the top, at least they were expected to be professionally qualified ... they would look down almost as if they were a social worker or whatever, but they're higher up so they're taking a broader view of it ... I don't have the sense that it's like that, now. I think firstly at the top you're not even expected to be a professionally qualified person. It's not required. There's a much greater divorce between that and what people are really doing, in the sense that at the top what you're doing is setting out what the objectives are, and broad strategies. But—and in a way this is good—you know, you're expecting other people below you, which sort of empowers them .. I'm employing you to know how to do that. You get on and do it ... it's not my concern exactly how you did it, providing you're not doing it in a way that comes back to my ears as being grossly unacceptable (OM1).

Managers feel they have wide-ranging, if unofficial freedom, but that this tends to be a limited freedom to be pragmatic. Procedures and guidance are seen as over elaborate and there is believed to be a tacit acceptance from senior managers that local managers can be selective in applying them:

> ... there are so many rules and procedures and everything else that ... you know, no-one's got the memory of an elephant, so everybody's got a whole load that they can't remember. So there's a sort of ignoring of certain things ... And in a sense I think that's quite tolerated (OM1).

Procedures must be tailored to the day-to-day conditions of practice within the organisation:

> I think what happens a lot is that the written policies and procedures are almost over the top on the side of the worthiness and including everything under the sun and every consideration—in a way that is totally unrealistic, given the resources that are actually devoted to doing the assessments ...You'd get through about two a week if you do them like that (OM1).

In this respect, local managers are as subject as street-level practitioners to the conditions of policy uncertainty and insufficiency of resources. In these conditions, they too make discretionary decisions about policy operation and implementation, and about which policies to follow through. Local managers are acutely aware that their flexibility is constrained by the core concerns of the organisation—the 'must dos':

> ... the must-do things is [*sic*] very much centred round money. Anything that causes a problem around money is a definite no-no! Getting expenditure properly authorised and things like that. Making proper orders and so on. Must-dos will be around doing assessments in a fairly recognisable sort of format, a fairly acceptable way of doing it (OM1).

Financial pressures connect with the need to attract central government funding by meeting performance targets, and feed into the requirement to capture performance measures through the correct processing of paperwork. However, even in relation to budgets, local managers have developed a system to allow some financial flexibility in mitigation of the more extreme aspect of this requirement. This relieves pressure on the margins, while the fundamental problem of financial restrictions remains a dominant issue.

Local managers' compliance with some of these 'must-do' procedures is related to their analysis of the poor PAF performance as primarily a recording problem; underlying practice is seen as sound. Accordingly, OPT managers focus on developing paperwork procedures, and see policing the paperwork as a major source of concern, particularly for the assistant managers:

> The PAF indicators get checked very regularly and we get feedback from people that deal with our stats ... There's extra pressure on that at the moment; our PAF indicators led to us being named and shamed. So we want to improve that, which is fair enough. But sometimes the professional bit doesn't seem to fit too squarely with the paperwork. [The team manager] says it does, but it doesn't quite feel right to me sometimes (OM3).

In order to present the team's work in a way that will be valued by inspectors, special efforts are made to ensure that paperwork is up to date and properly presented:

> There are some people working until three or four in the morning on various pieces of work and … We've got some help in, students helping to sort the files out, and a bit of overtime's available to cope with waiting lists (OM3).

In this context local managers make the point that they are 'playing the game' of senior managers and the government, but also seek to distinguish themselves from other players. They must negotiate, adapt and manipulate, and think about presentation of data:

> I don't think we live in a very numerate culture, and one of the things that I just noticed gradually by experience was that when you had to write reports about things, or report on things with figures, how impressed people are by any old numbers or percentages, regardless of how rubbish the methodology was by which you reached them! … Sometimes to get what you want—I almost feel that as long as you don't go so far that you kid yourself, that you really take yourself in with your rubbish figures … if you're using them to get what you need and what you want, why not? Everybody else is doing it … They're obsessed with having good percentages. Good places in league tables (OM1).

This manager distinguishes 'the game' from the reality of practice:

> For a lot of years I've looked at other things that go on and you learn not to say things, as well, in meetings, and … what you want to say is: but the emperor hasn't got any clothes on! … And after a while you learn that sometimes it's better not to … You work towards the same end but you kind of go round things in another way … So instead of coming straight out with it, you kind of work around while still keeping people's egos intact (OM1).

There seems to be a set of concerns that underpin local managers' criticisms of criticism of policy and procedures. This entails a mixture of commitment to older people as a disadvantaged client group; identification with professional status, and loyalty to the local team. It also entails a contrast with 'management': one local manager contrasts professional action to achieve improvement in resources, with managers, who are there to run systems efficiently:

> What's worrying is that we know we're doing this as a means to an end. What's going to happen when others come in to take over the system? You can see this in Health, where the new generation of managers see that the system is working in its own terms, and it becomes the end (field note: OPT, comment by manager).

While generally it has been possible to present the findings in terms of differences between local and senior managers, it is also important to acknowledge that pressure on the authority, in terms of management capacity, has tended to blur the distinction somewhat. Local managers describe being pulled in two directions—towards strategic planning, and as practitioners, stepping in to fill gaps in services. The authority is small and the team manager, particularly, is pulled into strategic work, leaving day-to-day management to the assistants:

> But some are like [team manager's name], for instance, doing an awful lot of development work and not … well, she's here, and we can refer to her, and she's very good, but it's sort of … I think she sort of passes down to us management and running of the office sometimes (OM2).

Meanwhile, the assistant managers talk of being drawn in to the practice role to deal with pressing problems, thereby blurring the distinction between managers and street-level bureaucrats:

> I do find my role is very much this front-line stuff … which needs to be done immediately. And then I'm also on … a 'lone workers' group looking at how we can protect ourselves; I'm on an EMI group looking at trying to develop services and create a service for older people with dementia or older people with mental health problems, and … various other groups, you know … I'm always pulled towards the immediate work, because it is immediate (OM2).

Mental Health Team

The two local managers in the CMHT have differing perspectives on their role in the organisation. The team manager sees the implementation of top–down policy as central to his role, while the assistant manager sees central policy as a sometimes helpful but more often frustrating element of the work environment.

The team manager, who, amongst all the managers interviewed, most closely meets Lipsky's characterisation of a manager, describes his role in terms of a chain of policy implementation, running down from the top via management to the front-line staff. However, he also describes a dual process of policy being communicated and being translated as it is passed down the hierarchy:

> It would be really good if the strategic goals of [Newunit] were the sort of things that every member of the team—from social worker, receptionist, community support worker—could see what they were doing as contributing towards those … I think the further down the structure you go, the less those strategic goals are apparent to you. So for my senior manager, the strategic goals of the council are bread-and-butter, day-to-day stuff. When you get down to my level, strategic goals make sense; perhaps what I'm doing is converting those into operational practice. And then the supervisors below me is [*sic*] about, you know—I won't say just my goals; my interpretation of what the strategic goals of [Newunit] are, and how we can make that a client goal (MM2).

For the team manager a key problem in the process is that managers at his level are not involved in advising and educating members about the 'business' of the authority:

> I see no evidence at my level of councillors being helped to understand the business … I think at my level and the first-line manager level, that's where perhaps the most valuable things can be said directly to them … "this is how our business works" … There are times when I wonder whether members are aware of our contribution towards people with mental health problems, or whether they see that as a wholly Health issue (MM2).

In contrast to this top–down view of policy implementation, the assistant manager, who manages the social work staff, is more critical of policy and sees the professional role (and her professional staff) adapting and interpreting policy creatively to make it workable:

> You can get very hide-bound and say, "the government says we've got to do this, so I'm only going to do that, and my manager says I've got to do this so I've got to do that". I think if you're sensible and if you take your profession seriously, I think you can, on a day-to-day basis, practise quite autonomously, really. It is dependent on having management structures that aren't overtly bureaucratic. And it's like anything else – you could actually, though, make yourself paralysed because you'd say, well, the bureaucrats say you've got to do this and this. So I think it's very much how you decide you're going to go for it (MM1).

In part, this approach to policy implementation is pragmatic; for instance, instead of using the formal caseload weighting system:

> I just do hassle-value, basically, one to five, you know, on the people I supervise. You know, I will do supervision, I look down, I say, "right: hassle value. Are you visiting once a week? Once every three weeks?"—whatever. But it's very crude. But it's better than nothing. And I'd sooner do that than wade through a load of paperwork (MM1).

But there is also a criticism of policy and of the bureaucracy and lack of trust of professional judgement:

> One of my big arguments—nobody will ever take me up on this—is a GP can write a prescription in three minutes and you know there's going to be a lot of problems with that prescription. They have quite a big budget and, OK, they have a lot of training, but now so do we … you know damn well that you go to see the clients, you know they need A, B and C and then you've got to go through all sorts of silly tricks to get it … I don't see why we have to write three-

page reports on everybody ... I let lots of things go as a manager. Somebody wants a community support worker—I just say yeah, you know. I just trust them (MM1).

The CMHT team manager is less involved in strategic management projects than the OPT team manager, and this is a source of frustration for him, as he believes that he should be more involved in strategic decision-making. However, like the OPT assistant managers, the CMHT assistant manager is also involved in practice, primarily as an Approved Social Worker—again, blurring the distinction that Lipsky emphasises between managers and street-level workers.

Conclusion

Local managers in both teams are critical of the policy context within which they operate. However, this evaluation arises from two quite different organisational experiences. In the OPT criticism focuses on senior managers' view of the service in terms of cost-cutting opportunities and meeting performance targets, rather than as a client group or profession to be valued. Local OPT managers express frustration that senior managers do not understand the practical difficulties of having a care management role without resources to care manage. However, they also cooperate with senior managers to achieve government-set targets. In the CMHT, managers feel marginal to the organisations in which they operate. They talk of a policy vacuum in relation to Health because of continuing structural changes. In relation to Social Services they talk of feeling 'semi-detached'. Managers in both teams (with the exception of the CMHT team manager) voice concern about the underlying values of the policy they must implement, which they contrast with their own commitment to their client group, and to the value of professional social work.

In both teams local managers see themselves as policy actors—in the sense of interpreting, adapting and choosing policy. In part, this was a role given within the organisation, but it is also a response to the situation in which they find themselves— having to juggle conflicting policy requirements and insufficient resources—rather like the street-level staff they manage. Most local managers criticise their senior managers' perceived policy stance and seek to use their discretion to reduce the impact of what they see as damaging policies. While one manager—the CMHT team manager—characterises his role (and that of the assistant manager) in terms of officers within a hierarchy, carrying out their instructions, the general picture that emerges here is of managers who do not conform to this picture of organisational compliance. These managers criticise policy, and seek to mitigate its impact in line with their professed commitment to service users and professional social work.

The distinction that Lipsky draws between managers and street-level practitioners is also problematic. Managers, like street-level practitioners, are subject to the discretionary conditions of street-level bureaucracy. Furthermore, the assistant managers in both teams straddle the divide between practitioner and manager, supervising staff but also working on cases to reduce the number waiting for allocation.

Chapter 6

Senior Managers and the Remote Control of Practice

Introduction

The preceding chapter considered the nature of the management chain of control within adult social services as an example of a form of organisation Lipsky describes as street-level bureaucracies. Rather than an unbroken chain of command and control peopled by like-minded managers, the research points to a fractured hierarchy, in which street-level managers view 'the organisation' and its senior managers as motivated by different principles and concerns. The 'domination managerialist' perspective can perhaps accommodate this finding. From this point of view, senior managers employ strategies of remote control that do not require local agreement: they are simply controlled from the centre, 'drilled' into obedience (Howe 1991a: 218).

The debate about the insertion of managerialism into public welfare bureaucracies such as Social Services reinforces this sense of a new iron cage containing practice and curtailing discretion.

Managerial reforms have been closely associated with rigorous budgetary control and the development of policies and procedures guiding practice. This chapter considers these strategies as techniques of remote control by senior managers. In the preceding chapter I outlined the fractured relationship between senior and local managers within the authority. The picture that emerged from the study suggests that 'management' is not a unified homogenous category and that different groups of management may have different interests and concerns. In understanding management relationships with street-level practitioners, it is useful to distinguish strategic management and local management. In this chapter I will consider how senior managers seek to control street-level discretion. Resources and procedures are the primary mechanisms by which senior managers seek to control local practices.

The question of managers' control of practice presumes a dissonance between managers' idea of what practitioners should do and practitioners' conception of their role: an assumption that is questioned by some of the critical literature (e.g. Carey 2008). Accordingly, I will first consider this point before examining the nature and effectiveness of management strategies in controlling discretion.

The Practitioner's Role: Conception and Control

The street-level bureaucracy perspective and domination managerialism emphasise the basic conflict between managers and street-level workers, with managers seeking to control and limit street-level practitioners' roles. There is clear conflict between some practitioners and the organisation in terms of their role. The OPT practitioners claim not to be allowed to practice as social workers, and are constrained by budgets and procedures into a much narrower care management role. However, the CMHT is less congruent with the picture of role conflict. In this team, the discretion of professional social workers is seen as acknowledged by the organisation, and practitioners' concerns revolve around fears of a change in the current situation (in which they retain considerable professional discretion) and (for a small group of practitioners) the current extent of officially recognised professional discretion.

The emphasis in Newunit is primarily on social work in terms of care management, as an administrative task, although there is greater acceptance of a broader social work role in the CMHT. Practitioners in both teams characterise senior managers' view of social work as primarily administrative care management. All, however, feel that social work is, in fact, a wider role, involving particular skills and a focus of interest that do not always sit comfortably with Newunit's version of care management. The role prescribed by Newunit is identified as an actual or potential limitation on their professional discretion.

Older Persons Team

In the OPT care management is seen as the role prescribed for social workers by the authority. Amongst practitioners in the OPT there is general disquiet that social work skills and values are being squeezed out by a narrow and administrative form of care management. Here the issue is not necessarily care management itself—which many practitioners see as having positive aspects: 'In some ways I think because of the care management there is more variety available, because people have got one eye on the cost. The good side of that is that I think it has improved the range of services available to people' (OS4). Frustration is chiefly expressed about the highly administrative version of care management involved, focusing on crisis work; all the practitioners contrast this with social work, which is seen as more wide-ranging in terms of skills and of goals and values.

These concerns are reflected in two strands of comments from practitioners. The first is that care management restricts their deployment of interpersonal skills, which they see as central to their professional identity:

> So as a care manager, I think I tie it up to services and arranging those services; whereas as a social worker it's what I'm bringing as an individual to, say, my relationship with the client (OS1).

> I think with care management it's very focused on assessment, care planning, care implementation, monitoring, reviewing, and that there is quite a pressure, I suppose, to close cases when they're stable and move on to new work. And there isn't so much room for perhaps the counselling role (OS3).

The other concern is the way in which care management changes the nature of practitioners' relationship with service users. One practitioner explains the nature of this shift as concern for money intruding into care for the person:

> I was trained as a social worker, not as a care manager. I think the management of the whole package for me involves—that's what takes you over into the finances, into the commissioning of services and costing the package, which I certainly wasn't trained in. I was trained in much more looking at what a client needed and trying to find it (OS4).

The financial context is also a prevalent issue, in terms of time and resources. A widespread concern is the increasing withdrawal from preventative work. When care management was first introduced in Oldshire, councillors—against the advice of senior officers—required inclusion in the care managers' role of responsibility for 'preventative' work and a budget for this (Oldshire Social services Committee Papers May and September 1993). However, following the move to the unitary authority, the preventative element of the care management role has been lost in the tightening of eligibility criteria and this was a source of frustration for the practitioners:

> Because [Newunit] has designed an eligibility criteria [*sic*] which is very high threshold, and ... is not doing any preventative work ... it's a vicious cycle, because there's no preventative work, so people whom we could have helped when their needs were not complex, their needs escalate and they become worse. And we are actually taking those people when they reach crisis point (OS5).

This shift is felt to weaken practitioners' ability to practise in accordance with fundamental professional principles:

> Going back to when I applied for my CCETSW training ... I suppose I saw [social work] in terms of empowering people and facilitating and advocating for people ... And I still see those roles as being relevant. But working, for instance, in the kind of field I'm working now, with ... older people and increased eligibility criteria ... you're limited in some things you can do, so you become a bit more of a sort of agent of social control, in a way (OS2).

The general impression among OPT practitioners is that their employing authority fails to understand or value them as professional social workers, and seeks to restrict significant aspects of the freedom they consider necessary to do their job, by casting their role in terms of narrow, administrative care management:

> For me social work is about supporting people and enabling people and empowering people to help themselves, and to sort out their own problems without me taking over from them. And that is by means of giving them information, directing them to the right places and, obviously accessing them to services which they're entitled to, and looking at ways of being able to help themselves ... I think [Newunit] has got a certain different concept of what a social work person is, in that the social worker is really very constrained with policies, and with the guidelines and with what the local government expects social services as a department to do for the community. Because most of that is resource-led, most of the time it doesn't actually look at what social work is all about. So a lot of times, a social worker feels as if they're [*sic*] negotiating and dealing with money, and dealing with things like getting resources for their clients, but not really doing the actual social work itself, which is about being with people and actually enabling people (OS5).

OPT practitioners see their freedom to act in terms of their professional role, constrained by policies, procedures and resources that focus their work on the much narrower care management role; and they see the emphasis on managing resources within care management as sitting uncomfortably with professional values.

Mental Health Team

The situation in the CMHT is quite different. As seen above, social workers' professional role is both acknowledged and resourced in mental health. Practitioners see care management as a strategy to which the organisation is committed, but one which is not applied strictly within the mental health setting. However, the organisation's commitment to care management is an issue of dispute within the staff group, in terms of the continuing necessity for professional discretion. It is possible to identify two different stances on this issue.

One group—three practitioners—sees care management as a restriction on professional social work discretion; but these practitioners, who identify themselves as social workers, indicate an ability to work in line with their own ideas of practice, because of the more flexible idea of care management within the CMHT than in the rest of the adult service. This flexibility, they claim, allows practitioners to continue in the role of direct service-providers:

> I'm probably much less orientated around care management, and more orientated around direct intervention. So rather than ... purchasing care, or purchasing packages of care, to make direct provision for people through other agencies, I

would be tending to, through the referral system, take on clients who I feel that I could do direct work with (MS1).

This group believes that practitioners are given the space and flexibility by their managers to act professionally, because of the complexity of mental health work and the specialist nature of services within this area of work:

> … there was a very strict care management model a few years ago. We weren't supposed to do anything other than care management. It's a bit of a misnomer, because there's not much to care manage. And in most situations, particularly in mental health, you're actually still the main resource—your relationship with the client or the family or the provider—so you're actually still doing what you've always done in social work: you get to know somebody, get the relationship going and negotiate (MS2).

The other two practitioners evaluate the relationship of care management and social work from another perspective. They positively identify themselves as care managers: 'I think I see myself more as a care manager than the majority of social workers' (MS4). One claims that social work is no longer relevant: that care management offers a clearer and more focused role for practitioners, reducing responsibility in constraining freedom, and making the role more amenable:

> … social workers are dinosaurs. There are no social workers any more. It's just come down to a title on a piece of paper … It stopped with care management. So we're not overly concerned any more with what I call "care". We are far more governed by financial constraints and matrices and the old-fashioned social worker that worked within a margin of welfare just doesn't exist any more. I like care management. I always have done, because my recollection of social workers was that they were always over swamped … I think care management actually empowered social workers, and clarified the role of social workers, and gave us some direction and more focus and more policies, procedures and there were more rules (MS5).

Across both teams, social workers contrast 'social work' with 'care management'. While in the OPT care management is consistently seen in negative terms, in the CMHT a small group of practitioners portrays it in a positive light, as more focused and practical than 'social work'—although these practitioners express concern that they are not supported by the organisation to practise as such. This contrast is within a context of a more widely defined idea of care management than that in the OPT. However, for other social workers in the CMHT, it is still seen as a potential limitation on their practice.

Practitioners also talk of the strategies used by the organisation to control and constrain the social work role, and point to the central role of the control of resources, in terms of purchasing services (especially in the construction of eligibility criteria), doing the job (resources for staffing), and procedures and guidance for practice. This area is examined in more detail below.

Remote Control of Practice

The use of resource management and procedures is not the same across all adult services. Within the OPT, both resource management and procedural guidelines have greater significance than in the CMHT. This seems to reflect the more significant place of the OPT in the authority's budget, and perhaps a greater recognition in the CMHT of a professional social work dimension to care management. Supervision plays an equally important but different role in both teams.

Resource Management

Older Persons Team

Restriction on funding is seen by OPT practitioners as a fundamental constraint on their discretion:

> ... everything is resource- and money-led, so you really have got, each and every time, have to check what you can use money on, or what you can't use money on ... You have to conform with what the procedure says and what the system says and what the department has agreed to (OS5).

The OPT has been increasingly subject to financial constraints by the authority, and as a result, not only are resources more restricted, but financial decision-making has been shifted up the organisational hierarchy from team managers to a service-led resources panel.

Qualified social work practitioners tend to deal with complex cases that often involve costly care packages. Due to tighter budgets, the Social Services funding process entails exhausting all other funding sources before committing Social Service money. The process for fund approval is, in part, integrated into care management procedures: team managers must endorse practitioners' decisions on eligibility following assessment, but also obtain permission from a higher level within Social Services, via the resources panel for most Social Services funding, and via the Health hierarchies for any joint funding.

Eligibility criteria are the primary means of controlling expenditure within Newunit's care management regime, and these have been increasingly tightened. The service uses a matrix: type/area of need on the horizontal axis; and level/urgency of need on the vertical axis, ranging from 8 (low-level need) up to 1 (urgent need). Recently the level identified by the authority as need that will be met has moved from level 3 to level 2.

However, even within the constraints of these tightened eligibility criteria, OPT practitioners see room to exercise discretion. Eligibility criteria are seen by all practitioners (and local managers) as open to interpretation. The criteria rely heavily on professional knowledge and judgement to be put into effect, and this allows for professional discretion:

> I think in practice, because they [eligibility criteria] are so broad and open to interpretation, if we as the care managers strongly feel that a particular client needs our service, we would give them a 2 and make them eligible (OS4).

> In one sense I think it's clear, in that it's trying to give examples of "this is the sort of level of dependency we're looking at in order to provide a service". But then there's still, I think, scope for interpretation. So it's like with anything that's written down: you could interpret it slightly differently, or perhaps you might interpret the risk somebody is at in a slightly different way … I can't remember all the wording, but I think it's like with anything, it's a substantial amount of care, but what do you mean by that word "substantial", or "imminent", a situation that's imminently going to break down? (OS3).

Practitioners adopt two stances with regard to their discretion in interpreting and applying the criteria. One position focuses on understanding the criteria in terms of justice and fairness, and is uncomfortable about practitioners' *de facto* discretion. The two practitioners adopting this position recognise scope for interpretation, but are also concerned about the inconsistency this creates in applying the rules:

> … my impression is, the eligibility criteria has [*sic*] been laid down and for me it has to be looked at in the light of that … there might be people who have a need, but whether or not we can act upon that would always be seen in the light of the eligibility criteria (OS3).

However, three other practitioners' approach to the interpretative discretion is guided more by a sense of seeking to achieve their own perception of just outcomes:

> … a leaflet came out that said changes to eligibility criteria, round the clients, which said if you've got a carer who does this, this probably means that we won't be able to support you. But I've always treated it that you're looking at the needs more of an individual … So there is a judgement there, I think, that we make, about how we apply those criteria. Because, I mean, if I had a client who, all they wanted was help with shopping and their daughter was doing it and the daughter was managing and wasn't under tremendous pressure … I would use that eligibility criteria [*sic*] as my defence. But there might be other times when I may treat it a bit more subjectively (OS2).

In this context, team managers are generally seen by practitioners as supporting their eligibility determinations:

> And that comes down to my professional judgement, I suppose. I think, well, I can see that if we don't do something about this we're going to have a problem, you know. Or that client will continue to deteriorate ... there may be the straw that breaks the camel's back ... And I think we're allowed to operate a bit of discretion there, and I think our supervisors will go along with that quite happily (OS2).

Both groups acknowledge that local managers encourage flexibility in their approach to eligibility criteria, in the sense of achieving 'sensible outcomes', but they express different views about this freedom in terms of the emphasis on outcomes over process. The first group expresses disquiet about the encouragement of practitioners to apply eligibility criteria in a flexible way, seeing this as unfair to those clients who do not receive the same degree of flexibility:

> And the word that was used at the time was "it's like adopting a pragmatic approach". I like to think that it's a level playing field, personally, but there we go ...
>
> Q: Who described it as a pragmatic approach?
>
> A: It was a manager who said that (OS1).

The other group is more comfortable with *de facto* discretion and its endorsement by local managers: 'It is actually working at the moment, and ... our managers are agreeing with who we're classifying as 1s and 2s' (OS4).

However, there is a limitation to practitioners' willingness to operate with *de facto* discretion. Several interviewees refer to a situation in the preceding year, when, alongside the published eligibility criteria, instructions came down by word of mouth from senior managers that the criteria should be applied in a tighter and narrower manner than officially acknowledged:

> When the decision was made that we would be providing services for matrix 1 and 2 clients, that wasn't supported by a policy, like a written document to support that. It was a policy decision that was agreed with local councillors. So we had a verbal directive. We had no written statement to support that, which made the job ... of having to share that information with clients and support people with that information—it made it much harder, because I think people could give different accounts of that policy (OS1).

Practitioners were concerned about this, not least because of their position with clients who met the formal criteria but were below the line set by the informal criteria. They objected to the authority's failure to acknowledge its tighter criteria publicly, and its perceived use of practitioners to mask a political problem with funding. The practitioners as a group wrote to senior managers to register their disquiet and demand that the authority formally acknowledge the tighter criteria it was seeking to operate. The authority, in line with the law, eventually published the tighter criteria and cases were reassessed against it (Brayne and Carr. 2005).

One of the local managers describes senior managers' reaction to the re-assessment exercise:

> There was quite a lot of suspicion when the matrix changed from only providing services for 1 to 2, 1 to 3; suddenly every client became a 2. I'm sure there was a lot of suspicion in terms of the [senior] management. But it [practitioner's reassessment] wasn't just about people saying, oh, I'll have to move you to a 2 because you won't get a service otherwise. It was a lot to do with the fact that they had been 3 throughout the years but nobody'd put the change in the matrix as they'd deteriorated, you know, because it wasn't important (OS2).

This quotation reinforces the sense of different relationships between different levels of management and street-level workers. It indicates suspicion of senior managers and distrust of local decision-making. This, perhaps, has contributed to the insertion of an additional decision-making level within the care management process, alongside the new, tighter criteria: a resources panel to manage budget cuts for adult services. The panel receives applications from practitioners who have assessed service users as eligible, to decide on the allocation of resources.

One local manager in the team explains the panel process as follows:

> … to get a lot of resources people have to go through our resource panel, and through their assistant team manager, and I think things will be put back to people if they're not that clear, and I suppose the kind of questions that we're pushing people to ask themselves is … what will happen if we don't do anything? What is likely to happen? You have to say, OK, how likely are they to have a fit, what will happen if they have one, what difference will it make if we put the—will it make any difference? And if so, what? Whereas I think in the past when resources are not so tight you just think, oh, yes—bit risky, that, you know (OM1).

Practitioners criticise the panel process for the delay created in providing service and the unfairness and distress created for clients awaiting resources. One practitioner, in describing the process of presenting cases, claims that applications are usually returned with requests for further information:

> It's usually very simple things like "have you explored Health funding for this particular client? If not go away and do so, and if it's not appropriate bring it

back". Again, it's not usually a case of turning things down; just wait, on the whole, just wait (OS4).

Related concerns voiced about the panel process are the amount of paperwork involved, and the knowledge required of how to present paperwork for positive and quick decisions:

> It's got to be seen by the team manager, then it goes to the service manager to be signed, then the service manager, sometimes he hasn't even read the paperwork, because there's a huge wad of work ... But he's got to sign it, then back to you. And then you can look for all the other assessments, and he's also got be sent those: the nurse's assessment, the consultant's assessment—and they have got to be put together, sent off to him, then they come back to you, and then that's when you can actually forward them to the PCT [primary care trust]. But before you do that you've got to collate all these assessments ... By the time it gets to the PCT, they look at it and they decide, Oh, this is nothing to do with us, we're not going to fund this—so effectively you've lost about two weeks running around trying to look for funding. So when the PCT says, No, this doesn't meet our criteria, then the papers come back to you, then you have to start over again because then the resource panel meets only once a week. So if you've missed that week it means now you're going to have to go in the third week to put it in to go to the panel. So effectively you're going through the systems for about three weeks, before you can know whether you're going to get this funding or not (OS5).

Another concern, expressed across the board, is about the role given to practitioners of communicating panel decisions to users and carers waiting for services. This is referred to as 'the Thursday chore':

> "Sorry, your care package didn't get agreed this week". You think, Oh, don't tell me that, what am I expected to do? And you as a social worker have got to deal with it. We're always at the rough end of that (OS5).

Overall, practitioners see this process as a severe limitation on their discretion and ability to meet clients' needs in line with their professional judgement. Serious misgivings are voiced about the panel process, even in terms of the narrower, care management role.

Despite these misgivings, practitioners work with the panel process beyond the passive sense of making their cases on paper; they are involved actively in comparing the urgency of cases and prioritising those going forward to the panel:

> ... it's when you've got people in hospital needing residential nursing beds. That's when we do negotiate, very amicably, between ourselves ... when [the assistant manager] knows there's a vacancy coming up she'll say, Well, your

client is actually at the top of the list, but [name of colleague]'s client has got X reasons why, or whatever, and we usually resolve it … it wouldn't be suggested if there wasn't a very real reason why. And then again, if I felt strongly that my client's needs were greater then that would be respected as well (OS4).

While practitioners do not discuss their reasons for working with the panel process in this way, one of the OPT managers believes that the local nature of the panel, including team and assistant managers, makes a difference:

… it's because you have to keep the process fairly open … I think if you took the process even one more step, so that the people making those decisions weren't in day-to-day contact with their team … it's almost people don't feel too uncomfortable—I won't say without exception—the fact that they know, if they're really worried about something, they can come to [name of other team manager] or me easily. We're here. We're people they know. We're not people they're going to find difficult to approach … (OM1).

Practitioners, too, note that they can present an argument for urgent funding to local managers, who were involved in setting up the panel system and built in the flexibility to use short-term money for pressing cases:

What happens in this team for home care, is, if it's urgent it will be agreed on a temporary basis and it will carry on being temporary until they've got sufficient hours to make it permanent. So in a sense they give you the package when you need it. It's just a way of working the system, which I respect (OS4).

Mental Health Team

Practitioners in the CMHT present their resource situation in a more positive light than those in the OPT. They express concerns about shortfalls, which are viewed in different ways by different groups of practitioners (see below). However, overall they present their position as better than that of other social workers in adult services, both in the level of resources and in the process by which resources are obtained for service users:

Well, we've probably been really fortunate … I understand adult and disability always have to apply—they now have to go to a panel, which we don't have to do; for respite we don't have to go to a panel. So in that way I think we're very fortunate … And we have a community care budget, so if we want support to go in, then we have to get it authorised by our manager (MS3).

Working in a multi-disciplinary team and with new legislation gives practitioners access to new sources of funding:

> ... it's pooled budgets now. Under the NHS Act 1999, Health and Social Services now have the legislative power to pool budgets and resources and chop and change money, and ... increasingly so under the new PCT arrangements. So there has been a new core of money that has come into the service. But not necessarily for care management (MS3).

Alongside a recognition of an improving resource situation in some areas, there is concern about significant gaps in service and the fact that substantial mental health resources are tied up in particular services:

> I think we've got better resources now. They're developing, compared to when I first started. Got more accommodation. More day activities happening. But we're still lacking resources for young people with mental illness. ... We're not catering for particularly the young males, who really don't want to come to the day centre, that kind of thing. We haven't yet tackled that (MS3).

In response to this situation those practitioners characterising themselves as 'social workers' conclude that: 'it's very much down to the individual worker to try and find something to replace that need, which is very difficult' (MS1).

However, as outlined in the case study outline, the level of funding for social work staff in the CMHT gives both professional freedom and time to act as direct service-providers, alongside care management:

> You're actually still the main resource—your relationship with the client or the family or the provider; so you're actually still doing what you've always done in social work: you get to know somebody, get the relationship going and negotiate (MS2).

In contrast, the two practitioners who identify themselves as 'care managers' emphasise the absence of resources to purchase services and see it as a more fundamental problem, limiting the service they can provide:

> We have very, very poor resources ... We have X number of hours with home care, which are not a good service for our clients, because they're not trained in mental health, and it's only the home carers that show a specific interest in working, you know, and they're few and far between (MS4).

They talk of having to respond to the situation by using their own time, but not in the sense of using a valuable resource, as expressed by the 'social work' group of practitioners. Rather: 'You use yourself a lot. You use whoever you can find, really' (MS4)—to create an informal economy of care which can be managed:

> But I will go out and do stuff. I will go out and do some shopping and I'll ... Simply because noone else to do it, it needs doing, it maintains that person and

it's easier to do it. Now I know that I shouldn't be doing those tasks, but I do it. … you know, you're running down town and thinking, "this is mad". I must be the most expensive shopper in [Newunit] (MS4).

This practitioner is concerned about having to use her own time to fill the gaps, as it risks undermining the argument for more resources to enable practitioners to act as care managers:

… and the thing that concerns me more than anything is, the more we do it, the more you accept, if you see what I mean, the more part of your work it becomes. Which to me is wrong. I should be able to pick up that phone and get somebody to do that task for me (MS4).

The key point here is the differing evaluations of the same resource context, in terms of its impact on discretion. The main resource is seen as social work time and those practitioners characterising themselves as social work professionals feel that they have professional discretion, backed up by the appropriate resource (i.e. time). Those who see themselves primarily as care managers see their freedom as limited by the lack of resources to purchase services, and use their time to create an informal economy of care and enable them to practise more as care managers.

In the CMHT the relationship between practitioners and the eligibility criteria within the service differs from that in the OPT. The CMHT is a specialist secondary service, accessible only by referral from primary care services. The primary role of eligibility criteria for these practitioners is to control access to them as a provider service. Within the CMHT two sets of eligibility criteria operate for the social work practitioners: Social Services criteria, and the NHS Mental Health Trust's criteria for identifying patients suitable for treatment by a specialist mental health service.

Practitioners in the team view the Social Services eligibility criteria in two different ways. One group emphasises their uncertainty, underlining problems in applying them to complex situations, which create room for interpretation:

They're not that clear. For instance, it would say something along the lines of "is this person at risk of being socially isolated?". Well, what does that mean? It's a very loose term. It could be somebody who just likes their own company and like many other people chooses not to socialise that much and have a limited circle of friends. Or it could be somebody who's developing a schizophrenic illness and is displaying negative symptoms and is staying indoors because they're worried that somebody out there is out to get them or they're being spied on (MS1).

and the volatility of mental health problems:

… you could have quite a few clients who, if you were just to look at them, it's not a picture of how they are today. You might say, well is she functioning? Yeah, she's functioning fairly well ... But you then set that against the broader picture of something—got a well-documented bipolar disorder, 10 admissions under Section 3—so they're actually well just now, but ... we wouldn't be closing that case. Whereas adult disability—they put in a package of care and it's fine and then close it, or put it onto a once-a-year sort of thing (MS2).

These practitioners see Social Services eligibility criteria as setting an appropriate general level of entitlement, while allowing them discretion and flexibility in their application.

The other view is that the criteria are clear and unambiguous. However, those who see the criteria in these terms differ in their understanding of the basis of this clarity. For one practitioner: 'Oh, it's very clear. It's written down. We have a matrix on it, setting down what it is ... Very specific, yes' (MS3). For her, the criteria are a restriction on practice. The remaining (two) practitioners claim certainty about what the eligibility criteria entail, rather than clarity in the criteria as such: 'I mean, it's very clear, the eligibility criteria; you know, completing that, they either meet it or they don't ...' (MS4). This certainty seems based less on a detailed knowledge of the criteria than on a personal understanding and commitment: '... gosh, I don't know when I last looked at the eligibility criteria. I think a lot of it for us is around suicide risk and self-harm and those sorts of ... there clearly is a need for a service if they're presenting as threatening' (MS4).

The main concern for CMHT practitioners is the impact of the wider NHS eligibility criteria on their role, which they identify as working with people with serious mental health problems. They express concern that the wider criteria will overwhelm them, and will prevent them from operating according to their professional judgement.

All practitioners agree that demand is outstripping their ability to provide a service. The main cause for this is seen as inappropriate referrals from GPs accustomed to referring all mental health cases, rather than just serious cases, to the Mental Health Team. Practitioners express frustration that GPs do not deal with minor mental health problems in the surgeries, in line with the national service framework (Department of Health 1999), but continue to refer them to the CMHT. As a result practitioners are asked to take on cases which do not meet Social Services eligibility criteria, but which do meet the Mental Health Trust's more inclusive criteria. Practitioners criticise this situation and the uncertainty and conflict caused—both within the team and across disciplines. They call for greater clarity:

CPNs have been so used to working to GP practices and just—can you see this person?—they would see the person, do an assessment and then say, no, we don't need to see them any more, we suggest this or that. So they're saying, a lot of them, how do we know this person doesn't need this service unless we see them? While some of us are saying—it's quite clear they don't need it ... really,

> I suppose, we should either be working to their matrix or they should be working to ours, or we should have a compromise and we go from 1 to 3 or 4 (MS3).

However, there is some disagreement about the source of the problem. For three practitioners (those who identify themselves as 'social workers'), it comes down to organisational management and agency politics. For this group the tighter use of eligibility criteria is a way of managing demand—an alternative solution would be a waiting list—and allowing them the time to focus on their work as service-providers and on a priority group of younger people with severe mental illness. They see the situation in terms of political problems between Health and Social Services and hiatus in policy development:

> ... there aren't any real strong protocols about what we do, and I think that is possibly deliberate, because it is so difficult to get a consensus of agreement between Social Services and Health. And when I say Health I include the GPs and consultants when necessary; at the primary care trust level, it's very difficult to get people to sign up. Because obviously the GPs are inundated; they want to offload onto us; we're saying, "hang on a minute, there's a Social Service organisation", we're saying "don't meet our criteria". But a consultant will say, "well, look, this person has been prescribed anti-depressants; the GP is concerned; we've got to see them". I think that's why it's very difficult to have these joint criteria (MS1).

For the other—'care management'—group the problem is managers' failure to take charge of the situation. They call for stronger team management to enforce criteria and to enforce care management procedures in the team:

> I mean we have our criteria, but we don't stick to it. We are still taking the lower end of the scale as well. And I think that's because management don't like to turn these people away. And fine, you know. I agree that these people could do with a service. But not from the Mental Health Team, because we've moved on from there now. We can only deal with the severe and enduring [mental health needs] (MS4).

This group is critical of managers' perceived inability to manage:

> ... our managers don't know how to manage because they don't have to manage ... We should be managed on the input of casework, allocation; we should be managed on the waiting list ... Because none of us want to do poor work. We try to do quality work. Quality work needs a certain time (MS5).

The control of resources to purchase services is less a focus of concern for CMHT practitioners than for the OPT—although there is a division amongst practitioners, as mentioned above, and for those who identify themselves as 'care managers' this is a more significant issue. However, there are two general areas of widespread concern about resource management in the team.

The first is the introduction of tighter controls on smaller and smaller amounts of spending. There is a view that controls are necessary for allocation of large amounts of money, but a feeling that the controls now in place for 'petty cash', requiring the approval of managers, places inappropriate limits on practitioners' professional discretion:

> Well, I think if I had to go through for that [funding for a placement], I'm not critical of them, because that is a lot of money … It's probably smaller things like getting support workers, getting home care, can you access some groups, things like anxiety management, anger management … I think then you're back to what model do you have for your team, how you're going to use your professionals (MS2).

The second concern amongst the practitioners, all of whom are ASWs, is their lack of discretion to commit resources to prevent compulsory admission under the Mental Health Act 1983, and the requirement for a manager to authorise the funding: 'I mean, to try and get hold of one of the managers here and say you want to do that. Because home care would say, whose budget is it coming out of?' (MS3). They express frustration that, while practitioners try to balance concerns with risk and liberty, the authority's prime concern seems to them to be control of expenditure and bureaucratic procedures.

Control of resources is a major focus of the management of discretion. Eligibility criteria have been developed to structure decision-making in both teams. However, eligibility criteria themselves are seen as open to interpretation and, in fact, requiring professional judgement—for instance, around ideas of risk and need—to make them operate. Within the OPT the pressure to control resource use is more acute: resources are actively being cut; whereas in the CMHT the main resource is the practitioner's own time, and additional resources are also being brought in to fund development associated with the national service framework. In the OPT, while eligibility criteria are being tightened, decisions about resource allocation are shifted up the management hierarchy to counter what senior managers see as practitioners' subversion of eligibility criteria.

Procedures

Alongside the management of resources, the other key mechanism of remote control of practice discussed by practitioners and local managers is the procedures developed under the auspices of senior managers. Procedures are often difficult to distinguish from financial management, particularly in relation to care management, where eligibility criteria are central to control of expenditure as well as assessment and provision of care. Here 'procedures' is used to refer to guidelines on the practice of key aspects of work.

In both the OPT and CMHT, formal procedures are identified by the organisation as an important part of the practitioners' context of work. In the care management procedures, which apply to children's and adults' services, it is stated that:

> This policy and procedures are [*sic*] designed to enhance our service to users, by promoting and enabling good practice in our interactions with people who come into contact with social services. Secondary to this, but also of vital importance to an efficient and effective service, is the need to fulfil local and national data and administrative requirements (Newunit Care Management Procedures: 4).

These procedures are a significant recent development. Care management policies across the organisation have been reviewed and relaunched, giving:

> ... much greater guidance through the structure of the forms as to what should be included in assessments, support plans and reviews (Newunit Care Management Procedures: 7).

However, a close examination of the care management document reveals that, while it talks of applying to all Social Services and includes a range of different matrices for children's services, mental health, older people and physical disabilities services, the pro-formas provided are more limited. The document distinguishes forms for children's services and adult services, but the adult services forms are headed 'elderly and physically disabled' (copies of this document were collected from both the OPT site and the CMHT site).

Local policies are also set in a wider framework of national policies and directives (Newunit Community Care Plans 1999–2000 and 2000–2001). On the ground, the national initiatives of direct concern to practitioners, and which they discuss as impacting on their practice, are the performance assessment framework for the OPT (Department of Health and Office of National Statistics 2001) and the national service framework for the CMHT (Department of Health 1999). In both teams the formal recognition of risk and the need to record assessments are also notable themes, including the development of vulnerable adults procedures.

As established ways of acting and prescribed modes of conduct, procedures are contained in written guidelines and policies. However, within teams, practitioners tend to talk of having to 'muddle through' in the face of the volume of and continuing changes and additions to these procedures. Here the understanding of procedures is largely located in informal knowledge and expectations within the teams:

> Care management procedures are being reviewed because we've recently had introduced the joint assessment form, which you've probably seen—the whole point of that is it's a joint assessment. ... it's a further change. It's a further adjustment. Another form to get used to. So if you were to follow me from start to finish with assessing a new client, you would find that I'm continually asking

other colleagues "Which form should I be using now? Have I covered this? Have I covered that?" And that's the feeling that I feel as an individual I'm left with all the time. So in terms of applying any policies and procedures, I never feel that I'm totally on top of it. It's always changing (OS1).

Older Persons Team

In the OPT procedures are seen as fundamental structures governing the work, but are characterised more as a framework than as a straightjacket:

> I don't think it is strictly specified. I think the core of the work is probably seen as the care management tasks ... the assessment, care planning. I don't think any sort of other aspects of the work are rigidly laid down, so I suppose that's where you'd bring your own skills and discretion in with regard to what you need to do in your work with your client (OS3).

However, in addition to the processes of obtaining funding outlined above, there is also increasing pressure to practise care management by the book. This seems to arise more from Newunit's concern to represent itself to central government than from a particular commitment among senior managers to enforce procedures as such. This was particularly evident during the interviews because they coincided with the 'naming and shaming' of the authority's adult services by the Department of Health for their poor performance against the performance assessment framework standards. In order to ensure better performance against the indicators in the next round, managers reviewed the way in which data on performance were captured within the department, and concluded that the problem was a failure to fill in the right paperwork at the right time and in the right way and the consequent failure to collect activity properly on the computer system. According to one practitioner, for instance:

> More recently it seems that a lot of our data collecting hasn't been that efficient, and that's influenced where we stand. So care management procedures will be reviewed from the basis that data is [*sic*] recorded accurately to record our performance (OS1).

Accordingly, managers are involved in a tighter enforcement of the care management process as a paperwork practice: making sure that forms are completed when they should be, and that the right form is used and is correctly filled in so that the activity can be recorded on computer for the PAF indicators.

Local managers and practitioners now regard following procedures by the book as a 'must do':

> There are certain expectations that in the assessment process you would use that paperwork and then you might need to go on based on your stage 1 assessment

to your stage 2 assessment if it was more complex, and—yeah, the actual paperwork you use is very much part of the [Newunit] structure (OS3).

There is an increasing emphasis on data collection. Forms used to be separate from data collection (for performance indicators); there would be a data form at the end to be completed. Now there are new forms—data collection is now in the body of the assessment—to ensure data are collected. Practitioners understand it's important to obtain good PAFs and how it will impact on finances for the department—'but as a social worker I feel it's not one of my primary roles to collect performance data. Now data boxes will need to be completed within the body of the care management forms. If they're not done there'll be a problem—it would be sent back to you or filled in by the senior. Things are being seen and signed more—back to accountability. For care management forms and data collection but not for social work' (Field note: OPT, information from practitioner).

However, even within this tightening focus on following procedures, practitioners still feel they can adapt the system:

I think there's always an element of interpretation, because if we talk together as a team, we sometimes find out we've used different paperwork for the same thing or you might find a way to cut a corner with the paperwork and think, well, I can miss out that form because I've got the same information on another form. I think to a certain extent people adapt the paperwork to what makes sense to them (OS3).

... some people might write up a support plan as soon as they've completed the assessment, so they would send to the client an assessment summary with the action they will be taking, which might be applying to a resource panel for funding for home care, for example; whereas some of us would actually carry out the action, and then write up the support plan at the time that you've got everything concretely in place ... So in that sense we would have all followed the procedure of doing a support plan and giving that written summary to the client, but we might have done it at slightly different stages (OS3).

Another recent development in the proceduralisation of work is the implementation of a vulnerable adults policy, in line with central government guidance (Department of Health and Home Office 2000). A point of interest here is the structural formality of the procedure itself but the lack of follow-through by the organisation in its implementation. The policy involves a bureaucratic procedure relying on a programme of training to give it effect but, following the establishment of the structure, the training required to bring it into effect was not carried out because of lack of resources, leaving the policy as an empty framework:

Social workers tend to deal with the more complex cases. With our vulnerable adults procedure that must be one of the department's expectations. The vulnerable adults policy goes across all adult services: I believe within all these procedures there's the expectation that the work is done by staff with appropriate training ... There is a vulnerable adults coordinator ... [who] ... runs case conferences and whose role it is to write procedures/training ... Although I should have had training I haven't. They developed the training but then decided it was too expensive so it's been done on a 'trickle-down' principle. I think that's poor practice (field note: OPT, comment by practitioner).

Mental Health Team

The CMHT characterises procedures as sparse and their role as low-key. Overall procedures are characterised as flexible and allowing for professional discretion.

We've got sort of a mission statement for the team about how we treat people, you know, and those sort of policies, but ... it is very much up to the individual worker how you determine the piece of work you do and in what way you do it. If somebody presents with depression, then it's up to you to decide how you want to work with that depression (MS4).

In contrast to the emphasis on strict adherence of pro-formas in the OPT, CMHT practitioners feel they have more flexibility:

It's carte blanche, really. All the pro-formas are doing is prompting you to ask the right questions. So it's a prompt to take a history, rather than a prompt to look at a specific level of need, or an absence of a service that would benefit ... There's no set format for presenting a level of need (MS1).

Paperwork is characterised as adaptable and allowing for individual approaches to come through—a useful guideline, but not a constraint:

I think the [risk assessment] policy is that there should always be an updated risk assessment on file, and that is it. It doesn't go in to explain what that means—you know, dated when, or how often or ... it's that simple. An updated risk assessment on the file. And people interpret that however they choose to interpret it (MS4).

Furthermore, practitioners believe they are afforded considerable freedom in terms of the style of work undertaken with clients:

I would think we're fairly autonomous ... my sense of professional responsibility is, if I felt there was somebody I was concerned about, somebody may harm themselves or harm somebody else, I would actually report that back. Or if I felt a person was vulnerable in some way, by a number of symptoms, I would kind of alert management to that, which is, I think, a sense of professional responsibility

... or [if] there are complaints coming in about something, anything like that. But outside of that I suppose we're fairly autonomous. I will make decisions on a day-to-day basis (MS3).

Practitioners within the team feel that they are afforded wide-ranging discretion by the organisation. Procedures are characterised as few and flexible. There is, however, a small group within the team (two of those who identify themselves as 'social workers', see above) expressing concern about the increasing impact of procedures on their professional freedom. One of these practitioners calls into question the level of management surveillance:

Lots of things have to go through your line manager and every time you do this, CPA, form goes through to be signed off by them ... After it's completed they're supposed to sign it before it goes through the computer system. I suppose that's a way of ensuring quality, I don't know. To me as a professional worker I don't think that's always necessary (MS2).

The other practitioner sees a degree of management oversight as important, but is concerned about increasing intrusion of management direction into professional discretion:

I suppose it's probably about right, although I think it's changing. I think because of accountability, people are feeling that managers have to be more on the ball in relation to what people are doing and not doing. And that's come from the government down. It's been very prescriptive about what you should and shouldn't be doing, and you have to meet ... my suicide rate's got to be cut dramatically by 30% or something. So I think from outside you're expected to meet certain targets, or perform in a certain way. So by its nature it would not always allow for autonomy or individual discretion (MS3).

Recent developments in the CMHT have included a requirement to see new referrals within a certain time scale, and a more formal risk assessment procedure. Other practitioners in the team, however, do not see these as constraining and even see increasing proceduralisation of practice as necessary to support professional good practice.

One area of day-to-day practice where policy is felt by practitioners to be prescriptive is that of response times to referrals, which falls within the requirements of the national service framework and national standards:

There are criteria in terms of ... the time scale between when you send that letter of appointment and when you actually see them. We have guidelines for that: we have to see people in a certain amount of time ... we are allowed to operate a waiting list, as long as you justify how your waiting list works and if people are prioritised within that waiting list. So people who need seeing quickly ... it's

> about how you prioritise who requires an urgent service and who doesn't ... but there is no rubric about how you prioritise. There is no written protocol about how you prioritise who will and won't receive a same-day service (MS1).

Another development is a policy on risk assessment:

> ... our assessment document's quite new. So ... before, we would do our own assessment and just make up our own typed-up assessment forms, in whatever format we chose to do it, you know, we'd always do different. And then we'd do a risk assessment separately. But in the assessment document there was no part to record risk ... Now we do a blue form [the risk assessment form] with the assessment document, so whenever we do an assessment the risk assessment goes with it ... the managers now expect that, and will ask you now, "where's the risk assessment?" (MS4).

Practitioners criticise what they see as unwieldy paperwork or bureaucratic intrusion into their practice and value the flexibility currently enjoyed, but they also welcome the introduction of policies and procedures which simplify processes or which support professional practice. For instance, one practitioner comments on the recent work undertaken by managers to integrate care management and Care Programme Approach procedures:

> We'd fill in a CPA form and then we'd have to fill in a [care management] review form, because it went on two different systems ... And we used to have to fill out care plans, plus the CPA, because we'd have our own set of forms. But in the last year ... they've agreed and brought somebody in to review everything (MS3).

Another notes that:

> ... there are some god-awful practitioners out there, and they're always the ones who come to the headlines ... is sort of increasing momentum for this sort of social work council to impose guidelines and guidance on social workers ... which I think is useful, because I think we all need to be working to a professional standard. But equally my concern would be that that would restrict our ability to decide how we work and who we work with (MS1).

While most practitioners feel positive about the level of discretion afforded in their work, some concerns are voiced. One sees the breadth of autonomy as an occasional burden:

> ... sometimes it feels as though you're expected to resolve something where you're not able to, really. Or you can end up feeling incompetent, that you don't have that effect on that person to resolve it (MS3).

Another has a wider concern about the level of professional discretion and accountability; for this practitioner, there is too much freedom, in the sense of demands on her time:

> We have far too much discretion. I would have to advocate strongly bringing back the old school approach. So what's wrong with clocking on and clocking off? At least I got an honest day's pay for an honest day's work. That's the taxpayer's money. So if I sit for an hour that's the taxpayer's money I'm sitting on (MS5).

Conclusion

The findings suggest that most practitioners and local managers occupy a different assumptive world from that of senior managers; but this is not uniform. Some practitioners clearly share the view of social work as a care management role, operating with management skills and priorities within a mixed economy of care. However, from the point of view of senior managers, the policy problem in relation to street-level practice is the assumption of an implementation gap—a void between the policy intention of the centre and policy practice at the periphery. Managerialist reforms over the past two decades in Oldshire/Newunit have involved classic strategies in the form of resource management and proceduralisation of practice to bridge the gap. However, this strategy has not been consistent across the two teams, and have been disproportionately focused on the Older Persons Team, both in the sense that they seem to have been formulated as if all practice were like that in the Older Persons Team (a restricted purchaser care management role); and in the concentration on resource-intensive services. Local managers use their own discretion to allow practitioners to stake their role in a wider professional manner than official policy would suggest in the case.

The Mental Health Team, meanwhile, operates in a zone of indefined and indeterminate policy, in which these policies lack relevance to professional practice, and so disregard them, with official and unofficial sanction.

In the Older Persons Team, practice is clearly constrained by resource management and procedures. However, what emerges from this study is that constraint is a matter of degree, not an absolute. The important sources of discretion identified by Lipsky are clearly present in terms of over-elaborate procedures having to be put into operation in a complex context: they have to be interpreted and practised. In addition to these pragmatic issues, there is a continuing assumption of officially sanctioned discretion in the operation of key management control strategies such as the eligibility criteria, which rely on professional judgements about need and risk.

Furthermore, street-level responses to 'control strategies' also raise questions about the way a strategy of control can itself be used to challenge control, (a) locating policital responsibility for rationing decisions embedded in eligibility criteria with senior managers and politicians; and (b) in the use of eligibility criteria by some practitioners within the CMHT to restrict their role to intensive work with a narrower group of people with severe mental health needs.

Chapter 7
Local Managers and Practitioners: Conflict or Collaboration in Supervision?

The Relationship between Practitioners and Local Managers

The preceding chapters have considered the strategies of managerial control of practice and professional responses to these. What emerges is a mosaic, rather than a clearly delineated picture.

Practitioners and local managers disagree with key elements of central policy (propagated by strategic mangers) as expressed through the management of resources and elements of procedures. Local managers support street-level practitioners in extending the discretionary potential of the interpretation and application of eligibility criteria etc. Furthermore, local managers use their discretion to extend the scope for street-level discretion, especially in relation to resource management, where they are able to use resources from different budget areas to circumvent restrictions in others; for instance, using short-term funding to resource long-term care while waiting for formal resources to be freed up through the panel process. But some practitioners may resist the offer to employ discretion in the operation of policies and procedures. They may also see the institution of managerial strategies as positive developments for their practice. The relationship between street-level practitioners and their local managers is clearly a key area in understanding street-level discretion and the findings in relation to this area will now be explored, primarily through an examination of 'supervision' and how this is viewed, and with particular focus on two questions: *to what extent is the relationship structured by the conflicting interests of managers and street-level bureaucrats and characterised as a managerial encounter in terms of organisational superior and subordinate? To what extent is it influenced by shared commitments and concerns, particularly around professionalism, in which practitioners are held to account for their practice but in a context in which the relationship is also seen as one of professional peers?*

Supervision

In formal organisational terms the relationship between local managers and street-level practitioners differs considerably in the two teams. Organisational documents and procedures indicate that practitioners in the CMHT have substantial formal discretion and are acknowledged as professionals; while in the OPT the practitioners' role is seen as less that of social worker and more a constrained role of care manager, bound by restrictions controlling their practice. This would suggest that relationships between managers and practitioners in the OPT might be more akin to Lipsky's model of relationships between managers and street-level bureaucrats, while those in the CMHT more closely fit the professional supervisory relationship characteristic of bureau-professional regimes.

However, the findings of this study suggest that professionalism is a significant element of the relationship between managers and practitioners in both teams, but that, because of the organisational context, this is expressed in a different, less formal way in the OPT than in the CMHT. In the OPT, practitioners appear to have a cooperative relationship with local managers. Their concerns focus on negotiating the pressures and requirements imposed both by senior managers and by councillors. There is an element of conflict in their relationship: local managers express concern that practitioners are not proactive decision-makers, and do not live up to the requirements of a 'professional'. In the CMHT there is disagreement among practitioners in their approach to supervision, and this mirrors disagreements about professional roles, and different attitudes to local managers and to the idea of 'management'.

Practitioners and local managers in both teams identify supervision as the focus of the management of discretion within the team. Supervision can be an informal, continuing relationship, involving exchange of information and advice, as well as a formal process. Here the focus will be on the formal process of a meeting in which supervisor and practitioner engage to review work—but there will also be reference to aspects of informal/ongoing supervision, as in the discussion of resource management and procedures above.

Local managers of both teams are located on site and are easily accessible to practitioners. In the OPT social workers are supervised by two assistant managers, themselves qualified social workers, as is the team manager. In the CMHT practitioners are supervised by the assistant team manager, who is a qualified social worker and a practising ASW. (One practitioner also has a specialist, forensic brief and is supervised in relation to this aspect of her role by a different manager, who is not part of the social work team.) The manager of the CMHT also has a social work background.

Older Persons Team

Practitioners in the OPT talk of supervision as a place where they engage with local managers in discussing professional issues, as well as considering the implementation of policies and procedures. Different practitioners focus on different aspects of supervision while, at the same time, outlining it as a place where their work is managed and as a professional space where they can explore their practice.

There is a strong organisational element for supervision, in the sense that cases are monitored and accountability sought:

... within supervision, or within part of the supervision, we'll be talking about what points we've got to, why we're doing something with a client, why we need to stay involved, what work we're doing with a client, and whether that needs to continue (OS3).

It is also a place where practitioners work with local managers and where organisational procedures are discussed and approached with a degree of pragmatism.

Supervision provides practitioners with an opportunity to review professional issues, and this is particularly valued:

... a good sounding-board, so that you don't become too prescriptive in: X has got this problem therefore you need A, B, C. It's good in supervision to say have you tried, have you thought of, have you spoken to, to make you a bit more creative. I think a very good balance, here (OS4).

While these three elements—organisational, professional and pragmatic—are present in supervision, the organisational element is seen as more prominent and as emphasising management concerns. There is no formal policy for caseload management, but there is an expectation that cases will be dealt with expeditiously. The idea of appropriate time spent on a case is linked to the pressure of cases waiting to be allocated, and an idea of practice that emphasises short-term, focused casework to meet a crisis and, once the problem was solved, withdrawal: '... And there is a kind of pressure to keep cases ticking through and moving on, rather than going for a very complex solution' (OS2).

While the general pressure is to close cases and move on to the next case, managers also claim to trust practitioners' professional judgement about their work:

If someone's performing really well and I would trust their judgement on when to close a case, I might not set a target date for when they should close a case ... Whereas someone I knew who was very slow and I thought a piece of work was actually complete, I'd say I want that closed by next time (OM3).

There is also a professional dimension to decisions about continuing a case:

Where people need ongoing social work support, they discuss that with me in supervision and, again, give me evidence as to why it's necessary to keep a case allocated to someone and I would generally say, yes, I agree: that person needs ongoing professional input (OM3).

These two factors are reflected in practitioners' accounts of discussion in supervision. Practitioners value the opportunity to continue with longer-term work, which they feel allows them to introduce social work skills alongside managing packages of care:

> I have kept about five, six cases now, for the last year, because they still need social work intervention. The ones which continue to need social work intervention are cases which you feel that they still need you to go in and advise on some aspect of care, or their needs change so quickly that this week they're all right, next week the whole support system is falling apart (OS5).

However, while believing that managers respect their professional judgement about the need for such work, practitioners also note increasing pressure from managers to close cases because of the level of demand for care management assessments:

> ... in supervision you discuss whether a particular case needs to remain and your judgement is respected. I think there's been pressure recently that you shouldn't have quite so many on-going cases. I mean, there were—I've been here just over six years and I certainly carried cases for over two years at one point ... There is this pressure to close cases, to bring you up, to take up more cases, otherwise the waiting list will just grow and grow, so there is that (OS4).

On the face of it, practitioners have a significant advantage in their relationship with their supervisor, in that they possess more detailed information about their clients. However, in the OPT, practitioners feel that the small size of the team and the role of supervisors in allocating cases and constantly signing paperwork make it impossible to undermine supervisory control by tailoring information about cases:

> I wouldn't just be looking to suddenly out of the blue to say this person needs residential care ... she's allocating work, so she knows what the referrals of information are; she's seeing the joint assessment form—all the way through there's a multitude of signatures going on this ... I don't think we get to the point where ... I'm saying we're looking for residential and all of a sudden she's going to disagree with that (OS1).

Nevertheless, decisions about how to work with people are based not only on facts and raw information, but also on the way this information is interpreted and contextualised: that is, on professional judgement. In supervision practitioners can use their claim to professional judgement to achieve what they see as appropriate results, or to enable them to work in their preferred way:

> I suppose you could potentially keep a client on forever. You could always create further issues, you know—well, you've got that home care, it's going well, but I'm not too sure, you know, there was a bit of concern a few weeks ago about

this … you could do, if you wanted, you could keep going and going into the minutest detail, if you became quite possessive about it (OS2).

This practitioner points out that the issue of trust in the relationship between practitioner and supervisor is central in this process:

> I think that one of the skills of work is knowing how, when to take things from clients and when to put them back, and I think if you can balance that, then our supervisors will give us quite a lot of autonomy, and they will trust us that what we were doing was at the right level. But if we were getting it wrong I imagine they would be a lot more rigorous, saying, no, you've got to give that back to the client and get that case closed (OS2).

During the interview process it became increasingly evident in the comments of both practitioners and managers that, while certain tasks are performed in supervision—management of caseloads, exchange of information and discussion of case issues—something less tangible but more significant takes place simultaneously, namely the negotiation of trust and respect between managers and workers. As can be seen above, managers are concerned with 'performing really well', 'judgement', and practitioners with 'autonomy' and 'doing … at the right level'—and both are fundamentally concerned with 'trust'. This seems to go to the heart of the nature of the relationship between local managers and practitioners.

One practitioner, for instance, describes a process of building trust with a supervisor which involves a changing and developing relationship, moving from close supervision to increased autonomy:

> I think when I started work obviously the monitoring was closer, but … once we got a kind of trust going and understanding, I think she trusted me and I knew her. It became more informal, and … I grew to having a bit more autonomy about how I pushed clients through the system. As long as I was being sensible and I was moving clients on (OS2).

This practitioner also recognises that the trust is not unquestioning: 'autonomy' continues only as long as decisions are 'sensible' (according to managers) and clients kept moving along:

> I think if you've got the right kind of relationship you get given the kind of responsibility, but … if I went into too much detail or I overstepped professional boundaries—if I was going round to a client's house and doing their shopping, you know … I'm sure there would be a lot more scrutiny and I'd have a lot less autonomy in what I do (OS2).

A manager explains this process of building trust and delegation and the constraints that apply to it:

I think it's probably fair to say here that I think authority and decision-making is delegated down to the lowest point it can go, almost. I mean, in a way, we would like to have the care managers deciding about the resources, but for reasons of having to amalgamate them—that's really the main reason we have it a tier up—because you can't amalgamate knowing what you've got and sharing it out on an individual basis, or it would probably bring things down to pots so small that nobody could use their pot, if you see what I mean. But I think there is quite a high level of support of expecting people to make decisions, and also, as long as they're reasonable ... of supporting them, even if afterwards you think they could have made a better decision.

Q: What's a reasonable decision?

A: I suppose it's something about expecting everyone to have a sense of judgement that's appropriate to their station, in a sense. So for the care managers, I suppose, or the assistant team managers, if they're qualified working, you don't expect to need to be on somebody's back. You expect them to be making decisions that are neither putting the authority at huge risk nor clients at huge risk nor themselves at huge risk, without you having to watch them every five minutes to make sure they're doing that (OM1).

This account of building trust, delegation and autonomy involves two elements. One focuses on practitioners as employees, workers—the agents of the authority in carrying out its responsibilities. There is a symmetry in the accounts of practitioners and managers that suggests an effective and accepted process. The other—professional—dimension to the relationship of practitioner and managers is professional supervision, a meeting of equals where the manager is not in control but acts in a consultancy capacity. Here, however, managers express frustration and concern about what they see as the limited sense of professional responsibility amongst some practitioners:

One of the things that worries me is the things that sometimes people ask me, as their boss ... almost to tell them what to do, in situations in which I would feel it's appropriate to consult me, but it's not for me to tell you what to do. That's what you're employed [for], to work out what to do; you're a professional person (OM1).

In part, this criticism is tempered by a perception of the impact of the declining evaluation of social work in Social Services and the historical emphasis on care management as the primary fieldwork role:

We don't do any supportive visiting generally speaking any more. There's less exploration of people's family history, if you like. I think sometimes they struggle to think about what they can do that's special. I think they do do things that are special: working with families; group work; counselling—not in-depth long-term counselling, but giving people in distressing circumstances time to resolve feelings and talk about things (OM3).

This view is echoed by practitioners, who refer to the impact on them of working within an increasingly resources-driven and resource-starved service, in which it is difficult to sustain the idea of professional practice. As one practitioner explains:

> [Social work values are] … kind of discussed in supervision, but the choices you make are still very limited by services. So I suppose we kind of always have the issues of user empowerment and choice and listening to the client up to a point. But at the same time it's kind of restricted by what realistically we can offer (OS2).

The pressure is felt not only from the upper tiers of the organisation, but also from within the professional peer group: as an awareness of demands on colleagues and the number of people waiting for a service:

> I think there's two things, really. Colleagues … the kind of peer pressure; colleagues are taking on cases, and that is keeping pressure up. Clients might be waiting for a service … I suppose if we gave them more of a Rolls-Royce service, we'd just have very few clients, and we wouldn't be able to work with the number of people we do. So there is a tension there as well—if we restrict our service and go down very complex solutions, then there isn't [*sic*] people who are coming through (OS2).

However, while recognising pressures on practitioners, one manager comments:

> I think social workers need to, perhaps, work a little bit more than they do on keeping up their professional standards, keeping up to date with changes in legislation (OM3).

Another manager also notes social workers' reluctance to challenge and question the authority's policies, contrasting this with her own experience as a social worker in the 1970s, working in a team where practitioners protested and challenged senior management and changed policy. While she now regards that level of activism as impossible, she still sees a critical role for professional social workers and expresses frustration at practitioners:

> … it almost seems that the whole job gets subsumed into carrying out the authority's instructions … I find it disappointing how little resistance there is to a lot of things. Why aren't you saying to me "You can't tell me to do that"? There doesn't be any sort of groundswell … it seems to me that part of our role

is to be advising the authority as social workers about things and saying: you're employing us as professionals, not as dogsbodies … I don't think we do enough of that. I think it's partly because it's easy and comfortable not to, really, and to have the good excuse of, oh well, I can't do that because I've been told to do this (OM1).

One explanation offered by this manager is in terms of individual motivation: that it suits some practitioners to limit their professional discretion, in order to avoid responsibility:

I think it quite suits some people, actually … to lose the sense that they have any autonomy or that they ought to be making professional decisions. "Oh, it's not my fault because" … I think it's a kind of screen for people to hide behind in some sense, and not take responsibility for their own professional development and thinking about things for themselves. … You know, it's quite nice to say, well, I haven't got any choice because they told me to; they take all the burden of responsibility of doing that. And just shed all the other bits that actually they're not telling you to do (OM1).

Mental Health Team

Within the CMHT the team manager does not directly supervise staff, but does deal with requests for funding. The assistant manager is employed by Social Services, practises as an Approved Social Worker and has responsibility for the day-to-day management of social work staff. These two local managers characterise the role of professional staff (and their relationship with them) in quite different ways.

The team manager (who has little contact with staff, except when they need agreement for funding) sees care managers as having a valuable and more focused role than 'old fashioned' social work:

It's much more focused and much sharper now. For me, where I was working at the time, the NHS Community Care Act did … ration the services much more. Not a bad thing, really (MM2).

He also emphasises the formal and discrete nature of the different roles of practitioners. Most social workers in the team have had extra training as Approved Social Workers (ASWs), and work within the team as both social work practitioners and ASWs. (All the practitioners interviewed are also ASWs, as is the assistant manager.) The team manager sees these roles as distinct, and does not see practitioners' ASW status and authority having any impact on their day-to-day social work role. In contrast, the assistant manager takes a wider view of the role of practitioners, and sees the ASW role as reinforcing the professional status of social workers. She criticises the narrowness of the care management role in mental health:

… sometimes I do think care management's not good for mental health, because … you get some workers who aren't comfortable with clients and they just get everybody else to do the sort of, if you like, the work, and they just oversee and care manage … social work is supposed to be a profession and you're supposed to have professional skills, so it's about how you value those and which direction you're going, really (MM1).

She emphasises the way in which social workers who are also ASWs carry that status into their other work:

[It] makes you think more legally, more laterally; you're more conscious about people's liberties—so I think it's just another layer, if you like, in the orange, really [*sic*] … I think you've got status as an ASW … I think you're more confident, because your general work's put you on that level of being quite a pivotal role in the assessment, and … So I think you just carry that round with you. You don't change. You're who you are when you're practising (MM1).

The role of ASW is different from that of day-to-day social work practice within the team, but practitioners' status and training as ASWs are seen both by them and by their line managers as contributing to their professional authority in other areas of practice and influencing supervision:

… the fact that you're an Approved Social Worker kind of adds weight to things, because they see straight away that you've had extra training and that you've had to have so much experience, should have so much experience before you go on to the training, so I think they see it that you're kind of much more up on that kind of thing … I can be more authoritative and say that I need to see this person … we need to get this organised (MS3).

Both managers identify a split in the team in how staff approach their work, one group seeing their role in terms of professional social work, the others in terms of care management:

I think historically the Mental Health Team thought that they were above such things as care management, because they did see it as devaluing their skills, really. So I think we have a mixture in the team. We have some that are reasonably pro-care management, and some that see … care management as a bit useless, because they've nothing to buy and they'll just do it themselves. So they're not that positive about care management (MM1).

The assistant manager, who is responsible for day-to-day management of the team, describes her management style as permissive and her relationship with practitioners as employing trust in them to act responsibly and professionally, but also managing with an idea of accountability (as opposed to control):

> ... the process is there to be accountable, because then I agree with them, I
> say "well, look, are we going to do that? Or are you going to have approached
> somebody by such a date?" And sometimes if they haven't I say, "well, come
> on, let's do it now". You know—let's write the letter now, get it out of the way.
> I'm not particularly for catching people out and saying, well, you didn't do it last
> time, so we're not going to do it now (MM1).

and enforcing her idea of their professional responsibility:

> Sometimes it's really difficult, because I very often find people are going out
> of our way to make sure people aren't in the matrix—you know, can we shove
> them to this place, can we put them to that place—and I'm thinking, no ... there
> are certain workers who I think do it more than others .. I'm saying, you mustn't
> keep passing them on; or they'll say "Well, I've done that, now. I've closed the
> case" ... but then in about two weeks Mrs Bloggs comes back ... and I feel like
> saying to the worker, "well, I'm sorry—you have to have them back. It's no
> good passing them to somebody else" (MM1).

The relationship between practitioners and the assistant manager—particularly
through supervision—is the main mechanism for the management of discretion
and accountability of professional social work staff. The primary areas of focus are
on professional practice and the management of caseloads. The assistant manager
sums up the purpose of supervision as follows: '... it doesn't matter who you are,
you get your monthly supervision; that's formal. That's your accountability stuff.
That's your cases' (MM1).

However, from the practitioners' point of view, the role and nature of supervision
is a point of conflict. Practitioners can be divided into two groups according to
their view of its purpose. One group (three practitioners) sees supervision as a
place where they are accountable and where they engage in consultation with their
manager as a fellow professional:

> In supervision, I suppose the role is and probably has been ... discussing any
> clients I'm kind of stuck on. And I suppose I see that as using some people with
> other ideas, coming in with professional ideas ... (MS3).

These practitioners—the 'social worker group' mentioned earlier—understand
supervision in terms of a relationship with their line manager entailing professional
interaction and negotiation, with 'trust' as a given:

> I think once you pick up the assessment through the allocations meeting, if you
> didn't want to raise that at your supervision with your line manager, you would
> not be asked why it hadn't been raised. You may be asked how you're getting on
> with that person. You'll say, fine, I've done the risk assessment, I've done all the
> paperwork, I'm seeing them every four weeks, and that would probably be the

end of the discussion. So from that point of view you're just ... acknowledging that this person is on your caseload, and that's usually sufficient (MS1).

They see their supervisor as a fellow professional, albeit in a supervisor's role. Local managers are not a source of great concern, but these practitioners are concerned about the idea of 'management': the spread of management control, intruding on professional discretion. One person, for instance, in discussing the wider supervision of practice, talks about managers checking paperwork, and feels 'as a professional' that it is not necessary for her work to be checked in this way.

Overall, practitioners in this group characterise the supervisory relationship in the same terms as the assistant manager who supervises them, emphasising their professional role, and tending to see themselves as partners, fellow professionals in supervision, where they are able to take the lead and set the agenda.

In contrast to this point of view the other two practitioners are critical of their supervisor, whom they describe as vague, and express a preference for supervision which is more management-led and directive:

My supervisor is ... always on the go, always getting caught up in this, so actually when we sit down I'm not sure who's supervising who ... A good manager should have an ear to things. They should be chasing up things and ... actually having it clear in their minds about the new role of the social worker (MS5).

They call for a clearer structure within which to work, and their primary concern is to be supported by managers in their role as care managers, with clarity and consistency, with the application of rules and the management of workloads across the team. They are critical of supervision as it stands, as a nebulous and diffuse process:

Because if you try to keep your supervisor down to a clear answer, you're not going to get one. I need to know yes or no, and I find that it's easier to go at her and say "I need a yes or no; I don't need that one-hour discussion whilst you think about this". I also need managers who can fight the good fight if there's an issue to be taken up (MS5).

These practitioners criticise the supervisor for not being, in their view, a business manager; they want more management and clearer direction:

Our biggest disservice is that all managers are professionals. We need managers for managers. Managers who have no idea how to manage social work—who manage people, who do not manage 'the issue', or get sidetracked. And we probably don't need all the managers to do that, but we do need one ... They're not looking at the matrix, they're looking at procedures, they're going to keep you on line. They're not going to get sidetracked into "get this person some help" (MS5).

I mean, at times I'm not very clear about my role ... So I think the management hasn't got their bit sorted out, really (MS4).

Caseload management is a point of contention within the team and an issue with which the supervisor is grappling. She explains that:

Our management have tried to introduce caseload weighting. Now we don't really strictly do that, but we're supposed to be looking at a weighting system which, then, each worker has a caseload of no more than so many points; no more than so many heavy cases. So that's kind of up here [pointing to her head] (MM1).

The assistant manager's view of supervision as a place for discussion of caseloads and of her approach to managing practitioners' workload as 'not draconian' presents no difficulty for the 'social work' group of practitioners, who see caseload management as a matter to be dealt with in the context of trust and professional discussion:

There's no caseload waiting procedure. It's very much left up to the individual person about whether they can take additional referrals or not ... how you actually manage your own caseload, that's usually a supervision matter and negotiated in supervision ... If you felt that you were particularly busy and couldn't take any more cases on ... you'd have to justify why you felt you would not be able to take any more of those on, but there would be no caseload audit. That doesn't take place (MS1).

However, for the 'care management' group this situation is not satisfactory. They would prefer a more formal system, and express distrust of colleagues and concern that managers are not policing the situation robustly enough:

... my point's always been that you can't, in mental health work, you can't just talk about numbers. Because one can have five clients and one can have 25, and the one with five can be as busy or busier. So I think it needs a system where it's much fairer distribution (MS4).

The assistant manager claims to have a good grasp of practitioners' work because the team is small and because of her day-to-day contact as an ASW:

Well, I've got a quite good memory, so that's really good. And I think I've got my finger pretty well on the ball for most things. There are some things that just slip me by, and I think, "my word" ... But I think generally I'm pretty red-hot, because my supervision's ongoing up here (MM1).

However, practitioners generally see themselves as the experts in the cases they manage, and best placed to decide how to present their cases in supervision:

> ... I suppose you have discretion in yourself when you decide whether you'll talk it over with a line manager just now, whether you'll wait until next week or whether you'll wait until the next supervision (MS2).

This is, nevertheless, understood within the context of accountability and responsibility to Social Services:

> I remember a colleague who'd been a nurse saying one of the differences was that any information that as a social worker we had actually belonged to the local authority, whereas the Health staff—information could be kept between them and the client. I think that affects what you mean by discretion as well. A lot of things—because Social Services is a managed—in a lot of things you don't have discretion (MS2).

Another practitioner recounts a story to illustrate the way accountability can include decisions about where to pass information, and when not to pass information to the line manager:

> I had a client who both had a mental illness and a physical illness. ... I remember one time I saw him at a day centre and he was in love—super. Then I realised it was one of his carers that he was in love with, and he was convinced that this relationship was reciprocated. ... My particular line manager—not anybody around just now—I knew was somebody who, because of things that had happened in her own life, would have immediately made it an enormous thing. And I didn't think that I could necessarily go by what that particular client was saying. I phoned and spoke to another senior manager who I knew very well, and we talked it over, and we decided there was no risk (MS3).

However, practitioners identify two strategies in relation to disclosure of information that seem designed to resist management intrusion into professional decision-making. These two strategies involve quite different rationales. One strategy available to practitioners (who identify themselves not just as professionals but also as clinicians with specialist skills) is to question the ability of their professional manager to supervise aspects of their work.

One practitioner notes the distinction between clinical and administrative supervision, indicating that aspects of this work are not liable to lay management, and the assistant manager discusses a similar point:

> I do think that the nurses hide behind clinical stuff, because they say, "oh, this is clinical supervision; it's different from line management supervision". And they don't understand how I can be a line manager and a ... practice supervisor

as opposed to a clinical supervisor. And now and again I can see their argument, because I'm not CBT [cognitive behavioural therapy] trained, so one of my workers is CBT trained, and he ought to get his CBT from somebody that can do that. But as his line manager and as an accountable person, as a rate-payer, I've got to make sure that that CBT is going the right way and it's not taking too long to develop and ... you know. So I actually think that I can just about justify being a line manager and a practice supervisor (MM1).

The second strategy is cruder, and involves the withholding or selective presentation of information. This is identified by the care management practitioners as a strategy used to obtain the desired decision in supervision.

I'd do my assessment and I'd just stick it in the file, and the manager would say, "but we need to see this". You know—why? It's OK ... You just make the decision, the sensible ones, you get on with your work the best you can and keep your head down and do what you know you do best (MS4).

Conclusion

Supervision is the stage at which local managers and practitioners make sense of the scripts provided by managerialism and professionalism.

Within supervision, local managers and practitioners consider their relationship to the wider organisation as well as to the immediate relationship of practitioner and manager/supervisor. This could involve any number of dimensions, but here the focus has been simplified to concentrate on the operation of discourses of managerialism and professionalism.

Local managers have sought to promote the idea of professionalism within supervision, both in the sense of a wider role for practitioners than care management and in having a degree of freedom to examine judgement. Many practitioners have welcomed this recognition of their professional role. However, this has also involved some tension: managers have felt that some practitioners have not recognised that professional status also entails responsibility beyond a nine-to-five work role (maintaining professional knowledge and skills, for instance); nor understood their responsibility to clients in terms broader than immediate problems or signposting services to close cases.

Some practitioners have felt comfortable with support for a wider professional role (wider than care management); but have demurred at the idea of exercising discretion in the operation of policies. Others have been critical of the lack of managerial intervention in their practice, and the encouragement to view their role in broader professional terms—although these practitioners have also been reluctant to give up the idea that they should also exercise discretion about the allocation and employment of services to their clients.

The relationship between social workers and their local managers is more complex than Lipsky's account suggests. Managers seek to ensure accountability to the organisation, but this is understood by them as a professional, as well as an organisational accountability. Practitioners speak of being encouraged and supported in approaching their work in professional terms and being professionally accountable. There is some conflict between managers and practitioners, but this is largely expressed by managers themselves in terms of their frustration with practitioners not behaving as professionally as managers think they should. Managerialism and professionalism seem to operate as cross-cutting discourses: resources for control and discretion. The next chapter will review and discuss the findings outlined in this and the preceding chapter, to consider how they can help us to understand the operation of discretion by professionals in contemporary welfare bureaucracies.

Conclusion: The Dynamics of Discretion

Introduction

My concern in this book is to examine the operation of discretion in welfare bureaucracies such as Social Services through a critical examination of the street-level bureaucracy perspective in relation to domination and discursive analyses of managerialism. In this chapter I want to consider these perspectives and the issues they raise for our understanding of discretion in relation to the findings presented in the preceding chapters.

Lipsky's account of discretion, set out in Chapter 1, suggests that we should look beyond formal accounts of roles and discretion to understand the extent of street-level workers' freedom in making choices about the delivery of services and policies. He argues that the difficult conditions of work in public service bureaucracies—street-level bureaucracies—give rise to greater discretion on the part of street-level workers than their formal role descriptions suggest. They are faced with choices about interpreting vague policy, and decisions about prioritising insufficiently funded policies. While their managers seek to control and direct their practice to ensure compliance with the spirit, if not the letter of policy, they are limited in their ability to direct work and often have to accept, reluctantly, a wider degree of street-level discretion than they would, in theory, allow.

Empirical research within the street-level bureaucracy perspective was also reviewed in Chapter 1. This research has tended to focus on demonstrating the extent of discretion of street-level workers, and in doing so has concentrated on non-professional officials. However, one study has compared white-collar with professional discretion within street-level bureaucracies (Kelly 1994) and suggests that professional street-level bureaucrats have a wider degree of discretion in their work than non-professional street-level bureaucrats. There has been little critical examination of Lipsky's characterisation of managers in street-level bureaucracies. He presents them as compliant organisational agents, seeking to implement policy and ensure that street-level bureaucrats comply with organisational objectives. There is evidence, however, that managers, like street-level bureaucrats, exercise discretion and influence the application of policy in line with non-organisational concerns (e.g. Weissert 1994, Keiser 1999, and Murray 2006).

The aim in undertaking the field study has been to consider these questions about the influence of professional status on discretion and the nature of management within public organisations, through the examination of a professionalised street-level bureaucracy in the form of social work teams in a Social Services department in England. Within this context it has also been necessary to address another argument: that is, that Lipsky's theory is no longer relevant, and that the organisation of Social Services has now moved on, with managers in charge and in control of practice to the extent that it is no longer sensible to talk about street-level discretion (Howe 1991a). Chapter 2 suggested that Lipsky's analysis of street-level bureaucracies is closer to the picture of managed bureaucracies than his critics recognise: his argument is that, although managers in street-level bureaucracies employ a range of managerial techniques to control street-level practice, the conditions of street-level bureaucracies essentially militate against this attempt at close and detailed control and give rise to significant informal discretion. Despite these differences, Lipsky and his critics share the view that managerialism has undermined professionalism as an important element in understanding discretion in the organisation of public services. However, as discussed in Chapter 3, while there is strong evidence pointing to the increasing strength of managerialism within the public sector, including Social Services, there is also evidence of the continuation of a professional discourse alongside managerialism in structuring street-level discretion.

In the discussion of these issues in Chapter 3, several areas were identified for particular attention. Lipsky (1980) characterises discretion in street-level bureaucracies in terms of particular conditions: resource scarcity and nebulous policy. Authors such as Howe (1986, 1991a) and Jones (1999, 2001), whom I have identified as domination managerialist analysts, have argued that managers now control organisations through budgets and policy specification, to the degree that the idea of street-level discretion no longer applies. In looking at Social Services generally, this view that discretion no longer exists has been called into question (Evans and Harris 2004a) and the importance of other factors, in addition to those identified by Lipsky (particularly the idea of professionalism), has been identified in understanding the extent and nature of street-level discretion (Clarke and Newman 1997). Lipsky and the domination managerialism perspective assign managers a central role in the operation of street-level discretion. However, their characterisation of management as an undifferentiated category, both in hierarchy and in motivation, has been called into question (Harris 1998a, 1998b). This, in turn, has raised questions about the impact on street-level discretion of management at different levels in the organisation. A persistent distinction in the empirical research looking at Social Services teams is between senior strategic managers, who set the context of work through their control of resources and development of procedures, and local managers, who are responsible for day-to-day management of staff, including the implementation of procedures and budgetary controls (Harris 1998a).

In considering the impact of these factors on street-level discretion, the importance of professionalism has been identified, in the degree to which managers accept practitioners' professional claims to manage their own work. This issue has been considered in terms of the extent to which professionals' claims to discretion are recognised; whether this applies uniformly within the organisation; and at what level and to what extent professionalism influences service managers' ideas about their role and that of the service they manage. The final area identified for investigation follows on from this: what is the nature of the relationship between street-level practitioners and managers, particularly local managers? Is it basically conflictual, as the street-level bureaucracy and domination perspectives suggest, or is there a cooperative dimension, relating to a shared commitment to principles of professionalism—a possibility identified by the discursive managerialism perspective?

The main themes to emerge from the findings will now be reviewed and related to the questions, identified from the review of the literature (Chapter 3), that have structured this study. My concern is to consider how the findings can contribute to advancing our understanding of the operation of discretion within a professionalised welfare bureaucracy.

The Environment of Discretion

The nature of Social Services as an organisation was further considered with the aim to consider the applicability and the 'fit' of the (American) street-level bureaucracy perspective to the analysis of social work discretion in the context of a contemporary (English) Social Services department.

In Chapter 2 the case for the appropriateness of applying the street-level bureaucracy perspective was set out, but within the context of recognising that some commentators are critical of the continuing relevance of the street-level bureaucracy perspective to managerialised Social Services and a separate argument pointing to the continuing recognition of professional claims to discretion within Social Services (an area of street-level theory identified as problematic in Chapter 1).

Lipsky's analysis of practitioners' discretion in public service organisations, and its relationship to two other accounts of discretion within contemporary Social Services—domination and discursive managerialism—were discussed in Chapter 3. The view that Lipsky's work is no longer relevant because of the increasing influence of managerialism within Social Services was critically examined in Chapter 2. The key issue of dispute between the two literatures is not, as Lipsky's critics suggest, the increasing influence of managerialism within public services (Lipsky's work assumes that street-level bureaucracies are managerialised organisations); but the extent to which managerialised public services live up to their billing—as rational and coherent organisations that have overcome problems of vague, imprecise policy, and the mismatch between policy objectives and agency resources; and the degree to which managers have the capacity and the tools to control practice.

On the surface, Newunit seems to conform to the picture of Social Services as the type of managerialist organisation suggested by Howe, namely Griffithian general management focused on financial management and clear lines of accountability and control (National Health Service Management Inquiry 1983, Griffiths 1988). Social Services in Newunit have been inherited from Oldshire. In its adult services, Oldshire embraced the community care reforms of the early 1990s in a way which reflected a strong commitment to the introduction of market reforms and managerial strategies for Social Services provision. The authority introduced a purchaser/provider split, locating social work teams on the purchaser side; and in this market context also sought to recast the role of social workers in terms of an administrative care management role, assessing and purchasing packages of care, and emphasising the need for managers to develop skills in financial management, goal-setting etc. (with, as one local social work manager comments, 'social work in brackets') (OM1). In this role social workers/care managers were part of a larger system in which resources and policies were, in theory, brought into alignment by clear lines of responsibility and decisive management, for instance using eligibility criteria to remove rationing decisions from the street level and to ensure that policies and resources were better matched.

However, as explained in Chapter 4, in addition to inheriting these reforms when it took over the county's Social Services, Newunit has also inherited Oldshire's difficulties in matching its resources with its policy and legal responsibilities. Within Newunit there are clear reasons for questioning the assumption that the management system has resolved tensions within the organisation, in terms of matching policy and practice goals and the resources available to meet them. Newunit has tried to reduce Social Services expenditure in line with its more limited resources through the imposition of cuts in the older persons service. However, in this process it has promoted policy confusion, e.g. publishing more generous eligibility criteria than those it informally sought to impose. Furthermore, the policy of reducing expenditure has increasingly come into conflict with other goals—to provide a welfare service, and to meet legal obligations and government targets.

The picture of Social Services presented by Newunit runs counter to the characterisation presented by the domination analysis of managerialist organisations as a well-run machine, in which managers prescribe policy to be put into effect by drilled and docile workers. Policy and resources in Newunit create work conditions of uncertainty and resource inadequacy—a situation reflecting Lipsky's portrayal of the corrupted world of work, which is characteristic of street-level bureaucracies. This impression is further supported when Newunit's situation is considered in the wider national context of Social Services outlined in Chapter 2, which also reflects concern about policy uncertainty and resource inadequacy.

Lipsky's analysis, however, also raises questions about the limitations on managers' capacity to control, seeing management as a limited resource with limited reach. This view conflicts with many domination managerialism analysts, who portray managers as ready, able and eager to take control in Social Services (Nixon 1993). This view assumes that the power and capacity of management to control practice is self-evident; but findings suggest that the capacity of management within Newunit is severely limited.

An external review of older people's services raised serious questions about the capacity of management both to run the organisation and to cope with the demands for continual change by central government. Management is a scarce resource, stretched almost to breaking point: in the OPT, for instance, the team manager is pulled up into a more strategic role, while the assistant managers take on more team management responsibilities. Alongside this, managers are drawn into reviews and audits of their services, in addition to their day-to-day mangement work.

Information technology (IT) is also identified as an important tool employed by managers to take control of and dominate the workplace (Jones 1983, Harris 1998). The move from shire to unitary was identified by senior officers in Oldshire as likely to undermine key aspects of top-down control, such as IT, and within Newunit the IT system it inherited was broken up between the six unitaries and has not been developed as a financial control system but is largely used to store basic records. The IT system, while being developed within Newunit the better to monitor practice, has been identified in a joint review as insufficient for the purpose. Some of the problems concerning management capacity and ability to control though the use of IT are particular to the local government reorganisation— an experience shared with many other Social Services departments in England (Craig and Manthorpe 1999). However, increasing diversion of management from control of practice to the performance of audit (Power 1997) and implemention of the modernisation agenda supports Lipsky's characterisation of management as struggling and limited in capacity, in contrast to the domination view of omnipotent, intrusive managers who dominate and control practice.

While Newunit therefore conforms to Lipsky's picture of a street-level bureaucracy, this is only half the picture. Other factors emerge as significant in understanding the organisational context of discretion which point to the limited nature of the street-level bureaucracy perspective's analysis. In Chapter 3 it was argued that managerialism's impact has not necessarily been to eliminate professional ideas, claims and assumptions, although it might modify them. Rather than assume a deprofessionalised workplace (as seems to be the approach of domination managerialism and the street-level presepective), the discursive analysis recognises that managerialist discourse can overlay and interact with an existing bureau-professional discourse, rather than replacing it (Clarke and Newman 1997). Both the street-level bureaucracy perspective and the domination managerialist analysis tend to play down the significance of professionalism in the analysis of street-level discretion.

Community care reforms such as care management and eligibility criteria are closely associated with the rise of managerialism within Social Services (Harris 2003), but their impact has been felt unevenly across adult services. Their implementation nationally (Lewis and Glennerster 1996) and within Oldshire and, subsequently, Newunit has focused on determining eligibility for public support for services and purchasing care packages in a mixed economy of care, and the financial control of this process. Chapter 4 considered the impact of these reforms on the OPT (and its predecessors in Oldshire) and the CMHT. Comparing these two sites, it is clear that reforms arising from the implementation of community care in the 1990s had a much more significant impact on the OPT than on the CMHT, giving credence to the discursive managerialist view that 'the impact of the developments is likely to be uneven and, at least in some cases, may be open to negotiation ...' (Harris 1998a: 858).

Control of spending is a priority for Newunit (as it was for Oldshire), and this is reflected in a different emphasis in the two teams and the role of budget management and procedural controls. The OPT has been a particular focus for senior management intervention, as a major user of community care spending; the CMHT, in contrast, is marginal in expenditure terms, and the impact of managerialist activity is less evident. Local managers and practitioners within the CMHT portray the strategic level of the local authority (and Health management) as constantly being reorganised and marginal; historically, mental health services have not been seen as a significant local authority responsibility—a situation reinforced by central government's identification of mental health as an NHS-led responsibility (Department of Health 1999a). In this context mental health social workers not only retain a sense of their professional identity but also receive recognition of this from the authority, which acknowledges that their role is a broader one than care management, involving a social work contribution to mental health care (Newunit Community Care Plan 1999–2000).

Harris argues that the dominant mode of organisation within Social Services departments prior to the community care reforms was bureau-professionalism (Harris 1998), but that this has been increasingly overlaid in Social Services by a managerial regime. While data from the OPT would support this view, data from the CMHT suggest another conclusion. Bureau-professionalism has continued to be an important factor in the official characterisation of the role of social workers in the CMHT and this is reflected in a recognition of the social work staff's professional role—a broad and wide-ranging role in which they can exercise their discretion in their practice.

Data from the two teams suggest that the impact of managerialism in Social Services is not uniform across adult services. Its particular penetration perhaps reflects Sabatier's observation that, while policy claims may be characterised widely and as far-reaching, they tend to be implemented with vigour only in areas that reflect the core strategic concerns (Sabatier 1993)—and in the case of community care that means the management of financial resources (Lewis and Glennerster 1996).

However, managerialism's uneven penetration of the organisation also seems to reflect the nature of the local economy of care, and how this supports (or not) the recasting of social work roles in terms of the purchaser/provider split and care management. The OPT has been able to purchase services appropriate to the client group: there is a local market of care. The model of administrative care management adopted by the authority can operate in this environment and is seen as necessary to manage expenditure. The CMHT, on the other hand, does not fit this model very well. In the mental health context, the market for social care services is much more limited by both demand and supply factors. Practitioners are, then, limited in their ability to act as care managers—the care management model adopted by Oldshire and inherited by Newunit not only reinforces but also requires purchasing budgets—and are also, in the absence of specialist social care services, required to retain their traditional social work role as providers, as well as purchasers, of services.

I do not mean to suggest, however, that the impact of managerialism is total in the OPT and absent in the CMHT. Professionalism is a factor in the OPT in a number of ways: managers are professionally qualified, as are the field social workers, and the professional dimension is an important aspect of their relationship. (This will be explored further below.) Furthermore, from the point of view of the Social Services management hierarchy, there appears to be a dual process at work in relation to professionalism. A recent audit commission review report criticises the high level of qualified staff in the team and calls for the reduction in qualified staff and their replacement by unqualified staff. At the same time, alongside deprofessionalisation at the team level, there is a growing recognition of the role of professionally qualified staff in working with people with complex needs and at risk, particularly those identified as vulnerable adults. The vulnerable adults policy identifies this area of work as requiring professionally qualified staff, particularly social workers. Within the CMHT practitioners and managers talk of being subject to performance standards, budgetary controls and care management procedures, but tend to characterise these as adaptable and flexible, recognising professional discretion.

A factor that might help explain the differential impact of managerialism relates to the impact of concern about risk on the organisation of services. Hood *et al.* have argued that management of risk, and of the risk of blame to the organisation, is an important factor in understanding the organisation of services that carry out risk work (Hood *et al.* 2001). Over the past decade mental health has been a primary site for concern about risk in adult services (Reith 1998). The emphasis on professional practice within mental health may reflect the influence of the role of ASWs[1] in retaining a strong professional social work dimension in mental health social work (Rogers and Pilgrim 2001), but continuing professionalism may also be a strategy for senior managers in the organisation to guard against responsibility in this politically charged area, by emphasising the continuing role of professional decision-making and using the idea of clinical responsibility as a technique to distance managers from responsibility. In contrast, in the OPT, where there is a degree of risk to the authority in relation to vulnerable adults, this is a relatively recent development. Historically, as mentioned above, the most pressing concern for senior managers has seemed to be the risk to the organisation's finances in expenditure on older people's services. Nevertheless, organisational policies seem to be in the process of changing—and acknowledging professional skills—in that social work is seen as engaging with complex, risky cases, particularly vulnerable adults.

---

1 The study was conducted before the abolition of the role of ASW by the 2007 Mental Health Act and its replacement with the role of the Approved Mental Health Practitioner (AMHP).

In summary, the evidence from this research supports the application of the street-level bureaucracy framework to the examination of social work discretion within adult social services; but it also highlights the framework's limitations. It supports the widespread characterisation of Social Services as a setting within which managerial strategies are brought into play. Rather than exhibiting the rational coherence suggested by domination theorists, the workplace resembles the 'corrupted world of service', of policy imprecision, and stretched and inadequate resources, described by Lipsky as characteristic of street-level bureaucracies. However, the street-level perspective's argument—that such conditions are the primary factors in explaining the nature of street-level discretion (Brodkin 1997: 24)—is problematic. The continuing influence of dimensions of a bureau-professional culture is evident within the site, although to different degrees in the two different teams. The situation within Newunit suggests a complex and varied work terrain needing further exploration to identify the influence of these factors on the nature of management, street-level discretion and the relationship between managers and practitioners, and the way these factors relate to the broader issues and debates about social work discretion that underpin the remaining research questions.

The Nature of Management

I now want to look at what the findings of this study suggest about the nature of management in the context of social services. Lipsky and the domination managerialist perspective provide a limited account of managers' own discretion, emphasising their attempt to control and limit street-level discretion and to impose organisational priorities on practitioners. From the discursive managerialist perspective, they do not give sufficient credence to the possibility that management is subject to cross-cutting cleavages, to the active role that some managers may have in the construction of street-level discretion, or to the interpenetration of managerial and professional discourse in particular sites of management.

In contrast to the portrayal of managers as a cadre of obedient policy implementers by both Lipsky and domination managerialists, managers in both teams in this study are critical of strategic policy and strategic policy-makers. Local managers criticise aspects of the policy they are required to put into force. However, the culture within Newunit gives managers significant management (discretionary) scope as policy implementers and interpreters. For different reasons—complexity of policy in the OPT and its absence in the CMHT—local managers in both teams express concern about and distance from the policy decisions of senior managers, echoing a strong theme in empirical research in Social Services teams, which reflects the continuation of a fundamental fracture in concerns and identities between senior and local managers. In the OPT local managers express the belief that senior managers see their service as important, but primarily as a means to an end: as a way of managing and controlling the overspend across the adult Social

Services budget. Local managers express the view that senior managers devalue the older people's service and service users, seeing the service as a convenient way to cut the overspend. They also feel that senior managers devalue professional work with this client group. Local managers have sought resources to increase professional staffing numbers, but feel that their arguments are not heard and perhaps not even understood. In the CMHT local managers refer to mental health services as marginal to Social Services as an organisation. They see policies as developed for the main adult client group—older people—and mental health as difficult to fit into the assumptions informing the guidance. The assistant manager criticises senior managers who, she feels, are trying to distance themselves from responsibility for mental health services. (She talks about this primarily in terms of avoiding cost by relying on the local NHS provision.) The critical comments from these managers echo the NISW study, which finds many managers disillusioned and critical of the objectives of their departments (Balloch *et al*. 1995). While feeling that they now have greater discretion as policy implementers and interpreters, these local managers—particularly in the OPT—feel under the scrutiny of audit and performance indicators. This suggests a level of distrust within management hierarchies of subordinates (O'Neill 2002), including senior managers distrust of subordinate managers.

Both teams had been subject to audit or inspection and the research findings reveal, alongside a sense of being 'checked up', a shared interest in the successful performance of audit. Local managers, warned by senior managers about the internal audits and inspections, had time to get their paperwork in order. The OPT was also subject to external inspection—an experience that seems to have contributed to a sense of joint purpose between street-level workers, local managers and senior managers. The impact on the team of these inspections is significant, and is highlighted particularly by local managers, because of the amount of work created by preparation for the inspections in checking files and bringing them up to date, and the resources spent on preparation and drafting in help. The whole sense of the inspection process seems to be one of presenting the best face possible to the world. Underlying this effort is real concern among managers about the impact of poor performance because of the threat of external managers being introduced to run the service if the performance is not adequate. The sense emerging from interviews with local managers is of a fractured management hierarchy, in which shifting relationships between levels are characterised by shifting relationships of trust, distrust, antagonism and alliance (e.g. in a common cause in the face of central government pressures).

Team management is no longer seen by local managers as part of a professional line of direction of practice (which characterised traditional bureau-professional regimes—Harris 1998a), but is now regarded more as an interface between two different cultures, characterised as the 'business planning' culture of senior managers and the world of professional practice within the team. This change has given rise both to new freedoms and to new constraints. In one way it is felt that this change has freed local managers from hierarchical control and direction of their own work: senior managers are not concerned with the way goals are achieved, according to local managers, but purely with outcomes. Local managers identify this as a freedom, not previously known, to manage their staff. However, this freedom is within limits: that is, the core concerns around financial management—control of spending, staff time as a scarce resource and the achievement of performance standards through key procedures (the 'must-dos'). In this respect the fundamental constraint on discretion, as suggested by Brodkin (1997), is the resources context. Over and above this, policy and procedures are extensive, but local managers believe that they have the tacit support of senior managers to exercise discretion in their application and use. Local managers are not simply mechanical implementers of policy; rather, they seem to conform to a picture of managers as active policy interpreters (Weissert 1994, Keiser 1999, Grattet and Jenness 2005, Murray 2005).

Generally local managers tend to identify themselves with practitioners as professional social workers—they share 'their assumptive worlds' (Murray 2005). All the local managers of the OPT, and the assistant manager of the CMHT, identify themselves as professional social workers who are managers and from this position are critical of the authority. They see themselves as promoters of professional practice, which includes sometimes being critical of staff who they considered not to be operating professionally. Within the OPT particularly, there is a sense of managers trying to maintain a professional dimension to the work of practitioners, both acting as advocates of professional practice within the organisation and encouraging practitioners to develop the professional dimension of their role. These managers express cynicism and are pragmatic about management processes, and about the increasing emphasis within the authority on characterising the service in numerical and financial terms. They talk about having to 'play the game', but distinguish this from their underlying commitment to and idea of professional integrity, which involves commitments to clients, social work as a valuable profession and the locality. Particularly striking is the team manager's concern that she is playing the numbers game, and her feeling that new managers are coming along whose view of the service focuses on the managerial calculus (Clarke and Newman 1997). The team manager in the CMHT is an exception to this general trend, emphasising the practitioners' roles in formal organisational terms, and focusing on their role as subordinates.

In summary, the research findings challenge the view of managers in street-level bureaucracy literature and present a different picture of managers from that in the domination managerialist literature. Local managers tend to distinguish themselves from senior managers within Social Services not simply in terms of position with the management hierachy. While managers are sometimes drawn into strategic decision-making, this seems to emphasise rather than reduce the distinction, with local managers critical of senior managers' concerns. One local manager—the CMHT manager—seems to conform to Lipsky's portrayal of managers in street-level bureaucracies. He identifies himself with the organisation, distances himself from practice, sees practitioners as the servants of policy and believes that his level of management should be more involved with strategic policy-making. He is, however, the exception. The other managers' practices and ideas raise questions about Lipsky's picture of street-level bureaucracy management. They are sceptical about management initiatives, and express concerns for the client group and for professional practice. They are critical of organisational policy and employ their discretion in ways that are sometimes unsympathetic to official policy. In the OPT, for instance, local managers view the social work role in ways that challenge the official emphasis on a narrow administrative care management, and are concerned with maintaining a professional social work dimension to the care management role, in contrast to the organisationally defined role, perceived by them as minimising professional potential.

Contrary to the tendency of Lipksy and domination managerialists to characterise managers as 'other' *vis-à-vis* the workers they manage—not only in terms of role and commitments but also in terms of day to day activities— the assistant managers in both teams are often drawn into direct work with clients, because of the pressure of waiting lists, and, in the case of the CMHT, because of the manager's role as an Approved Social Worker. This makes it difficult to distinguish clearly their work role from that of the street-level practitioners whom they manage, and reflects Causer and Exworthy's (1999) observation about the mixed nature of many management roles in welfare services.

I will now turn my attention to the remaining two research questions, which relate specifically to the operation of practitioner discretion. Evetts (2002) has argued that the idea of discretion as autonomy—that is, absolute freedom—is a myth: discretion is freedom within constraints. Here I will examine the extent of freedom and the nature of the constraints on this freedom experienced by the professional street-level bureaucrats in the two social work teams in Newunit. Management control of discretion can be exercised in a number of ways. The first question focuses on the extent and effectiveness of 'remote' control through the management of resources and use of procedures. The second looks at more direct management of practice through the examination of the relationship of supervisor and supervisees in the teams.

Strategic Managers' Control of Street-Level Practice

Domination managerialism, in contrast to the street-level bureaucracy perspective and the discursive managerialist analysis, characterises managers as not only seeking control but also being in control.

Managers' need to control practice implies the actual or potential absence of compliance amongst practitioners. Across adult services, the prescribed care management role is seen as sitting uncomfortably with the broader role of a professionally qualified social worker. In the OPT, in particular, this constraint is felt acutely because the authority emphasises the care management role to a much greater extent in older people's services than in the CMHT, where it continues to acknowledge a more formal professional social work role.

The domination managerial perspective suggests that managers use, with great success, a range of strategies to curtail practitioner discretion. Howe and Carey, for instance, suggests that managerial ideas of practice have become hegemonic and constrain not only social workers' behaviour but also the way they see their role and their ability to conceive of practice outside a managerially prescribed role (Howe 1986, Carey 2008). The findings from this study question this view of management control in older people's and other adult services.

Prescribing and Resourcing Roles

The care management role has been identified by many commentators as central to management strategies of control. However, rather than accepting it as the natural social work role within community care, as Carey's (2008) view would suggest, the practitioners are critical of it.

In the OPT, care management is the role prescribed for practitioners in official policies. It is defined as a largely administrative role, assessing and constructing care packages. Practitioners within the team feel both constrained and uncomfortable with this role. Though not against care management as such—they see it as a useful technique—practitioners are concerned about the way in which social work is equated with a narrow administrative notion of care management, particularly in view of the impact of tightening eligibility criteria. They express frustration that pressure to restrict resources leads to crisis situations, when earlier intervention could have led to preventative work. Related to this, there is also criticism of the way in which the purchaser/provider split structures their role and prevents them from using their social work skills to the extent they feel to be appropriate. The care management role in the authority, they claim, is driven by concern for control of resources, and does not allow them sufficient room to engage with concern for people and their care needs. From practitioners' standpoint, the authority neither values nor understands social work.

In the CMHT, the official construction of the social work role is quite different, and perhaps represents the sort of role to which many of the social workers in the OPT aspire. The organisation recognises mental health social workers as both service-providers and service-purchasers, and recognizes a 'clinical role' and traditional social work skills, such as counselling, within their role. Within the team, staff respond to this situation in different ways. One group sees it in positive terms, though expressing concern about the level of demand; another group criticises the role's vagueness and would prefer a clearer care management role to clarify practitioners' responsibilities.

The literature discussed in Chapter 3 suggests that strategies of management control within adult services focus on using procedures to govern practice and using eligibility criteria to control access to services; and also on restricting the social work role. However, as is also discussed in Chapter 3, there are divergent views about how effective and extensive these strategies are likely to be. The domination managerialist perspective suggests that they are both effective and extensive, identifying little continuing space for social work discretion. The street-level perspective, on the other hand, suggests that, while extensive, these strategies are limited in effect, and that discretion, far from being curtailed, often arises from the imprecision and contradictions embodied in management tools such as eligibility criteria. Practitioners can use these problems to create extensive *de facto* discretionary space. From the discursive managerialist perspective, practitioner discretion is contingent upon local circumstance and draws on a range of resources and alliances specific to locations. It shares the street-level bureaucracy perspective's view of the possibility of *de facto* discretion, but also points to the possibility of professional discourse as a resource in creating discretionary space.

Resource Management and Procedures

Generally, procedures play a more significant role in structuring practice in the OPT than in the CMHT. However, the strategy of remote control of practice in this area is problematic, and supports Lipsky's view that procedures and guidance, while designed to constrain discretion, often give rise to it.

Within the OPT, not all policies are followed. The distinction is made between general procedures, which are seen as extensive, constantly accumulating and impossible to keep up with or even, necessarily, apply; and core, 'must-do' procedures, which are significant in structuring practice. These 'must-do' procedures relate to finance and the recording and ordering of care management paperwork, specifically to generate performance data for the national performance assessment framework. In relation to performance, practice also seems to be increasingly colonised by audit (Power 1997) but this is a constraint as much on local managers as on practitioners. Managers talk about their frustration with the paperwork but are anxious to ensure that practitioners present paperwork both in the right format and at the right stage in the care management process. To achieve this, the care management process within the team is increasingly integrated with organisational monitoring/data-collection. The care management procedures (which have recently been reviewed) demonstrate further this emphasis on care management as a monitoring, administrative exercise, with, for instance, several pages of the guidance document taken up with lists of data and budget codes (Newunit Care Management Procedures). However, while practitioners are constrained in the format required for presentation of assessments and cases for funding, they still feel that they have some freedom to use the forms to achieve their professional aims. Practitioners still retain flexibility in relation to the contents of assessment, as will be discussed in more detail, with reference to eligibility criteria, below.

In the CMHT, procedures are seen as more marginal to practice and where they do apply practitioners largely do not view them as onerous. They also welcome management initiatives to integrate care management and Care Programme Approach paperwork as simplifying previous duplication. Generally, practitioners portray paperwork and procedures as flexible: a loose framework, allowing significant professional freedom. The major exception is the requirement that every case should have a risk assessment, but this is itself a minimal requirement, and does not specify the form or frequency of any assessment. Another requirement mentioned by practitioners is a national standard requiring response to requests for assessment within a fixed time. Within the team, practitioners are generally positive about their freedom, although some describe it as too wide-ranging, and raise questions about the need to clarify accountability for use of professional time. Practitioners also characterise procedures as sometimes necessary, as Robinson found (Robinson 2003), not to restrict professionalism, but to set professional standards and enforce them against poor practice.

The evidence considered so far offers some support for the domination managerialist view of the curtailment of discretion. While it is possible to identify areas in which practitioners have resisted these strategies, it would be disingenuous to describe them as other than marginal. However, this conclusion relates largely to the OPT. In the CMHT the situation is different, with more limited penetration of managerial techniques. Here practitioners are freer to define their role in terms they feel to be consistent with professional social work, and do not feel constrained by policies and procedures. This finding is consistent with the discursive managerialist argument that the impact of managerialism and continuing influence of bureau-professionalism will vary from site to site.

The care management role is centrally concerned with the 'balancing of scarcity and resources' (Challis 1994) through the use of eligibility criteria to govern service users' access to services. In this area a picture emerges from the findings which questions the domination managerialism argument and points to extensive and significant practitioner discretion.

In the OPT the primary means of controlling discretion in resource allocation within the formal care management system is the matrix of eligibility criteria. This provides the threshold against which the authority's responsibility to meet assessed needs is set. In Newunit's OPT the matrix is a detailed framework setting out thresholds of entitlement to support from the authority. These thresholds have become increasingly restrictive to the point where service users are entitled to a service only where there is a pressing need or extreme risk. However, the matrix is seen by practitioners as essentially open to interpretation, especially around the definition of the key terms 'need' and 'risk'. The authority does not provide a definition of these terms, and this is understood within the team to be due to the need for interpretation by professionally qualified practitioners with particular expertise in the analysis and application of these concepts. Local managers encourage practitioners to be pragmatic in implementing the eligibility criteria— to interpret them 'sensibly'; 'sensible' being defined in terms of the professional concerns shared by practitioners and local managers, rather than organisational concerns. Within the practitioner group there are two approaches to the local manager's request for pragmatism. One group sees it as an opportunity to use the criteria in a way which better reflects their understanding of professional values, and to ensure that people receive services identified by practitioners as necessary, for example, by extending the idea of risk beyond immediate crisis to anticipate potential deterioration. The other group expresses disquiet about pragmatism, which it sees as leading to special pleading, rather than consistency of services, and as undermining equality of provision and accountability. Nevertheless, this adaptation of the criteria takes place, with the active support and knowledge of the local managers, and seems to conform to Lipsky's idea that managers will encourage the discretion necessary to do the job.

This evidence confirms the research informed by the street-level bureaucracy perspective, which has identified the continuation of extensive practitioner discretion within adult Social Services—and points to some degree of ambivalence on the part of practitioners towards this form of discretion (e.g. Ellis *et al.* 1999). The basis of this discretion is not clear. From the street-level bureaucracy perspective, it is available to any worker in a similar situation, because of the essential messiness of policy. Its imprecision requires workers to make choices, and managers collude with this to get the job done (Lipsky 1980). However, the centrality of terms such as 'need' and 'risk'—key terms in the professional social work discourse (Barnes 1998)—and encouraging interpretations in line with professional commitments, suggests a significant professional element to the basis of this discretion. This issue seems to turn largely on the nature of the relationship between the practitioners and the local managers, and will be examined in more detail below.

Eligibility criteria tend to be presented in the literature as a largely managerial tool. The relationship between practitioners and eligibility criteria in the CMHT illustrates the way in which they can be subverted by practitioners and used as a strategy of resistance to managerial pressures. The issues of resources and practitioners' relationship to eligibility criteria are different in the CMHT from those predominating in the OPT. Within mental health the mode of practice is more akin to traditional social work than care management. The main resource input of Social Services into the CMHT is the time of social workers. This is an important factor to consider when examining the relationship between eligibility criteria and managerial control. In contrast to the OPT, the efforts of practitioners in the CMHT are focused on narrowing the eligibility entitlement—excluding the lower NHS eligibility threshold in favour of the higher Social Services eligibility threshold. The role of Social Services eligibility criteria in mental health is about access to social work as a provider service and practitioners see their role as focusing on people with severe mental health problems, in line with national policy statements (Department of Health 1999a). In contrast, local managers in the CMHT seek to apply broader eligibility criteria. The team manager's motivation concerns the politics of working with Health, and social workers being seen to work with the same range of clients as the CPNs. The assistant manager, on the other hand, is concerned that practitioners should be working preventatively, as well as targeting services on clients in crisis. Eligibility criteria, as a mechanism for management control, need to be viewed, then, in relation to their context. Practitioners, in seeking to restrict eligibility, talk of focusing on those most in need and being able to sustain the ability to use their own time to meet people's needs as best they see fit. They seek to retain their discretion (to work in the way they feel to be appropriate). The conflict here seems to be about the team manager's approach to the uniformity and intensification of labour, seeking to obtain more from the resources already committed to staffing, while, for the assistant manager, the extension of eligibility criteria reflects her idea of professional practice and her critique of senior managers' policy, in terms of narrowing of mental health services.

In the older people's service, alongside tighter eligibility criteria, senior managers have established a resources panel to micro-manage team expenditure and decide on the release of resources to meet needs already established as eligible for help. The panel is made up of local and senior managers. Practitioners express concern about the panel process at a number of levels. At a personal level they are annoyed at having to report to service users—who have been told they are eligible—that there are no resources to meet their needs. They also express professional frustration at identifying needs and seeing people's situations deteriorate, while waiting for service provision. However, it is interesting to note the absence of concern expressed in terms of the authority's failure to meet its legal responsibilities and respect service users' rights, especially given the protests made by practitioners to senior managers about the instruction to operate a higher eligibility threshold than publicly acknowledged. Once eligibility is established, the local authority has a legal responsibility to provide a service (Brayne and Carr 2005); but in this case the practitioners interviewed do not seem to identify for themselves a role in challenging and questioning the legality of the authority's actions. In fact, informally, despite their misgivings about the panel process, the practitioners as a group participate in prioritising clients for the panel, agreeing between themselves on the most pressing cases and advising their managers of this. While practitioners are formally excluded from making these decisions within the panel process, they are given this power to decide which cases should be given priority—that is, to exercise discretion—by local managers.

Again, this raises questions about how to interpret their behaviour. Is it an example of what Leonard identifies as apparently free but ultimately unfree action (Leonard 1997), because of the way in which managerial discourse constrains practitioners' freedom of choice? Or is it a strategic choice, seeking to ensure that professional concerns are reflected in the decision-making process, which involves strategic decisions about compromise (Healy 2000)?

In considering practitioner discretion, a continuing theme has been the role of local managers in supporting and encouraging aspects of discretion. I will return to this issue in the next section. This reinforces the earlier observation that 'management' needs to be approached as a complex set of fractured layers and alliances, rather than as an homogenous and monolithic entity, as suggested by domination managerialism. In the discussion of Lipsky's analysis of the relationship of line managers in Chapter 1, it was noted that Lipsky identifies, in passing, the problems of layers in management, but brackets them off in his analysis. In the preceding section this point was made in relation to managers as active policy interpreters, but the discussion here points to another dimension of management discretion: managers' role in recognising in their staff, or ascribing to them, a discretionary role. Lipsky argues that managers may collude with discretion to get the job done, but the findings summarised here suggest that they do more than collude in street-level discretion; they can actively promote it for fellow professional staff. This also suggests that local managers perceive their role as having an element of the bureau-professional peer/supervisor role, rather than the controlling and directing manager. In fact the role of local managers as discretionary agents themselves, and as supporters of professional discretion, has perhaps contributed to the development of the panel process in Newunit's older people's services, reflecting senior managers' distrust of both practitioners and local managers. Control of expenditure is a clear priority for senior managers, and is focused on the older people's service as a prime target for service cuts to reduce the department's overspend. Practitioners and local managers work in a context in which financial control is increasingly tightened, as represented by the eligibility criteria. Senior managers are reported by a local manager to have expressed suspicion about practitioners' allocation of eligibility levels, characterising them as too inclusive and seeking to undermine service rationing. This local manager denies the senior manager's reported view and interprets practitioners' actions as recognition of increasing need. The introduction of the panel (an unusual step within local authorities—Bauld *et al.* 2000) seems to be an acknowledgement on the part of senior managers of the failure of eligibility criteria as a managerial technique of control. It also suggests that they do not trust local managers to enforce the tighter criteria.

Within Newunit there is clear evidence of the use of managerial techniques to govern the discourse of professional practice. However, they are more heavily located within the OPT. There is also evidence of resistance to a number of these controls, not by practitioners alone, but by practitioners in alliance with local managers to subvert the remote control techniques of senior managers.

Managerial control of practice is not only an issue of directing practitioners' activities; it is also about trying to cast the role of the practitioner in a way which meets organisational needs. Professionalism becomes compliance with organisational expectations and priorities. The language of professionalism is commandeered by a managerial discourse (Fournier 1999, Evetts 2006). An aspect of the government of the professional role by strategic managers is the resources which are made available to the team for professional staffing. Hadley and Clough (1996) identify care management, combined with the purchaser/provider split within Social Services, as key techniques for management control of social work. This strategy is evident in the OPT but not in the CMHT, where practitioners are still recognised as social workers in organisational statements and in terms of relatively generous funding of social work input. Furthermore, practitioners seek to use eligibility criteria as a means to manage demand and to reinforce a clinical notion of their professional role. In the OPT, practitioners feel restricted in their ability to challenge the official framing of their role as care managers. A key constraint here is funding (Brodkin 1997). Demands on practitioners to assess clients and restricted staffing levels severely limit their capacity to redefine their role. This is recognised by local managers, who have sought additional funds to support more professional work. Pressure to take on new cases and close existing cases is immense and is felt by practitioners both from local managers and as peer pressure. However, within this constraint, practitioners and local managers seek to maintain a professionally defined dimension of practice, providing direct social work services to maintain a small number of clients on their caseloads with whom they are undertaking preventative, counselling and long-term work. Of course it may be that, rather than being an act of joint professional resistance, this is a skilled strategy on the part of management, allowing minor elements of 'professional' social work to persist while requiring practitioners to conform to the constraints of care management in most of their work (Fleming and Spicer 2003).

The Relationship of Local Managers and Practitioners

In this final section I will look at the nature of the relationship between street-level practitioners and their local managers, and how this influenced their discretion. Aspects of this relationship, particularly the sense of professional alliance between practitioners and local managers (and against senior managers), have been discussed above. In this section the focus is on the relationship between practitioners and local managers through the prism of supervision: is there conflict, and about what? How extensive are alliances and on what basis are they built?

Supervision is an important site within which to explore these questions (Seden and Reynolds 2003). It is, for instance, the key location in which discretion is reconstructed in the OPT. Here, accountability is examined, procedures are checked out, interpretations tested and professional status recognised. The discussion of resource management and procedures in the preceding section emphasised the importance of the resource context as a mode of control of the local environment of work for senior managers. However, the local work context should not be characterised as an iron cage—not only because practitioners identify room for manoeuvre within procedures and guidelines, but also because local managers tend to lend their support to practitioner discretion. It is within supervision that the effective limits of discretionary interpretation—or the acceptable range of interpretations—are established with local managers, as, for instance, when local managers in both teams encourage the professional social work dimension of practitioners' roles.

The street-level bureaucracy perspective characterises the relationship of line managers and practitioners in terms of conflicting interests, with pragmatic compromises necessary to get the job done (Baldwin 2000). This latter point is the essential difference from the domination managerialism perspective, in which managers' and workers' interests are seen as essentially in conflict, but managers are sufficiently powerful to impose their will (Howe 1991a, Carey 2008). Carey, for instance, sees this power involving not only the use of overt techniques such as procedures and monitoring but also a more subtle mode of control over practitioners' view of their work, where they take on management concerns and prespectives on practice as natural (hegemonic). The third view of the supervisory relationship, the discursive managerialism perspective, characterises supervision as a site of conflict and transition: managerialist discourse influences and changes the relationship between managers and practitioners, but alongside the continuing influence of bureau-professionalism, the balance between these two influences varying in specific sites. The dynamics of the relationship between local managers and the practitioners they manage reflect different areas of conflict and co-operation within the supervisory relationship between local managers and practitioners in each team.

Older Persons Team

In the OPT the areas of tension within supervision raised by interviewees are, for practitioners, the narrow and limiting eligibility criteria and their task of communicating to service users panel decisions to postpone funds for care packages; and, for managers, aspects of practitioners' professional practice. Those tensions identified by practitioners reflect common concerns amongst street-level workers about managers, but the concerns raised by managers remain relatively unexamined.

A key example of conflict between managers and practitioners over eligibility criteria is the instruction which came down the management hierarchy to run a narrow, covert eligibility threshold alongside the more generous but superseded public threshold. While local managers passed these instructions on to practitioners, it is interesting to note that they characterise this as a dispute with senior managers. In this situation the practitioners were prepared to challenge this practice and to point to the responsibility of the authority to act according to its published eligibility threshold.

Another area of conflict over eligibility arose in relation to the panel process introduced to decide on the release of resources to service users assessed as eligible for local authority assistance. The nature of this conflict spreads some light on the relationship of local managers and practitioners. Unlike the preceding issue of the overt and covert eligibility criteria, practitioners have not actively challenged the panel process. They dislike it, but continue to work within it. What is the basis of this practice? Is it acceptance of the need to integrate concern for resources into professional decision-making—professional subordination to managerialism (Clarke and Newman 1997)? Or is it strategic resistance (Healy 2000), or one of the strategies of resistance described by De Certeau as 'tactics', by which actors—

in this case both practitioners and managers—can transform their experience of a dominant culture into something better, reflecting their own commitments through their day-to-day practices (Ahearne 1995)? Evidence from within the case study points to the latter interpretation: both practitioners and their local managers talk of using their discretion to make the system work as best it can for service users.

In a sense the ability of local actors to resist the panel process—as they resisted the covert eligibility criteria—is more difficult, because the location of possible dispute is less clear. Part of practitioners' dislike of the process is having to break bad news to eligible service users—and a sense that local managers, rather than they, should be 'taking the flak'. Other studies have also identified this as an area of conflict between practitioners and their line managers (e.g. Carey 2008). Nevertheless, this does not preclude the possibility of an alliance here between local managers and practitioners; and local managers themselves disagree with the system, citing, with approval, a recent legal opinion questioning the legality of the process.

What, then, is the basis of this co-operation? Is it, as Lipsky argues, simply a move by local managers to get the job done, or a strategy by dominant managers to take the sting out of practitioner resistance? The important question here is to what extent resistance is based on pragmatic concerns to ameliorate (but still perpetuate) a managerialist rationing logic, and to what extent the local practices are guided by a different set of professional principles outside this logic. Comments by the team managers about ethical and legal problems, and comments of local practitioners about the panel process, point to the second interpretation.

The other area of conflict within the supervisory relationship focuses on the nature of practitioners' professional responsibilities, a concern raised by local managers, who feel that practitioners sometimes shirk their professional responsibility, not only to act with professional discretion but also to speak up about problems within the service and to challenge practice. This raises interesting questions about the behaviour of practitioners. Practitioners talk about being professionals, which includes, for them, not only short-term crisis interventions, but also therapeutic and longer-term work with some clients, which allows them to employ social work skills such as counselling and preventative interventions. However, the managers do not feel that practitioners acknowledge their professional responsibilities within the role to maintain an up-to-date professional knowledge base, to work proactively and to question and challenge.

This picture of the professional passivity of practitioners comes from one source—local managers. The managers' frustration seems to be that the practitioners are too slow to anger. However, there is also a strong sense that the practitioners rely heavily on local managers for professional guidance. Local managers characterise this as withdrawal, not wanting to take responsibility, but local managers and practitioners also link it to a sense of hopelessness amongst practitioners; or perhaps as a reflection of the profile of experience within the team, where most practitioners are relatively newly qualified. It is unclear which of these factors lies behind the behaviours: whether withdrawal as self-interest, as Lipsky suggests, or as a form of 'covert resistance' (Leonard 1997: 94, White 2009); or relatively inexperienced professional practitioners who are not yet confident to operate within and extend their professional role (Maynard-Moody and Musheno 2003), or some combination of these factors.

This emphasis on the responsibilities of practitioners is also interesting in considering the dynamics of power between local managers and practitioners. Supervision is concerned with discussion of day-to-day work and the use of procedures, amongst other matters, but implicitly, through this discussion, it is also a place for managers and workers to establish trust as the basis of discretion in practice.

One interpretation of these data is that they represent a more sophisticated form of management control than a crude, overt control. Katz (1973), for instance, identifies a process where autonomy is used within organisations to control subordinates, permitting workers freedom, but within the context of informal understandings of its proper use. Managers can be seen as disciplining and directing practice by setting the framework of practice in a manner that disciplines street-level work, but at arm's length (Howe 1991, SSI 2001). A similar strategy of control through allowing discretion is identified by discursive managerialism authors (Leonard 1997).

However, a problem with this interpretation is that local managers are emphasising the need for practitioners to maintain professional knowledge, a key source of professional authority and one of the bases for the claim to exercise professional discretion. These local managers appear to be locating the idea of professionalism within a discourse of professional practice, rather than a managerial discourse emphasising compliance with organisational objectives (Fournier 1999, Evetts 2006). In emphasising the responsibility to keep up to date with current knowledge, local managers are also seeking to reduce a key power differential within the practice setting. An aspect of the relationship between street-level workers and managers that is central to the process of supervision is the exchange of information. For Lipsky, for instance, information is a key area of power and conflict between them. Practitioners, he argues, manage disclosure information about their work to influence management and achieve the outcome they desire. However, within the OPT, this is not a strategy discussed by practitioners or a topic of concern to managers. While there is some evidence that practitioners might consider how to present information to achieve their goals, the overwhelming picture is of a small professional team, with constant formal and informal contact between practitioners and managers about cases, in which the asymmetry of information is not as marked as Lipsky suggests. Furthermore, this asymmetry appears to be reversed in relation to how the facts about a case should be understood and interpreted. Managers within the team are significantly more experienced as professional social workers than the workers they manage, in terms of possessing knowledge and practice experience to interpret and understand 'cases'; the asymmetry of information argument operates in the (professional) managers' favour. In this context local managers seem to be seeking, in emphasising the need for practitioners to develop their professional knowledge bases, to make the balance of power between practitioners and managers more equal.

Practitioners and local managers are critical of the emphasis on economic values of efficiency and financial effectiveness, and subscribe to what Lapsley and Llewellyn describe as the traditional 'tribal' commitments of social work to helping people (Lapsley and Llewellyn 1998). This commitment echoes what Leonard has described as welfare-building: '... the ethic of organized caring ... an expression of emancipation still residing there in spite of its accompaniment by surveillance and control' (Leonard 1997). Local managers and practitioners appear to share 'assumptive worlds' (Murray 2006). They work within the clearly managerial vision of care management, but within these constraints they seek to subvert the financial monitoring, audits and increasingly constrained paperwork processes involved. Together they seek to extend access to services and mitigate what they see as the worst excesses of the restrictive eligibility criteria within which they have to operate. Managers' encouragement of practitioner discretion focuses on the idea of its 'sensible use', defined by managers in broad terms as advancing service users' interests and not putting the client or the worker at risk.

Mental Health Team

The relationship between local managers and practitioners in the CMHT differs from that in the OPT. This reflects the different commitments of the two local managers—the team manager, who identifies primarily with his organisational role, and the assistant manager, who emphasises her professional commitment— and the two groups of practitioners: those who identify themselves as professional social workers and those who, though qualified, identify themselves as care managers.

The two local managers characterise their role and their relationship with practitioners in very different terms. The team manager, who conforms more to the domination managerialism and street-level bureaucracy characterisation of a manager, emphasises his management role, distancing himself from the world of practice and describes practitioners as his subordinates, putting into effect his instructions. However, practitioners have little day-to-day contact with him, and their main management relationship is with the assistant manager, who is their direct line manager and provides them with supervision.

The picture of supervision presented by practitioners in the CMHT is consistent: as a space for accountability and professional discussion. However, they evaluate their experience of the supervisory relationship in quite different ways. The assistant manager questions the value of care management in a mental health setting, emphasising the role of more traditional social work skills in building relationships and delivering services. She also portrays the staff management process more as a consultative, supportive, professional exercise, but in which she is reluctant to direct their practice. This seems to reflect the continuation of a bureau-professional form of supervision identified by Harris in his study of social work managers (Harris 1998). As discussed above, professional discretion is recognised by the organisation as the appropriate mode of operation for practitioners within the team. However, within supervision the assistant manager encourages a wider sense of discretion—for instance, in a critical stance towards policy. The practitioners divide into two groups in relation to their response to the supervision they experience. One group, whose members characterise themselves as professional social workers first and foremost, portrays supervision as a meeting of equals, where professionals (manager and practitioner) meet on the basis of pre-existing trust (because of their professional status), emphasising the consultation element and a shared concern with the assistant manager. The assistant manager and the practitioners share a view of supervision as a place where they are also accountable to the organisation via professional review—for instance for major expenditure and safe practice—but, like the practitioners observed by Pithouse when he returned to his research site (Pithouse 1998), these practitioners are also wary about the possible management intrusion into practice. A contrasting view of supervision and the role of managers and practitioners is presented by those practitioners who characterise themselves as care managers. These practitioners are antagonistic towards 'professional social work', which they characterise as old-fashioned and unsuited to contemporary practice. They are critical of the assistant manager, whom they see as imprecise and ineffectual, for not taking control of the team and directing workers' practice. For these practitioners, social work and its management are insufficiently managerial. This minority group of practitioners represents the intrusion of managerialism into practitioners' view of their work—a phenomenon also found in a small number of the respondents in Lapsley and Llewellyn's study (1998). These practitioners seem to subscribe to a discourse of professionalism that is framed in terms of the concerns and responsibilities of the organisation. This is a discourse that subordinates and disciplines 'the "irresponsible" exercise of professional judgement' (Clarke and Newman 1997: 76). The conflict between these practitioners and the assistant managers is a mirror image of that portrayed in the substantial body of the research literature reviewed in Chapter 3: instead of practitioners seeking to resist management control to defend professional autonomy, these practitioners go beyond accepting organisational priorities; they actively seek a more managerialised work environment and a managerialised mode of practice and are in conflict with the assistant manager, who operates within a more bureau-professional conception of her role and that of practitioners.

In this context the issue of use of the asymmetry of information by practitioners to 'manage' or misguide managers, identified by Lipsky as a key element in the discretion achieved by practitioners, plays a more interesting role than his analysis would suggest. The assistant manager characterises herself as 'nosy', and aware of the progression of most cases—a claim that is not implausible in the small team which she manages. However, the two groups of practitioners use the idea of asymmetry of information to defend or challenge supervision, suggesting very different expectations of their relationship with managers. Within the professional social work group, the potential for control of information is evident in the assertion of special expertise and comments about commitment to particular values; this is not extensively used but is a resource available to practitioners in case managers move to a more directive supervision. The assistant manager seems receptive to this argument, and sees it as a potential limit on the degree of enquiry she can make about a practitioner's professional practice. This resource—the claim of expert judgement—is not used by the care management group of practitioners. Their characterisation of their role in a sense excludes this claim, because they call for managers to take a more active role in directing their work. Their strategy is more straightforward, and more closely resembles Lipsky's account of creating discretion in the face of hostile management through the selective presentation of information. They seek to control the effect of supervision on their practice by being careful about the information presented in order to limit scrutiny of their cases and their freedom of action—often to close cases they feel no longer require intervention. In turn, the assistant manager identifies 'unprofessional' practice, including the premature closure of cases, as a source of conflict between her and some of her supervisees.

In summary, the evidence from the fieldwork discussed in this section has explored the nature of the relationship between local managers and practitioners. It suggests that this relationship is different from that outlined by domination managerialism and the street-level bureaucracy perspective. The significant finding is the continuation of bureau-professionalism as a key structuring principle in the relationship between local managers and practitioners in both teams. Discursive managerialism presents local settings as sites for the interaction of discourses, and this is particularly the case in the CMHT, where one of the managers and two practitioners criticise the prevailing bureau-professional culture from a managerial perspective.

Summary

My goal in this book has been to consider a range of views of the nature and extent of discretion of professional staff within welfare agencies – here specifically of professional social workers within an adult Social Services department. Two of the approaches I have considered—street-level bureaucracy theory and the discursive analysis of managerialism—are sceptical of the claims of management extent and effectiveness of management control that can be found in the third perspective, domination managerialism.

The idea of managerial omnipotence put forward by the domination managerialist perspective characterises practitioner discretion as its mirror image. There is some support for its idea of the extensive nature of managerial forms of control within the teams, particularly in the OPT, in terms of systems of resource allocation and control. However, the full picture that emerges from the evidence is more complex, and calls into question managers' ability and willingness to control practitioner discretion, and the effectiveness of tools of control such as eligibility criteria and procedures to control street-level practice as well as highlighting practitioners' ability at street level to circumvent procedures and play a significant role in interpreting policy. On balance the evidence suggests, as Lipsky argues, that, despite the introduction by senior managers of increasingly structured and prescribed approaches to practice and service provision, there is still significant freedom of movement within these constraints, and practitioners retain extensive informal discretion in their day-to-day work. However, the study also raises questions about the limited nature of Lipsky's account of discretion in street-level bureaucracies, in relation to his characterisation of the nature and role of management and the insufficient attention given to the impact of professional ideas and practices on the construction of discretion.

In the street-level bureaucracy perspective's account of discretion, Lipsky casts managers in a particular role, according to which they seek to control street-level practice and policy implementation and to limit discretion; but recognising the complex work context of street-level bureaucracies, they reluctantly collude in allowing street-level discretionary practices, in order to get the job done. Lipsky is not alone in tending to present managers as an homogenous group. This can also be seen in the domination managerialist analysis. However, in line with a consistent body of research in Social Services, the data from this study point to local managers distinguishing themselves from more senior layers of management within the organisation. This distinction is not only in terms of hierarchical structure but also—in the view of local managers—in terms of their commitments. Overwhelmingly, local managers characterise senior managers as committed to cutting funds and rationing services, and not to the professional dimension of social care. In contrast, they characterise themselves, and are characterised by the practitioners they manage, as concerned with service users and professional issues and practices.

In contrast to Lipsky's focus on practitioners as the discretionary agents of public organisations, the data from this study show local managers using their discretion to adapt, change and subvert policy. Furthermore, as is mentioned below, these managers also encourage their staff to see themselves as professionals, and acknowledge their claims to discretion (while at the same time requiring accountability). Within the CMHT this view of staff as professionals is more in line with official policy than in the OPT, where it leads to a 'shadow professionalism', alongside the official care management role—in terms of a continuing element of traditional social work practice, sponsored by local managers, and a recognition of practitioners' discretion within the limits characterised by professional concerns and good professional practice.

The data on management in Newunit show that managers are under severe pressure, with an insufficient number of managers at all levels to manage effectively. This supports Lipsky's suggestion that management is a scarce resource and questions the picture of the powerful management cadre suggested by critics of Lipsky, such as Howe. However, in contrast to the firm line that Lipsky (and others) tend to draw between managers and workers, at street level the lack of sufficient resources has impacted not only on street-level workers but also on line managers, who are drawn into direct provision. Overall, the picture of managers in this study is of an internally fragmented group—divided hierarchically and in terms of their commitments. Furthermore, at street level the distinction between manager and street-level bureaucrat becomes increasingly difficult to sustain, as local managers are themselves obliged to operate in the corrupted world of work as street-level bureaucrats.

In both teams the discourse of social work professionalism plays an important role in establishing a claim to discretion, but it does so in very different ways. While there is some organisational acknowledgement that the OPT practitioners are social workers with a degree of professional autonomy—for instance, in determining need and specifying risk in decisions about resource allocation, and in complex cases involving vulnerable adults—this officially recognised discretion is more limited than in the CMHT. This is seen particularly in the definition of the OPT practitioners' role, which emphasises an administrative care management function, reinforced by a level of funding for staff and recent cuts in the number of professional staff, restricting the possibility of extending care management interventions in the light of broader social work concerns. However, this managerialised idea of the social work role and context of practice has been set primarily by senior managers; local managers express disagreement with many of the policy objectives of the organisation and talk about their commitment to service users and social work professionalism within their team, which they contrast with the concerns of senior managers. Practitioners and local managers see professional discretion as curtailed, but through a range of tactics they are able to reclaim some of its aspects. This discretion is largely constructed in negotiations between practitioners and local managers, as a cooperative enterprise.

In the CMHT, the official approach to practitioner discretion is quite different. There is a greater recognition of the social work role in official (senior management) accounts of the team and this role is wide-ranging, including the provision of services. This wider role is also recognised in relatively generous (compared to the OPT) provision for staffing. Within the CMHT there are two groups of practitioners. One group, whose members identify themselves as professional social workers, is largely content with existing discretion, but wary of the intrusion of management control. The other group, whose members see themselves as care managers, expresses frustration with the vagueness of the social work role and the very limited care management budget. This group is critical of what it characterises as confusion in the local manager's role between professional practice and management, and calls for a clearer and more proactive style of management within the team.

The picture of discretion that emerges from the case study does not fit easily into either the domination managerialist analysis or the street-level bureaucracy perspective. While each is useful in focusing on particular aspects of discretion, this focus seems to be achieved by bracketing off other significant elements of discretion and factors that explain its extent and variation. The discursive managerialist perspective is better able to analyse the topography of social work discretion in the two teams. This is, in part, because it can incorporate recognition of the growing influence of managerialist control and scepticism about its effectiveness, with a tentative analysis which recognises the continuing influence of other organising principles within Social Services—the focus being, in this case, on the continuing but varied influence of bureau-professionalism. In this context, while management is still a significant player (as domination managerialism argues), but limited in its capacity to control (as Lipsky argues), it is also influenced by a continuing professional discourse, in different ways at different management levels, in the shaping of practitioner discretion. The ability of senior managers to control and direct street-level practice is curtailed not only by practical limitations, but also by the practices of local managers, who promote professional street-level discretion, largely in alliance with local practitioners.

In the introduction I discuss the understanding of the existence of discretion as a precondition for the analysis and evaluation of its use. I have examined the extent of discretion and its differing natures within two social work teams. Understanding the topography of discretion is one aspect of appreciating discretion in practice; the other is the exploration of the evaluation of the uses of discretion. One way suggested by the street-level bureaucracy perspective is to assess discretion against policy; this is done, for instance, by Baldwin (1998, 2000). Another approach is to criticise practice using the researcher's own idea of appropriate use of discretion (e.g. Ellis *et al.* 1999). Both approaches are problematic. The argument about discretion operating throughout the organisation underlines the problem of identifying the policy by which practice should be evaluated and where it is located (Evans and Hardy 2010). Lewis and Glennerster (1996), for instance, use Sabatier's (1993) idea of core and peripheral policy goals to distinguish the overt and covert policy in the new community care, but also point to how local authorities often look to the overt policy to frame their responses. The other approach—researchers asserting a standard against which practice is to be assessed—raises questions about what justifies the application of these standards to the situation. Another, but less prominent approach to the examination of the use of discretion is to look at the evaluation of discretion in the same way that this book has sought to examine its extent and basis: by identifying and specifying the commitments cited by the actors involved as central to understanding and judging the exercise of discretion. This would be in line with forms of ethical analysis that emphasise an understanding of actors' own commitments as well as external criteria in assessing their actions (e.g. Williams 1993). How do citizens and service users expect discretion to be used? What are the expectations of practitioners? How do the latter understand, when their claim is to exercise professional discretion, what the professional requirements are? How do managers at different levels of the organisation evaluate the uses of discretion? Rather than seeking to impose external criteria of evaluation, this research would first seek to identify the values, commitments and aims of the different actors involved. The problem is, of course, that these standards of evaluation may be self-serving; but it may also be the case that they are not, or at least not exclusively so. What is clear is that the investigation of the evaluation of discretion is an area of work that follows from the identification of the extent and nature of discretion; and that, in evaluating the use of discretion, it would be best to take account of the wide range of perspectives on this issue.

Appendix

Presentation of Interview Data

In presenting the interview data, I have sought to use the interviewees' own words wherever possible. Often this has involved cutting verbatim quotations. Cuts are indicated with ellipses and usually involve extraneous, illustrative material and phatic statements. Where proper names have been used I have changed them and put the pseudonym in square brackets. For instance, the following statement:

> But I will go out and do stuff. I will go out and do some shopping and I'll … last week I had … doing some of the washing as well. Simply because noone else to do it, it needs doing, it maintains that person and it's easier to do it. Now I know that I shouldn't be doing those tasks, but I do it. I mean, when I'm running for the shopping for one of my old people because the carer has yet again failed to turn up and she had no food and I know she doesn't eat. I know she doesn't eat. And so I … you know, you're running down town and thinking, "this is mad". I must be the most expensive shopper in [name of unitary authority]

becomes:

> But I will go out and do stuff. I will go out and do some shopping and I'll … Simply because noone else to do it, it needs doing, it maintains that person and it's easier to do it. Now I know that I shouldn't be doing those tasks, but I do it … you know, you're running down town and thinking, "this is mad". I must be the most expensive shopper in [Newunit] (MS4).

The source of the quotation is given in brackets at the end of each quotation. The first letter indicates the team: O for the older persons team, and M for the mental health team. The second letter denotes whether the interviewee was a manager (M) or a social work practitioner (S), and the number identifies different individuals and is based on the order in which they were interviewed. The above quotation is ascribed to MS4: that is, the fourth social worker interviewed in the mental health team.

Bibliography

Ahearne, J. (1995) *Michel de Certeau: Interpretation and its Other*, Cambridge: Polity Press.

Alaszewski, A. and Manthorpe, J. (1990) 'Literature Review: The New Right and the Professions', *British Journal of Social Work*, 20, 237–251.

Allen, D., Griffiths, L. and Lyne, P. (2004) 'Accommodating Health and Social Care Needs: Routine Resource Allocation in Stroke Rehabilitation', *Sociology of Health and Illness*, 26, 411–432.

Anon (1981) 'Review Article: Street-Level Bureaucracy', *Michigan Law Review*, 79, 811–814.

Baldwin, M. (1998) 'The Positive Use of Discretion in Social Work Practice: Developing Practice Through Co-operative Inquiry', *Issues in Social Work Education*, 18, 42–48.

Baldwin, M. (2000) *Care Management and Community Care: Social Work Discretion and the Construction of Policy*, Aldershot: Ashgate.

Baldwin, M. (2004) 'Critical Reflection: Opportunities and Threats to Professional Learning and Service Development in Social Work Organisations' in Gould, N. and Baldwin, M. (eds) *Social Work, Critical Reflection and the Learning Organisation*, Aldershot: Ashgate.

Balloch, S. (1999) 'Education and Training in Social Work and Social Care' in Balloch, S., McLean, I. and Fisher, M. (eds) (1999) *Social Services: Working Under Pressure*, Bristol: Policy Press.

Balloch, S., Andrew, T., Ginn, J., McLean, J., Pahl, J. and Williams, J. (1995) *Working in the Social Services*, London: National Institute for Social Work.

Balloch, S., McLean, I., and Fisher, M. (eds) (1999a) *Social Services: Working Under Pressure*, Bristol: Policy Press.

Balloch, S., Buglass, D. and McConkey, W. (1999b) 'Introduction' in Balloch, S., McLean, I. and Fisher, M. (eds) (1999) *Social Services: Working Under Pressure*, Bristol: Policy Press.

Balloch, S., Fisher, M., and McLean, J. (1999c) 'Conclusion and Policy Issues' in Balloch, S., McLean, I. and Fisher, M. (eds) (1999) *Social Services: Working Under Pressure*, Bristol: Policy Press.

Balogun J. and Johnson, G. (2005) 'From Intended Strategies to Unintended Outcomes: The Impact of Change Recipient Sense-making', *Organization Studies*, 26 1573–1601.

Barnes, M. (1998), 'Whose Needs, Whose Resources? Assessing Social Care' in Langan, M. (ed.) *Welfare: Needs Rights and Risks*, London: Routledge.

Barret, S. and Fudge, C. (eds) (1981) *Policy and Action*, London: Methuen.

Bauld, L., Chesterman, J., Davies, B., Judge, K. and Mangalore, R. (2000) *Caring for Older People: An Assessment of Community Care in the 1990s*, Aldershot: Ashgate.

Beck, U. (1992) *Risk Society: Towards a New Modernity*, London: Sage.

Blackmore, M. (2001) 'Mind the Gap: Exploring the Implementation Deficit in the Administration of the Stricter Benefits Regime', *Social Policy and Administration*, 35, 145–162.

Bradley, G. (2003) 'Administrative Justice and Charging for Care', *British Journal of Social Work*, 33, 641–657.

Bradley, G. (2005) 'Movers and Stayers in Care Management in Adult Services', *British Journal of Social Work*, 35, 511–530.

Brayne, M. and Carr, H. (2005) *Law for Social Workers*, Oxford: Oxford University Press.

Bream, J. and Gates, S. (1999) *Working, Shirking, and Sabotage: Bureaucratic Response to a Democratic Public*, Ann Arbor: The University of Michigan Press.

Brodkin, E. (1997) 'Inside the Welfare Contract: Discretion and Accountability in State Welfare Administration', *Social Services Review*, March 1997, 1–33.

Brown, R. (1975) *The Management of Welfare*, London: Martin Robertson.

Burawoy, M. (1991) 'The Extended Case Method' in Burawoy, M., Burton, A., Ferguson, A., Fox, K., Gamson, J., Gartrell, N., Hurst, L., Kurzman, C., Salzinger, L., Schiffman, J. and Ui, S. (eds) *Ethnography Unbound: Power and Resistance in the Modern Metropolis*, Berkeley: University of California Press.

Burns, T. (1997) 'Case Management, Care Management and Care Programming', *British Journal of Psychiatry*, 170, 393–395.

Butcher, T. (1995) *Delivering Welfare: The Governance of Social Services in the 1990s*, Buckingham: Open University Press.

Cabinet Office (1999) *The Modernising Government*, London: Cabinet Office.

Carey, M. (2003) 'Anatomy of a Care Manager', *Work, Employment and Society*, 17, 121–135.

Carey, M. (2006) 'The Quasi-Market Revolution in the Head: Ideology, Discourse, Care Management', *Journal of Social Work*, 8, 341–362.

Carey, M. (2008) 'Everything Must Go? The Privatisation of State Social Work', *British Journal of Social Work*, 38, 918–935.

Causer, G. and Exworthy, M. (1999) 'Professionals as Managers Across the Public Sector' in Exworthy, M. and Halford, S. (eds) *Professions and the New Managerialism in the Public Sector*, Buckingham: Open University Press.

Challis, D. (1994) *Implementing Caring for People. Care Management: Factors Influencing its Development in the Implementation of Community Care*, London: Her Majesty's Stationery Office.

Challis, D. and Hugman, R. (1993) 'Editorial: Community Care, Social Work and Social Care', *British Journal of Social Work*, 23, 319–328.

Checkland, K. (2004) 'National Service Frameworks and UK General Practitioners: Street-level Bureaucrats at Work?', *Sociology of Health and Illness*, 26, 951–975.

Cheetham, J. (1993) 'Social Work and Community Care in the 1990s: Pitfalls and Potential' in Page, R. and Baldock, J. (eds) *Social Policy Review*, 5, University of Kent at Canterbury: Social Policy Association.

Clarke, J. (1996) 'After Social Work' in Parton, N. (ed.) *Social Theory, Social Change and Social Work*, London: Routledge.

Clarke, J. and Newman, J. (1997) *The Managerial State*, London: Sage.

Clarke, J., Gerwitz, S. and McLauchlin, E. (2000) 'Reinventing the Welfare State' in Clarke, J., Gerwitz, S. and McLauchlin, E. (eds) *New Managerialism New Welfare State?* London: Sage.

Craig, G. and Manthorpe, J. (1999) *The Impact of Local Government Reorganisation on Social Services Work*, York: Joseph Rowntree Foundation.

Davis, K. (1971) *Discretionary Justice: A Preliminary Inquiry*, Urbana, Ill.: University of Illinois Press.

Department of Education and Skills (2003) *Every Child Matters*, London: Department of Education and Skills.

Department of Health (1989) *Caring for People: Community Care in the Next Decade and Beyond*, London: Her Majesty's Stationery Office.

Department of Health (1991) *Care Management and Assessment: Practitioners' Guide*, London: Her Majesty's Stationery Office.

Department of Health (1995) *Building Bridges*, London: Department of Health.

Department of Health (1999) *National Service Framework: Mental Health*, London: Department of Health.

Department of Health (2001) *National Service Framework for Older People*, London: Department of Health.

Department of Health (2003a) *Fair Access to Care Services Guidance on Eligibility Criteria For Adult Social Care*, London: Department of Health.

Department of Health (2003b) *Fair Access to Care Services. Practice Guidance: Implementation Questions And Answers*, London: Department of Health.

Department of Health (2005) *Personal Social Services Staff of Social Services Departments at 30 September 2004 England*, London: Department of Health.

Department of Health (2009) *Personal Social Services Staff of Social Services Departments at 30 September 2008 England*, London: Department of Health.

Department of Health and Home Office (2000) *No Secrets: Guidance on Developing and Implementing Multi-agency Policies and Procedures to Protect Vulnerable Adults from Abuse*, London: Department of Health and Home Office.

Department of Health and Office of National Statistics (2001) *Social Services Performance Assessment Framework*, London: Department of Health and Office of National Statistics.

Diner, S. (1998) 'Social Welfare' in Shumsky, N. (ed.) *Encyclopedia of Urban America*, Santa Barbara, Calif.: ABC-Clio.

Dunkerley, D.J., Scourfield, J., Maegusuku-Hewett, T. and Smalley N. (2005) 'The Experiences of Frontline Staff Working with Children Seeking Asylum', *Social Policy & Administration*, 39, 640–652.

Dworkin, R. (1978) *Taking Rights Seriously*, London: Duckworth.

Edwards, A. and Talbot, R. (1999) *The Hard-pressed Researcher*, London: Longman.

Eisinger, P. (1998) 'Johnson Administration: Urban Policy' in Shumsky, N. (ed.) *Encyclopedia of Urban America*, Santa Barbara, Calif.: ABC-Clio.

Ellis, K. (2007) 'Direct Payments and Social Work Practice: The Significance of "Street-Level Bureaucracy" in Determining Eligibility', *British Journal of Social Work*, 37, 405–422.

Ellis, K., Davis, A. and Rummery, K. (1999) 'Needs Assessment, Street-Level Bureaucracy and the New Community Care', *Social Policy and Administration*, 33, 262–280.

Evans, T. (2009) 'Managing to be Professional' in Harris, J. and White, V. (eds) *Modernising Social Work*, Bristol: Policy Press.

Evans, T. and Harris, J. (2004a) 'Street-Level Bureaucracy, Social Work and the (Exaggerated) Death of Discretion', *British Journal of Social Work*, 34, 871–895.

Evans, T. and Harris, J. (2004b) 'Citizenship, Social Inclusion and Confidentiality', *British Journal of Social Work*, 34, 69–91.

Evans, T. and Hardy, M. (2010) *Evidence and Knowledge for Practice*, Cambridge: Polity Press.

Evetts, J. (2002) 'New Directions in State and International Professional Occupations: Discretionary Decision-making and Acquired Regulation', *Work, Employment and Society*, 16, 341–353.

Evetts, J. (2006) *The Sociology of Professional Groups: New Directions, Current Sociology*, 54: 133–143.

Fleming, P. and Spicer, A. (2003) 'Working at a Cynical Distance: Implications for Power, Subjectivity and Resistance', *Organization*, 10, 157–179.

Flynn, R. (1999) 'Managerialism, Professionalism and Quasi-markets' in Exworthy, M. and Halford, S. (eds) *Professionals and the New Managerialism in the Public Sector*, Buckingham: Open University Press.

Foster, P. and Wilding, P. (2000) 'Whither Welfare Professionalism?', *Social Policy and Administration*, 34, 143–159.

Foucault, M. (1981) *The History of Sexuality, Volume One: An Introduction*, Harmondsworth: Penguin.

Fournier, V. (1999) 'The Appeal to "Professionalism" as a Disciplinary Mechanism', *The Sociological Review*, 280–307.

Freeden, M. (1996) *Ideologies and Political Theory: A Conceptual Approach*, Oxford: Clarendon Press.

Freidson, E. (1994) *Professionalism Reborn: Theory, Prophecy and Policy*, Cambridge: Polity Press.

Gadamer, H.-G. (1975) *Truth and Method*, London: Sheed and Ward.

Gallie, W. G. (1955) 'Essentially Contested Concepts', *Proceedings of the Aristotelian Society*, 56, 167–98.

Gianakis, G. (1994) 'Appraising the Performance of "Street-level Bureaucrats": The Case of Police Patrol Officers', *American Review of Public Administration*, 24, 299–315.

Goldner, F. (1982) 'Review Article: Street-Level Bureaucracy', *Administrative Science Quarterly*, 27, 153–155.

Gostick, C., Davies, B., Lawson, R. and Salter, C. (1997) *From Vision to Reality in Community Care: Changing Direction at the Local Level*, Aldershot: Arena.

Gouldner, A. (1957) 'Cosmopolitans and Locals: Towards an Analysis of Latent Social Roles', *Administrative Science Quarterly*, 2, 281–306.

Grattet, R. and Jenness, V. (2005) 'The Reconstitution of Law in Local Settings: Agency Discretion, Ambiguity, and a Surplus of Law in the Policing of Hate Crime', *Law & Society Review*, 39, 893–941.

Griffiths, R. (1988) *Community Care Agenda for Action*, London: Her Majesty's Stationery Office.

Hadley, R. and Clough, R. (1996) *Care in Chaos: Frustration and Challenge in Community Care*, London: Cassell.

Halliday, S., Burns, N., Hutton, N., McNeill, F. and Tata, C. (2008) 'Shadow Writing and Participation Observation: A Study of Criminal Justice Work Around Sentencing', *Journal of Law and Society*, 35, 189–213.

Harris, J. (1998a) 'Scientific Management, Bureau-Professionalism and New Managerialism. The Labour Process of State Social Work', *British Journal of Social Work*, 28, 839–862.

Harris, J. (1998b) *Managing State Social Work*, Aldershot: Ashgate.

Harris, J. (2003) *The Social Work Business*, London: Routledge.

Harris, J. and White, V. (eds) (2009) *Modernising Social Work*, Bristol: Policy Press.

Harrison, S. (1999) 'Clinical Autonomy and Health Policy: Past and Futures' in Exworthy, M. and Halford, S. (eds) *Professionals and the New Managerialism in the Public Sector*, Buckingham: Open University Press.

Harrison, S., Hunter, D., Marnoch, G. and Pollitt, C. (1992) *Just Managing*, Basingstoke: Macmillan.

Hartley, J. (2004) 'Case Study Research' in Cassell, C. and Symon, G. (eds) *Essential Guide to Qualitative Methods in Organizational Research*, London: Sage.

Hasenfeld, Y. (1981) 'Review Article: Street-Level Bureaucracy', *Social Service Review*, 55, 155–156.

Hawley, W. and Lipsky, M. (1976) 'The Study of City Politics' in Hawley, W. and Lipsky, M. (eds) *Theoretical Perspective on Urban Politics*, Englewood Cliffs, NJ: Prentice-Hall.

Healy, K. (2000) *Social Work Practices: Contemporary Perspectives on Change*, London: Sage.

Henderson, J. and Seden, J. (2003) 'What Do We Want from Social Care Managers? Aspirations and Realities' in Reynolds, J., Henderson, J., Seden, J., Charlesworth, J. and Bullman, A. (eds) *The Managing Care Reader*, London: Routledge.

Hill, M. (1982) 'Street-Level Bureaucracy in Social Work and Social Services Departments' in Lishman, J. (ed.) *Research Highlights 4: Social Work Departments as Organisations*, Aberdeen: Aberdeen University Press.

Hill, M. (2000a), 'What are Local Authority Social Services?' in Hill, M. (ed.) *Local Authority Social Services: An Introduction*, Oxford: Blackwell.

Hill, M. (2000b), 'Origins of Local Authority Social Services' in Hill, M. (ed.) *Local Authority Social Services: An Introduction*, Oxford: Blackwell.

Hill, M. (2000c) 'The Central and Local Government Framework' in Hill, M. (ed.) *Local Authority Social Services: An Introduction*, Oxford: Blackwell.

Hill, M. (2000d) 'Organization within Local Authorities' in Hill, M. (ed.) *Local Authority Social Services: An Introduction*, Oxford: Blackwell.

Hill, M. (2003) *Understanding Social Policy*, Oxford: Blackwell.

Hogwood, B. and Gunn, L. (1984) *Policy Analysis for the Real World*, Oxford: Oxford University Press.

Hood, C., Rothstein, H. and Baldwin, R. (2001) *The Government of Risk: Understanding Risk Regulation Regimes*, Oxford: Oxford University Press.

Hopkins, J. (1996) 'Social Work Through the Looking Glass' in Parton, N. (ed.) *Social Theory, Social Change and Social Work*, London: Routledge.

Howe, D. (1986) *Social Workers and their Practices in Welfare Bureaucracies*, Aldershot: Gower.

Howe, D. (1991a) 'Knowledge, Power and the Shape of Social Work Practice' in Davies, M. (ed.) *The Sociology of Social Work*, London: Routledge.

Howe, D. (1991b) 'The Family and the Therapist' in Davies, M. (ed.) *The Sociology of Social Work*, London: Routledge.

Howe, D. (1996) 'Surface and Depth in Social Work Practice' in Parton, N. (ed.) *Social Theory, Social Change and Social Work*, London: Routledge.

Hudson, B. (1993) 'Michael Lipsky and Street-Level Bureaucracy' in Hills, M. (ed.) *The Policy Process: A Reader*, Hemel Hempstead: Harvester Wheatsheaf.

Hudson, B. (2000) 'Conclusion' in Hudson, B. (ed.) *The Changing Role of Social Care*, London: Jessica Kingsley.

Hugman, R. (1991) *Power in Caring Professions*, London: Macmillan.

Hussey, R. (ed.) (1999) *Dictionary of Accounting*, Oxford: Oxford University Press.

Huxley, P. (1993) 'Case Management, Care Management and Community Care', *British Journal of Social Work*, 23, 366–381.

Irving, J. and Gertig, P. (1999) 'Brave New World: Social Workers' Perceptions of Care Management', *Practice*, 10, 5–14.

James, A. (1994) *Managing to Care*, London: Longman.

Jamous, H. and Peloille, B. (1970) 'Changes in the French University-Hospital System' in Jackson, J.A. (ed.) *Professions and Professionalization*, Cambridge: Cambridge University Press.

Jewell, C. and Glasser, B. (2006) 'Toward a General Analytic Framework: Organizational Settings, Policy Goals, and Street-Level Behavior', *Administration & Society*, 38, 3: 335–364.

Joffe, C. (1981) 'Review Article: Street-Level Bureaucracy', *Harvard Education Review*, 51, 333–336.

Johnson, T. (1972) *Professions and Power*, London: Macmillan.

Jones, C. (1983) *State Social Work and the Working Class*, London: Macmillan.

Jones, C. (1999) 'Social Work: Regulation and Managerialism' in Exworthy, M. and Halford, S. (eds) *Professionals and the New Managerialism in the Public Sector*, Buckingham: Open University Press.

Jones, C. (2001) 'Voices From the Front Line: State Social Workers and New Labour', *British Journal of Social Work*, 31, 547–562.

Kadish, M. and Kadish, S. (1973) *Discretion to Disobey*, Stamford, Calif.: Stamford University Press.

Katz, F. (1973) 'Integrative and Adaptive Uses of Autonomy: Worker Autonomy in Factories' in Salaman, G. and Thompson, K. (eds) *People in Organisations*, Harlow: Longman.

Kaufman, B. (1998) 'Carter Administration: Urban Policy' in Shumsky, N. (ed.) *Encyclopedia of Urban America*, Santa Barbara, Calif.: ABC-Clio.

Keiser, L. (1999) 'State Bureaucratic Discretion and the Administration of Social Welfare Programs: The Case of Social Security Disability', *Journal of Public Administration Research & Theory*, 9, 87–106.

Kelly, M. (1994) 'Theories of Justice and Street-level Discretion', *Journal of Public Administration Research and Theory*, 4, 119–140.

Kirkpatrick, I. (2002) 'A Jungle of Competing Requirements: Management "Reform" in the Organisational Field of UK Social Services', *Social Work and Social Sciences Review*, 10, 24–27.

La Valle I. and Lyons K. (1998a) 'The Social Worker Speaks I—Perceptions of Recent Changes in British Social Work', *Practice*, 8, 5–13.

La Valle I. and Lyons K. (1998b) 'The Social Worker Speaks II—Management of Change in the Personal Social Services', *Practice*, 8, 63–71.

Laffin, M. and Young, K. (1990) *Professionalism in Local Government*, Harlow: Longman.

Langan, M. (1998) 'The Contested Concept of Need' in Langan, M. (ed.) *Welfare: Needs Rights and Risks*, London: Routledge.

Lapsley, I. and Llewellyn, S. (1998) 'Markets, Hierarchies and Choices in Social Care' in Bartlett, W., Roberts, J. and LeGrand, J. (eds) *A Revolution in Social Policy*, Bristol: Policy Press.

Law, J. (1986) 'On the Methods of Long-distance Control: Vessels, Navigation and the Portuguese Route to India' in Law, J. (ed.) *Power, Action and Belief: A New Sociology of Knowledge?* London: Routledge & Kegan Paul.

Leonard, P. (1997) *Postmodern Welfare: Reconstructing the Emancipatory Project*, London: Sage.

Lewis, J. and Glennerster, H. (1996) *Implementing the New Community Care*, Buckingham: Open University Press.

Lincoln, Y. and Guba, E. (2000) 'The Only Generalization is: There is No Generalization' in Gomm, R., Hammersley, M. and Foster, P. (eds) *Case Study Method*, London: Sage.

Lipsky, M. (1971) 'Street-Level Bureaucracy and the Analysis of Urban Reform', *Urban Affairs Quarterly* 6, 392–409.

Lipsky, M. (1976) 'Towards a Theory of Street-Level Bureaucracy' in Hawley, W. and Lipsky, M. (eds) *Theoretical Perspective on Urban Politics*, Englewood Cliffs, NJ: Prentice-Hall.

Lipsky, M. (1980) *Street-Level Bureaucracy: The Dilemmas of Individuals in Public Service*, New York: Russell Sage Foundation.

Lipsky, M. (1991) 'The Paradox of Managing Discretionary Workers in Social Welfare Policy' in Adler, M. (ed.) *The Sociology of Social Security*, Edinburgh: Edinburgh University Press.

Local Government Association (2002) *Local Authority Social Services: Budget Survey*, London: Local Government Association.

Local Government Association/Association of Directors of Adult Social Services (2009) *Report on Adults' Social Services Expenditure 2008–9*, accessed 14 March 2010 at http://www.lga.gov.uk/lga/aio/1853692.

Lord Laming (2003) *The Victoria Climbié Inquiry: Report of an Inquiry*, Norwich: Her Majesty's Stationery Office.

Lovrich, N., Steel, B., Majed, M. (1986) 'The Street-level Bureaucrat—a Useful Category or a Distinction Without a Difference?: Research Note on Construct Validation', *Review of Public Personnel Administration*, 6, 14–27.

Lupton, D. (1999) *Risk*, London: Routledge.

Lymbery, M. (1998a) 'The Development of Social Work in Britain 1969–1996' in Kwak, A. and Dingwall, R. (eds) *Social Change, Social Policy and Social Work in the New Europe*, Aldershot: Ashgate.

Lymbery, M. (1998b) 'Care Management and Professional Autonomy: The Impact of Community Care Legislation on Social Work with Older People', *British Journal of Social Work*, 28, 863–878.

Lymbery, M. (2000) 'The Retreat from Professionalism: from Social Worker to Care Manager' in Malin, N. (ed.) *Professionalism, Boundaries and the Workplace*, London: Routledge.

Macdonald, G. (1990) 'Allocating Blame in Social Work', *British Journal of Social Work*, 20, 525–546.

Magnusson, W. (1981) 'Review Article: Street-Level Bureaucracy', *Canadian Journal of Political Science*, 14, 213–214.

Malin, N., Wilmot, S. and Manthorpe, J. (2002) *Key Concepts and Debates in Health and Social Policy*, Buckingham: Open University Press.

Marchant, C. (1993) 'Crock of Fools' Gold', *Community Care*, 1 April, 14–16.

Marshall, T. and Rees, A. (1985) *Social Policy*, London: Hutchinson.

May, P. and Wood, R. (2003) 'At the Regulatory Front Line: Inspectors' Enforcement Style and Regulatory Compliance', *Journal of Public Administration Research and Theory*, 13, 117–139.

Maynard-Moody, S. and Musheno, M. (2003) *Cops, Teachers and Counselors: Stories from the Front-line of Public Service*, Ann Arbor: University of Michigan Press.

McDonald, C. and Marston, G. (2005) 'Workfare and Welfare: Governing Unemployment in the Advanced Liberal State', *Critical Social Policy*, 25, 374–401.

McLean, J. (1999) 'Satisfaction, Stress and Control over Work' in Balloch, S., McLean, I. and Fisher, M. (eds) (1999) *Social Services: Working Under Pressure*, Bristol: Policy Press.

McNay, L. (1994) *Foucault: A Critical Introduction*, Cambridge: Polity Press.

Mead, L. (2005) 'Policy Research: The Field Dimension', *The Policy Studies Journal*, 33, 535–557.

Meyers, M., Glaser, B. and MacDonald, K. (1998) 'On the Front Lines of Welfare: Are Workers Implementing Policy Reforms?', *Journal of Policy Analysis and Management*, 17, 1–22.

Mitchell, S. (2000) 'Modernising Social Services' in Hill, M. (ed.) *Local Authority Social Services: An Introduction*, Oxford: Blackwell.

Muijen, M. (1996) 'Scare in the Community: Britain in Moral Panic' in Heller, T., Reynolds, J., Gomm, R., Muston, R. and Pattison, D. (eds) *Mental Health Matters*, Basingstoke: Macmillan.

Munro, E. (1998) 'Improving Social Workers' Knowledge Base in Child Protection', *British Journal of Social Work*, 28, 101–102.

Munro, E. (2004) 'The Impact of Audit on Social Work Practice', *British Journal of Social Work*, 34, 1075–1098.

Murray, C. (2006) 'State Intervention and Vulnerable Children: Implementation Revisited', *Journal of Social Policy*, 25, 211–227.

National Health Service Management Inquiry (1983) *Report*, London: Department of Health and Social Security.

Netten, A. (2005) 'Personal Social Services' in Powell, M., Bauld, L. and Clark, K. (eds) *Social Policy Review*, 17, Bristol: Policy Press.

Newman, J. and Clarke, J. (1994) 'Going About Our Business? The Managerialization of Public Services' in Clarke, J., Cochrane, A. and McLaughlin, E. (eds) *Managing Social Policy*, London: Sage.

Newton, J. and Browne, L. (2008) 'How Fair is Fair Access to Care?', *Practice*, 20, 235–249.

Nixon, J. (1993) 'Implementation in the Hands of Senior Managers: Community Care in Britain' in Hill, M. (ed.) *New Agendas in the Study of the Policy Process*, London: Harvester Wheatsheaf.

Noon, M. and Blyton, P. (2002) *The Realities of Work*, Basingstoke: Palgrave.

Noordegraff, M. (2007) 'From "Pure" to "Hybrid" Professionals – Present-day Professionalism in Ambiguous Public Domains', *Administration and Society*, 39, 761–785.

O'Neill, O. (2002) *A Question of Trust*, Cambridge: Cambridge University Press.

Ovretveit, J. (1993) *Co-ordinating Community Care: Multidisciplinary Teams and Care Management*, Buckingham: Open University Press.

Pahl, J. (1994) 'Like the Job but Hate the Organisation: Social Workers and Managers in Social Services' in Page, R. and Baldock, J. (eds) *Social Policy Review*, 6, University of Kent at Canterbury: Social Policy Association.

Parry, N. and Parry, J. (1979) 'Social Work Professionalism and the State' in Parry, N., Rustin, M. and Satyamurti, C. (eds) *Social Work, Welfare and the State*, London: Edward Arnold.

Parsloe, P. and Stevenson, O. (1978) *Social Services Teams: The Practitioner's View*, London: Her Majesty's Stationery Office.

Payne, M. (2005) *The Origins of Social Work*, Basingstoke: Palgrave.

Perlman, R. (1981) 'Street-Level Bureaucracy', *Social Casework*, 62, 446.

Pithouse, A. (1998) *Social Work: The Social Organisation of an Invisible Trade*, Aldershot: Ashgate.

Pollitt, C. (1993) *Managerialism and the Public Sector*, Oxford: Oxford University Press.

Postle, K. (2001) 'The Social Work is Disappearing. I Guess it Started with Us Being Called Care Managers', *Practice*, 13, 13–26.

Postle, K. (2002) 'Working Between the Idea and the Reality: Ambiguities and Tensions in Care Managers' Work', *British Journal of Social Work*, 32, 335–351.

Power, M. (1997) *The Audit Society*, Oxford: Oxford University Press.

Preston-Shoot, M. and Wigley, V. (2002) 'Closing the Circle: Social Workers' Responses to Multi-Agency Procedures on Older Age Abuse', *British Journal of Social Work*, 32, 299–320.

Prottas, J. (1978) 'The Power of the Street-Level Bureaucrat in Public Service Bureaucracies', *Urban Affairs Quarterly*, 13, 285–312.

Ragin, C. (1987) *The Comparative Method: Moving Beyond Qualitative and Quantitative Strategies*, Berkeley: University of California Press.

Reith, M. (1998) *Community Care Tragedies: A Practice Guide to Mental Health Inquiries*, Birmingham: Venture Press.

Reynolds, J. (2003) 'Becoming a Manager: Acting or Reacting' in Seden, J. and Reynolds, J. (eds) *Managing Care in Practice*, London: Routledge.

Rhodes, R.A.W. (1997) *Understanding Governance*, Buckingham: Open University Press.

Rhodes, R.A.W. (2008) 'Understanding Governance: Ten Years On', *Organization Studies*, 28, 1243–1264.

Robinson, G. (2003) 'Technicality and Indeterminacy in Probation Practice: A Case Study', *British Journal of Social Work*, 33, 593–610.

Rogers, A. and Pilgrim, D. (2001) *Mental Health Policy in Britain*, Basingstoke: Palgrave.

Sabatier, P. (1993) 'Top-down and Bottom-up Approaches to Implementation Research' in Hills, M. (ed.) *The Policy Process: A Reader*, Hemel Hempstead: Harvester Wheatsheaf.

Satyamurti, C. (1981) *Occupational Survival: The Case of the Local Authority Social Worker*, Blackwell: Oxford.

Schofield, J. (2000) 'Increasing the Generalizability of Qualitative Research' in Gomm, R., Hammersley, M. and Foster, P. (eds) *Case Study Method*, London: Sage.

Scott, J. (1990) A Matter of Record: Documentary Sources in Social Research, Cambridge: Polity Press.

Seden, J. and Reynolds, J.(2003) 'Introduction' in Seden, J. and Reynolds, J. (eds) *Managing Care in Practice*, London: Routledge.

Shaw, I. (2000) 'Mental Health' in Hill, M. (ed.) *Local Authority Social Services: An Introduction*, Oxford: Blackwell.

Simic, P. (1995) 'What's in a Word? From Social "Worker" to Care "Manager"', *Practice*, 7, 5–18.

Smith, G. (1981) 'Discretionary Decision-making in Social Work' in Adler, M. and Asquith, S. (eds) *Discretion and Welfare*, London: Heinemann.

Social Services Inspectorate (2001) *Modern Social Services—A Commitment to Deliver: The 10th Annual Report of the Chief Inspector of Social Services*, London: Department of Health.

Stevenson, O. (1978) 'Practice: An Overview' in *Department of Health and Social Security, Social Services Teams: The Practitioners' View*, London: Her Majesty's Stationery Office.

Stone, C. (1983) 'Whither the Welfare State? Professionalization, Bureaucracy, and the Market Alternatives', *Ethics*, 93, 588–595.

Strauss, A., Schatzman, L., Ehrlich, D., Bucher, R. and Sabshin, M. (1963) 'The Hospital and its Negotiated Order' in Freidson, E. (ed.) *The Hospital in Modern Society*, New York: Free Press.

The Guardian, 'Social Services Hindered by Lack of Cash, says Inspector', John Carvel, Social Affairs Editor, 1 December 2005.

Turbett, C. (2009) 'Review: Iain Ferguson Reclaiming Social Work—Challenging Neo-liberalism and Promoting Social Justice', *Journal of Social Work*, 9: 239–240.

Walton, J. (1992) 'Making the Theoretical Case' in Ragin, C. and Becker, S. (eds) *What is a Case? Exploring the Foundations of Social Inquiry*, Cambridge: Cambridge University Press.

Weissert, C. (1994) 'Beyond the Organization: The Influence of Community and Personal Values on Street-level Bureaucrats' Responsiveness', *Journal of Public Administration Research and Theory*, 4, 222–254.

Weitz, M. (1977) *The Opening Mind*, Chicago: University of Chicago Press.

Wells, J. (1997) 'Priorities, Street-Level Bureaucracy and the Community Mental Health Team', *Health and Social Care in the Community*, 5, 333–342.

White, V. (2009) 'Quiet Challenges? Professional Practice in Modernised Social Work' in Harris and White (eds) *Modernising Social Work*, Bristol: Policy Press.

Williams, B. (1993) *Ethics and the Limits of Philosophy*, London: Fontana.

Winter, S. (2002) *Explaining Street-level Bureaucratic Behaviour in Social and Regulatory Policies*, Paper prepared for the XIII Research Conference of the Nordic Political Science Association, 15–17 August 2002: Aalborg.

Wittgenstein, W. (2001) *Philosophical Investigations*, Oxford: Blackwell.

Yates, D. (1982) 'Review Article: Street-Level Bureaucracy', *The American Political Science Review*, 76, 145–146.

Yin, R. (2003) *Case Study Research*, Thousand Oaks, Calif.: Sage.

Index

Printed in Poland
by Amazon Fulfillment
Poland Sp. z o.o., Wrocław